BORDERLINE
PERSONALITY
DISORDER and the
CONVERSATIONAL
MODEL

The Norton Series on Interpersonal Neurobiology

Allan N. Schore, PhD, Series Editor

•

Daniel J. Siegel, MD, Founding Editor

The field of mental health is in a tremendously exciting period of growth and conceptual reorganization. Independent findings from a variety of scientific endeavors are converging in an interdisciplinary view of the mind and mental well-being. An interpersonal neurobiology of human development enables us to understand that the structure and function of the mind and brain are shaped by experiences, especially those involving emotional relationships.

The Norton Series on Interpersonal Neurobiology provides cutting-edge, multi-disciplinary views that further our understanding of the complex neurobiology of the human mind. By drawing on a wide range of traditionally independent fields of research—such as neurobiology, genetics, memory, attachment, complex systems, anthropology, and evolutionary psychology—these texts offer mental health professionals a review and synthesis of scientific findings often inaccessible to clinicians. These books aim to advance our understanding of human experience by finding the unity of knowledge, or consilience, that emerges with the translation of findings from numerous domains of study into a common language and conceptual framework. The series integrates the best of modern science with the healing art of psychotherapy.

A Norton Professional Book

BORDERLINE PERSONALITY DISORDER and the CONVERSATIONAL MODEL

A Clinician's Manual

Russell Meares
Nick Bendit
Joan Haliburn
Anthony Korner
Dawn Mears
David Butt

W. W. Norton & Company
New York • London

For information about permission to reproduce selections from this book, write to
Permissions, W. W. Norton & Company, Inc., 500 Fifth Avenue, New York, NY 10110

For information about special discounts for bulk purchases, please contact
W. W. Norton Special Sales at specialsales@wwnorton.com or 800-233-4830

Manufacturing by IBT/Hamilton Printing
Book design by Charlotte Staub
Production manager: Leeann Graham

Library of Congress Cataloging-in-Publication Data

Borderline personality disorder and the conversational model : a clinician's manual / [edited
by] Russell Meares ... [et al.].
    p. cm. — (The Norton series on interpersonal neurobiology) (A Norton professional book)
Includes bibliographical references and index.
ISBN 978-0-393-70783-0 (pbk.)
1. Borderline personality disorder. I. Meares, Russell.
RC569.5.B67B687 2012
616.85'852—dc23
                    2012024203

W. W. Norton & Company, Inc.
500 Fifth Avenue, New York, N.Y. 10110
www.wwnorton.com

W. W. Norton & Company Ltd.
Castle House, 75/76 Wells Street, London W1T 3QT

1 2 3 4 5 6 7 8 9 0

CONTENTS

Expanded Contents

Acknowledgments

Many people have been involved in the creation of this book. We wish to thank those who preceded us in this endeavor. The first group of people that attempted to develop a "practical guide" for the practice of the Conversational Model (CM) was composed of the faculty and the candidates of the Master of Medicine (psychotherapy) course at Sydney University. These individuals were followed some years later by another group from the Australian and New Zealand Association of Psychotherapy (ANZAP). It was found, in each case, despite a great deal of work, that these efforts had not captured the essence of the model. What was lacking was the vitality and immediacy of the real-life situation. For this third attempt, that deficiency has been rectified. We would like to thank those patients, and their therapists, for permission to use their conversations to illustrate main aspects of CM. These extracts make a crucial contribution to this volume. Since the contributions of patients, therapists, and authors of the book could not be given relative "weights," the royalties from this book will go toward a scholarship for training in CM with ANZAP.

Secondly, I want to thank our editor, Deborah Malmud, who had the imaginative realization that this book's companion—*A Dissociation Model of Borderline Personality Disorder*—needed a partner to describe the treatment method designed to overcome the core deficit of the borderline condition: a lack of cohesion of self. I also thank Allan Schore for his constant support. His seminal idea concerning a right-brain-to-right-brain entrainment in mother–baby interaction is a perfect fit with the Conversational Model. All the authors, particularly myself, wish to express our profound gratitude to Michelle Phillips, secretary to the Mental Health Sciences Centre, Cumberland Hospital, Sydney. Her patience, competence, and herculean labors in many directions were essential to the achievement of this publication.

BORDERLINE
PERSONALITY
DISORDER and the
CONVERSATIONAL
MODEL

Chapter 1

Introduction

Russell Meares

NOT SO LONG AGO, the diagnosis of borderline personality disorder (BPD) was one of despair, bringing with it the implication that the condition was intractable and untreatable. A series of reports, however, of the outcome of various forms of specific treatments, appearing first in the early 1990s (Linehan, Armstrong, Suarez, Allman, & Heard, 1991; Stevenson & Meares, 1992), suggested otherwise. These findings, together with evidence (also accruing during this period) of the severe morbidity associated with BPD—its high suicide rate, its effect upon the families of patients, and the heavy burden it placed on the health system—have led to the establishment of specialized programs for BPD in many countries.

The health professionals involved in such programs are varied in their training and their experience in dealing with BPD. This book is written as a practical guide to be of relevance for this whole group, ranging from the consultant psychiatrist with a career specialization in working with BPD to those who are about to enter the field, perhaps with some trepidation, say, as a community nurse or trainee psychiatrist. Because of this intended broad audience, we have tried to write relatively clearly and simply about a complex and difficult condition. There is little use of technical language, and references are kept to a minimum here; however, they can be found in abundance in the companion volume to this, *A Dissociation Model of Borderline Personality Disorder* (Meares, 2012), which, together with Hobson (1985) and my earlier works (Meares, 2000a, 2005), make up the essential background to this guide. My two previous volumes (2000a, 2005) explore the experience of BPD, its dynamics, and its developmental basis. The references given in this present guide are limited to those that, in the main, allow some elaboration of the ideas expressed in these earlier texts.

LACK OF COHESION: THE CENTRAL DEFICIT OF BPD

At present, as authoritatively noted by Leichsenring and colleagues (Leichsenring, Leibing, Kruse, New, & Leweke, 2011), further studies are required before one particular therapeutic approach to BPD can be considered preferable. Evolution toward a more effective means of treating BPD will involve a focus upon what is found to be the primary disturbance that brings forth its manifestations. A logically constructed system of treatment must be based on data concerning this central deficit and directed toward its rectification. The Conversational Model (CM) is such a treatment.

In the parallel text (Meares, 2012), it is argued, using a variety of evidential sources (including our own), that the primary disturbance in BPD is a failure of cohesion of the sense of self, and that this disconnectedness among the elements of psychic life is a reflection of a disconnectedness, or lack of coordination, between areas of brain function that usually operate together. This disconnectedness of brain–mind function is associated with neurophysiological evidence of relative failure in higher-order inhibitory function (Meares, 2012, Chapter 4; Meares et al., 2005). It is related to underactivity of cortical midline structures, notably the prefrontal orbitofrontal cortex and anterior cingulate.

The second part of the argument concerns the way in which lack of cohesion is overcome. Its basis is developmental and dependent on the idea that the first forms of the cohesion of personal existing are found in early life in particular kinds of interplay between the child and his or her caregivers, exemplified by "protoconversation" and "symbolic play," which are briefly described in a later section.

BPD is largely identified by affect and impulse dysregulation. Five of the nine diagnostic criteria in the *Diagnostic and Statistical Manual of Mental Disorders—Fourth Edition* (DSM-IV; American Psychiatric Association, 1994) refer to these behaviors, either directly or indirectly. This group of behaviors is currently conceived by many authorities to compose the core of the disorder and to be its primary source of disturbance. When, however, the outcome of the grouped features of dysregulation is compared with the outcome of the three criteria making up the so-called *self-triad*—a nebulous sense of self/identity, emptiness, and intolerance of alone-ness—the latter grouping is relatively enduring, unless treated by specifically de-signed therapy, whereas the former grouping (related to dysregulation) improves (Meares, 2012, Chapter 3; Meares, Gerull, Stevenson, & Korner, 2011). Since endurance is the cardinal feature of personality disorder, it is inferred that this grouping, which can be understood as reflecting disturbances of self experience, is primary and that, to a large extent, dysregulation is secondary to it. In short, as cohesion increases, dysregulation wanes.

It is assumed that dissociation is part of the self-disturbance grouping of DSM criteria. The self *is* a coordination; dissociation is its opposite (Meares, 2012, Chap-ter 7). It is proposed that this state, in varying and fluctuating degrees, is the core of the borderline condition.

OUTCOME STUDIES ON BPD AND THE CONVERSATIONAL MODEL

Advocacy of a particular treatment must depend upon suitable evidence and the effectiveness of that therapy. For this reason, it is worthwhile spending some time on an account of our outcome studies, which give us confidence that CM is at least as effective as other methods of treating BPD that are currently employed.

The first outcome study arose out of a training program, established in 1983 at Westmead Hospital, Sydney, for the treatment of patients with borderline condi-tions. In order to judge whether the trainee therapists were able to deliver effec-tive therapy, the training system was also set up as a research project, in which Janine Stevenson (J.S.) was the research psychiatrist. The methods involved are described in detail in our publication (Stevenson & Meares, 1992) and are not repeated here. One issue only is considered: the problem of the comparison group.

The patients entering the study were severely ill. One, for example, had un-dergone over 30 hospital admissions, often for extended stays. We had planned to make as a comparison group a cohort of patients being treated by object-relations-oriented therapists. This group, however, withdrew from the study. We therefore had to devise an alternative comparison, and we decided to make the patients their own controls. This method was based on the common idea at the time that BPD was an intractable condition unlikely to change over a 3-year pe-riod. The study became a 3-year one, in which 1 year was devoted to the treatment, and the year before the treatment was compared with the year after the treatment in terms of a "morbidity budget" consisting of the following:

- An inventory of behavioral measures that included amount of time away from work (in months)
- Use of medical facilities (number of outpatient visits to a medical facility each month)
- Quantity of drugs (prescribed and illegal) used on a daily basis
- Self-destructive behavior and outwardly directed violence (number of episodes over a 12-month period)
- Number of hospital admissions and time spent as an inpatient (in months)

Information was obtained from the patient, friends or relatives, medical records, and referral sources. Such methodology reduces errors that may be inherent in patients' own reports. All assessments were performed by the research psychiatrist (J.S.), who was not involved in the therapy process.

The differences in these behaviors in the year following treatment compared with the year before were highly significant. The number of episodes of self-harm, for example, dropped to less than a quarter of their previous occurrence; violence dropped nearly the same amount; drugs, both prescribed and illicit, were used at only 13% of the previous rate; and time away from work fell by two-thirds. We also compared a score (comprising DSM features) at the end of the year's treatment to the score at the beginning. Once again, the change was highly significant ($p < .001$).

When we submitted the paper to the *American Journal of Psychiatry* in 1990 we believed, as stated in the article, that this report described "the first prospective study of its kind." The beneficial effect of the treatment, involving 2 hours of outpatient therapy per week, seemed remarkable at the time. Certain assessors of the paper found it hard to accept the data presented to them because the findings were at odds with the prevailing belief in the intractability of BPD.

The paper was published, after a delay, in 1992. In the meantime Marsha Linehan and her colleagues (1991) published data showing that episodes of parasuicide significantly fell during a year of dialectical behavior therapy (DBT), which was designed specifically for chronically parasuicidal patients. The two forms of treatment have very different theoretical bases and a different therapeutic approach, yet there are certain commonalities between them, particularly in the management of what I understand to be the intrusion of unconscious traumatic memory.

The study attracted some attention in the years following its report. Our comparison method, however, was generally disregarded and the study taken to be a simple "before and after" study, whereas only the DSM index was used in this way. Nevertheless, another comparison method fortuitously became available. The clinic, which was the only one in the state, had developed a waiting list, and some patients had had to wait for over a year before being admitted to the program. These patients were continuing in treatment with their referring practitioners. This group of "treatment as usual" (TAU) patients were compared with our CM treatment cohort. The condition of the patients in the TAU group was slightly, but not significantly, less severe than the condition of those in the CM cohort, and they were demographically indistinguishable. Their condition changed very little over a year (Meares, Stevenson, & Comerford, 1999).

The publication of the findings concerning a control group helped secure initiatives to achieve greater governmental support for the treatment of BPD and related conditions. Health administrators, however, objected that replication of our program would be too expensive. Accordingly, we published preliminary data showing that our treatment saved the health system about $8,000 per patient (Stevenson & Meares, 1999). This study, however, was not ideal in that we ourselves conducted it. By means of a grant, a team of health economists from Sydney University, operating at "arms length" from us, conducted a more detailed study. Even greater savings were demonstrated—about $18,000 per patient (Hall, Caleo, Stevenson, & Meares, 2001).

Meanwhile our control data were criticized on the grounds that the TAU group was not contemporaneous, nor was it randomly selected. In reply, a replication study was mounted. Once again, the CM group changed very significantly over a year of treatment while the condition of the contemporaneous TAU group did not alter. The amount of improvement in the CM group was very similar to the change in the first study (Korner, Gerull, Meares, & Stevenson, 2006).

The TAU group was not selected by standard methods of randomization, such as a random numbers sheet, because that approach was not strictly possible. However, we did use a "naturalistic" method of randomization that produced a sample that could not be distinguished from the CM group on clinical or demographic grounds by basing patients' inclusion in this group upon the chance event of a therapist being available at the clinic. We had no evidence of a selection bias causing the CM group to be easier to treat than the TAU patients. The naturalistic method, then, achieved the outcome that is the objective of standard randomization methods.

Our reasons for not employing a formal randomizing procedure were both practical and ethical. Since we were functioning at a hospital clinic, not as a research unit, it was unacceptable to the administration to turn away patients when a therapist was available. It was also impractical, since the clinic was also a training program that required therapists to be actively engaged in therapy. Finally, it was unacceptable on ethical grounds since we had good reason to suppose that the CM was superior to TAU.

The replication study was published in several parts. It included a consideration of Cloniger's (1987) Harm Avoidance Scale, whose scores, we believed, might reflect the activity of unconscious traumatic memory. The level of harm avoidance was found to be high in BPD but to fall following treatment by means of CM (Korner et al., 2006).

Another aspect of the replication study focused on length of treatment. We were concerned that our outcome evidence about the effect of 1 year's treatment might give grounds for limiting treatments to this length when there was no evidence to suggest that this duration was optimal. Accordingly, 1 year of treatment was compared with 2. It was found that the same gradient of change shown during the first year of treatment was continued into the second year. However, in those patients for whom treatment had ceased after 1 year, the severity of BPD, as indicated by DSM features and as computed by our scale, remained on a plateau, persisting at the level achieved after 1 year of treatment (Korner, Gerull, Meares, & Stevenson, 2008).

A third aspect of the replication study concerned depression. Linehan and her colleagues (1991) had found that her patients, after receiving a year of DBT, did not change significantly in terms of "depression, hopelessness, suicidal ideation, or reasons for living" (p. 1064). We found, on the other hand, that depression scores changed significantly after a year's treatment with CM (Meares, Gerull, et al., 2011).

MAIN FEATURES OF THE TREATMENT APPROACH

The first sketch of the CM approach to BPD was given in our initial outcome paper. Although this outline has since been greatly elaborated, it is useful to reproduce here, since it provides a summary of the basic ideas that are expanded upon in the following chapters:

> The treatment approach is based on the notion that borderline personality disorder is a consequence of a disruption in the development of the self. The principal assumption is that a certain kind of mental activity, found in reverie and underlying symbolic play, is necessary to the generation of the self. This kind of mental activity is nonlinear, associative, and affect laden. In early life its presence depends on a sense of "union" with caregivers, in which they are experienced as extensions of the developing individual's subjective life (Piaget, 1959, p. 243). Development is disrupted through repeated "impingements" of the social environment, which have an impact on the child rather like that of a loud noise. This effect arises through actual stimuli (abuse of various kinds is common in the early lives of borderline patients), through high anxiety, and through responses that do not connect with the child's immediate reality and so seem to come from "outside."
>
> The aim of therapy is maturational. Specifically, it is to help the patient discover, elaborate, and represent a personal reality, i.e., a reality that relates to an inner life and has an affective core. (Stevenson & Meares, 1992, p. 358–359)

This passage contains several key ideas. Firstly, it implies that a particular kind of mental activity, which we characterize as "right-hemispheric," is deficient in patients with BPD, consistent with neurophysiological evidence that BPD may be a particularly right-hemispheric disorder (Meares, Schore, & Melkonian, 2011). This kind of mental activity is reflected in a form of language that the therapist seeks to foster with CM. Secondly, the therapist aims to develop a representational function of a particular kind that is discussed in some detail in later sections. I call these representations *analogical*. An *analogue* is a thing that resembles, but does not replicate, another thing. The first analogues that represent an individual's personal and immediate reality are those displayed in the mother's face and conveyed by her voice.

Thirdly, this passage implied that in BPD we are dealing with two main psychic dynamisms, one relating to self and the other to trauma. The aims of therapy are (1) to potentiate the emergence of self and (2) to integrate into the form of consciousness we call *self* those unconscious traumatic memory systems that repeatedly intrude into healthy mental function and, at times, overthrow it.

Nearly all forms of effective therapy for BPD approach the malignant intrusion of traumatic memory, usually without using this language. Traumatic memories, for example, are reflected in the concepts of maladaptive cognitions (Linehan et al., 1991), distorted transferences (Clarkin & Posner, 2005), and faulty schemata (Giesen-Bloo, 2006). No therapy, however, is directed toward that which we believe is the primary and fundamental disorder: that of self. We define *self* in an experiential and phenomenological way, according to William James (1890), and as a hierarchical organization of psychic life reflecting evolutionary history, as suggested by Hughlings Jackson (1958). The experience of self—the flow of thoughts, images, memories, sensations, feelings, imaginings, and so forth—was not born with us but develops during life. Its identifying feature is a reflective awareness of inner events (James, 1892). *Reflection*, however, is not the same as *self*; it arises out of self, as Jackson pointed out (see Meares, 2012, Chapters 4 & 6). Reflection is the outcome of an increased cohesion, or coordination, to use Jackson's word, of psychic life.

POTENTIATION OF THE "NONSPECIFIC EFFECT"

The developmental emergence of the cohesion of self depends, we believe, on a particular style of conversation that caregivers naturally adopt as part of our biological heritage. Like any phylogenetically given propensity, it is not equally distributed. Some people are very good at this conversation. It is this group of people, I am suggesting, who provide the powerful "nonspecific" effect demonstrated in numerous studies and psychotherapeutic outcomes. It has long been known that particular therapists achieve good therapeutic outcomes regardless of the mode of therapy used (Beutler, Machado, & Neufeldt, 1994). Moreover, these effects often outweigh the "specific" effect of the particular strategies used in a mode of therapy. CM might be seen as a model of therapy in which the therapist has been trained to develop, refine, and enhance a natural capability by potentiating the so-called *nonspecific* effect. The process might be akin to training an individual to hit a ball with a stick, which anyone can do, compared with the skill of a champion golfer, which depends upon more than a natural ability. Training is necessary in honing what is given to us as part of evolution. A systematic approach to the potentiation of self experience, in addition to a second focus upon the integration of traumatic memory, provides an extra dimension to the care of those with BPD not, in the main, encompassed by other therapeutic approaches. It may be that this primary focus makes CM more powerful than therapies lacking this dimension. As yet, evidence necessary to support this hypothesis has not been generated. It may be significant, however, that 2 hours of outpatient CM therapy per week produces for those with BPD beneficial changes, which seem to be much the same as those effected by greater amounts of therapeutic time. In DBT, for example, 3½ hours per week per patient are required.

Since the therapy described in this book seems "natural," many people reading it will say to themselves, "But I do that already!" That is the point of CM. It seems natural because it *is* natural, in a highly disciplined and attentive way. The word *conversation* implies this naturalness. It is not like a *dialogue*, for example. It is conducted in ordinary vernacular, avoiding the stilted or formulaic. This style of conversing, we believe, may contribute to CM's more ready acceptance by patients with BPD who are often resistant to, or even contemptuous of, attempts at treatment.

ORGANIZATION OF THE BOOK

This introductory chapter is followed by a chapter dealing with the theoretical bases of CM. Chapter 3 very briefly touches upon some key aspects of the language that is used in the therapeutic conversation.

In Chapter 4, in order to give a sense of the feeling and flavor of CM, a 2-year treatment is described in which a therapist works with her first patient with BPD: a woman severely disabled by her condition, repeatedly hospitalized after suicide attempts, and despairing of her particular health-care system. Over the 2-year period, a transformation is effected.

In the fifth chapter the general characteristics of a coordinated system of mental health care for dealing with BPD is described. Although in many cases of BPD a single therapist is involved, in the more severe cases a number of facilities and health professionals are caught up in the patient's illness. Effective management of this network is an important element in the total therapeutic approach.

Chapters 6 and 7 deal with the "nuts and bolts" of the CM approach. First, general principles are described, and then particular issues and situations are briefly considered. The account in both cases is not exhaustive but touches upon the more significant aspects of the therapeutic conversation.

In the last chapter, the team of linguists that has been working with us to develop CM gives a short account of an approach to the study of mental process that moves beyond, but complements, such research instruments as neuroimaging. Although we cannot view psychic life, the way words are used gives us a window through which we can "see into" the mind.

An appendix follows with a suggested adherence scale that we hope will be useful both to practitioners and to those undertaking future research.

THE PROBLEM WITH A MANUAL

It may be asked, since CM has been used as a form of treatment for BPD for some 30 years, why this manual, or practical guide, has taken so long to produce. The answer is that, whereas particular therapeutic strategies and maneuvers are relatively easy to describe, it is extremely difficult to characterize the crucial form of conversation that I call *analogical relatedness* because in no case is it the same. Every conversational dyad creates its own unique "culture" and its own language. Two previous, monumental efforts to encapsulate the nature of this kind of conversation failed.

It will be apparent to the reader of this guide that feeling tones and how they arise in particular forms of relatedness are of major significance in the CM approach. "Meanings," out of which comes the valuation of personal experience, frequently arise in these shifts in mood and emotion. Conversations are not merely made of words and their literal meanings. Their subtleties and complexities cannot be properly encompassed in a written work. We hope that these chapters will be read with this caveat in mind.

Finally, in this kind of account there is also a danger of creating a sense of fixity. CM is not a closed but an open theory, evolving on the basis of new data generated in such fields as neurophysiology, child development, linguistics, memory research, trauma studies, and, most important, accounts of personal experience, coming not only from the clinical setting but also from expressions found in art, literature, and philosophy.

Chapter 2

Basis of the Conversational Model

Russell Meares

IN THIS CHAPTER I describe how the Conversational Model (CM) was developed as a way of treating people suffering from mental illnesses that seemed intractable and which could not be effectively treated by standard methods. Many of these people would now be called *borderline*. This chapter outlines a theory of how the condition is to be understood.

EARLY BACKGROUND

The project began in the 1960s, pioneered by the late Robert Hobson (1920–1999) who had set up a ward at the Bethlem Royal Hospital, London, devoted to the care of these patients. I joined him during this time.

I had been inspired to consider a career focused on the care of this group of people by the story of a young woman, given the name of "Jennifer," who had a severe psychotic illness involving hallucinatory phenomena. Her illness was diagnosed as schizophrenia and did not respond to any of the treatments available at that time, the 1950s. The story was told by my father, Ainslie Meares (1958), her psychiatrist/therapist. In retrospect, it seems that she may have been suffering from borderline personality disorder (BPD), a condition that was unrecognized in those days. She had a history of sexual abuse, consistent with the background of those suffering from BPD.

Jennifer recovered from her illness after about 7 years of treatment. Therapy was difficult at first because she was terrified and almost mute. One day she brought a painting to the session, out of which developed a conversation between her and my father. This was followed by a series of paintings. The conversation that evolved was of a particular kind. My father seemed to be simply trying to understand what was being conveyed to him. Specifically, he made no psycho-analytic interpretations, despite the urgings of his colleagues to whom he presented her case.

Jennifer's remarkable recovery, together with some similar experiences with other patients, led my father to write a paper, published in *The Lancet* (Meares, 1961), in which he suggested that in these cases the therapeutic effect was achieved by the therapist's capacity for "understanding." He believed that interpretation directed at insight had little to do with it. This article seemed to have little influence, and my father did not continue this line of work, as his interests turned to the introduction of meditation as a mode of psychiatric treatment (Meares, 1967). Although I could not have imagined it at the time, however, the story of Jennifer contained the first seeds of my contribution to the development of CM.

In 1962, when I came to my first posting in psychiatry in Melbourne, the first patient I was given would now be diagnosed as *borderline*. I realized that she was given to me because nobody else wanted her. Without seeming to do very much, she preoccupied the nursing staff, in a negative way. I became aware that her diagnosis was a mystery. I was supervised by a Tavistock-trained Kleinian at that time. The theory in which I was instructed was intriguing, but I could gain no guidance from my supervisor about a therapeutic approach. Neither could I gain guidance from any other staff member. The principal aim in the patient's management was to achieve her discharge.

I was lucky in my consultant, Dr. Ron Kingston. He understood the direction of my interests, which was to gain skills in a form of psychotherapy involving the notion of unconscious mechanisms but different from those forms of treatment governed by the prevailing orthodoxies of the time. He suggested that, if possible, I should try to work with Robert Hobson.

I started work with Hobson in 1965. His outstanding characteristics were his warmth and humanity, and his personality, interests, and background are reflected in CM. His aim was to develop a "humanistic" therapeutic approach that went beyond the limitations of "a positivist, mechanistic, atomistic view of human behaviour" (Hobson, 1985, p. 228).

One of my first patients was a prickly, intermittently aggressive young man, who I sensed had great promise, even though we were not getting anywhere.

Despite the copious and meticulous process notes I presented to him, I could not convey to Bob the essence of what was going on between me and my cantankerous patient, who seemed always on the verge of blowing up. I had come 12,000 miles and wanted to get something out of the experience. I asked Hobson to listen to audiotapes of my sessions. So this is what we did. Although we did not know it at the time, this was the beginning of the project to develop what Hobson later called the *Conversational Model* (Hobson, 1985).

We found the tapes fascinating. In the "minute particulars" of the therapeutic conversation (Hobson, 1985) could be found, in microscopic form, not only systems of destruction of the sense of personal being but also "moments of aliveness" that are the seeds of self. These minute particulars provided the experiential data that became the basis to the theory developed in the following decades, and which is outlined in this chapter. They are also the essential components of training programs in CM set up in the north of England by Hobson and in New Zealand and most states of Australia by me.

The project finally began in 1970 with a publisher's contract for Hobson as editor and myself as author. The outcome was a book giving a preliminary account of some features of the model, which were more fully developed in later publications (Meares, 1977). The essential idea is that the patients we were working with suffered, as their primary and fundamental disturbance, not symptoms, conflicts, and so forth, but a disruption and stunting of the ordinary experience of personal existing—of the ongoing flux of feelings, sensations, images, memories, and imaginings that we sense as uniquely our own and which William James called *self* (James, 1890). The second main idea is that self is not an isolated system. Rather, it is "part of a larger organism which includes the social environment" (Meares, 1977, p. 20). "The psyche and its world are interrelated, constantly nourishing and recreating each other" (p. 27). The psychic state of self arises through a form of relatedness that involves the feeling of a "fit" between psyche and world.

The kind of relatedness necessary to the experience of a fit is seen as one of "congruity between inner and outer," a state of "harmony" (pp. 54–55) that depends upon a "matching" system, reflected at its simplest and most fundamental level in the phenomenon of habituation. *Fit* is a state of well-being that is not merely psychic but felt in the totality of self experience, including the body. There is an enhancement of boundedness, rhythm, substantiality, and coherence (Meares, 1980), combined with a sense of "flow," a feeling of the movement of

William James's "stream of consciousness." It is an aspect of a form of relatedness that has paradoxical qualities. An enhanced sense of one's own experience and its boundedness is, at the same time, part of a feeling of at-oneness with another. It is a form of relatedness Hobson called "aloneness–togetherness" (Hobson, 1971, 1985). I have used the term *intimacy* to describe this kind of relatedness. Intimacy is understood, in this context, as a technical term referring to an interplay between people involving the exchange of "inner" experience—that is, thoughts, feelings, imaginings, and so forth that are usually regarded as part of "private" experience. This kind of conversation can be compared with another kind of interplay, which might be called *dialogue*, in the context of public events.

There is a contrasting psychic state in which self is lost, a condition of "non-being" (Meares, 1977, p. 55) in which there is a disconnection between self and other, between inner and outer, such that *fit* is lacking. The experience of boundedness is one of diminishment and contraction. The perceived density of the body is attenuated, such that substantiality is lost. There is a sense of having nothing inside, of nothing happening, of unease, of boredom; there is an absence of well-being, and the feeling of flow is gone. The form of relatedness in which this condition is found is paradoxical in the opposite way to that in which self arises. There is a coexisting fusion and disconnection or alienation (Meares, 1980, 1984). It is apparent that this latter state resembles that of BPD, in which chronic dysphoric feelings of emptiness and boredom prevail, and the "broken-upness" and disconnection of psychic life are aspects of a persisting and subtle disconnectedness in ordinary relationships. Intimacy is not achieved.

These observations lead to an inference of major importance: *The therapeutic approach to BPD must be relational.* In order to bring about a change in those with BPD in which the elements of selfhood begin to appear in psychic life, the aim will be to transform a persisting form of relatedness, characterized by fusion and disconnection, or alienation, into one of aloneness–togetherness. Hobson proposed such an objective in a paper that launched the CM project and in which he announced the hope for a "testable model of psychotherapy." He wrote: "Much of the work of psychotherapy is concerned with establishing the state of aloneness–togetherness, by resolution of an 'idealized' fantasy of fusion which goes together with social isolation" (Hobson, 1971, p. 97). These early ideas provided the essential basis of the Conversational Model.

THE ESSENTIAL PRINCIPLES OF THE CONVERSATIONAL MODEL FOR BPD

- The central disturbance of BPD is an inadequate development of the experience of self.
- Self is abstraction. As a form of consciousness it cannot stand alone as an isolated entity.
- Self always arises from a particular activity of the brain.
- A brain is also an abstraction. There is no such thing as a brain, standing alone as an isolated entity, unless it is a dead brain.
- A brain is always in an interplay with the total sensory environment, the most important part of which, in terms of BPD, is the social environment.
- This interplay creates a brain state that is the origin of a particular state of mind or consciousness.
- Each interplay, or form of relatedness, is then an aspect of a state of consciousness. It not only manifests but also constitutes a form of consciousness; for example, the relatedness of fusion and disconnection both manifests and constitutes the psychic state of dissociation.
- Each form of relatedness/form of consciousness involves a feeling.
- The components of this system of interplay—the form of consciousness, the feeling, the form of relatedness, the brain state—can be seen as a kind of ecology.
- Any change in one of these components causes all the others to change; conversely, one component cannot change unless the other components also alter.
- In working with BPD, therapeutic transformation of the characteristic state of mind depends upon a relationship.
- It is the form of relatedness that changes the form of consciousness.
- Since the main disturbance of BPD is seen as disconnectedness among the elements of psychic life (Meares, 2012), the therapeutic form of relatedness must involve, as its central characteristic, the feeling of connection between the therapeutic partners.
- A form of relatedness is conducted by means of conversation.
- Each form of relatedness is conducted by means of a particular form of conversation.
- The therapeutic aim in treating BPD is to transform one kind of conversation, which is characteristic of BPD and that both constitutes and manifests intrapsychic and interpersonal fusion and disconnectedness (Meares, 2012, Chapter 8),

into another kind of conversation involving interpersonal connectedness and a feeling of personal cohesion.

This line of reasoning makes evident why the Conversational Model has been given such a name, which those who first hear it often consider banal and too "ordinary" for the exalted practice of psychotherapy, conceived as a skilled technical operation. However, the name is precise. The essential proposal is that the experience of self arises in the context of a specific kind of conversation. As Hobson put it: "I can only find myself in and between me and my fellows in human conversation" (Hobson, 1985, p. 135). An old definition of the word *conversation*, provided by the Oxford English Dictionary (O.E.D.), is: "The action of living or having one's being *in* a place or *among* persons."

An interchange of words that induces the feeling of connection, or fit, is not adequately described by terms such as *dialogue* or *discourse*. The requisite language must be familiar, and have the sense that it is one's own speech, and not the language of others. Conversation, then, is "ordinary" and includes the vernacular. It is "familiar discourse" (O.E.D.) and has associations with that zone of experience we call intimate—that is, relating to that which is inner.

LATER DEVELOPMENTS IN THE CONVERSATIONAL MODEL

Although the foundation of the model was in place by the 1970s, there was a great deal of work still necessary to the building of a scientific theory of psychotherapy and more specifically, a theory of treatment relating to BPD.

A main issue to address was the role of trauma. I had suggested that at the core of individual existing there are threads of ideas, images, memories, imaginings, and so forth, which are sensed as intensely personal and to which a special feeling is attached that gives them value (Meares, 1976, 1995). William James described this area of psychic life in the following way: "If the stream as a whole is identified with the self far more than any outward thing, a *certain portion of the stream abstracted from the rest* is so identified in an altogether peculiar degree, and is felt by all men as a sort of innermost centre within the circle, the sanctuary with the citadel, constituted by the subjective life as a whole" (James, 1890, I, p. 297, italics in original).

The word *sanctuary* implies a certain feeling of value and also an area kept safe. Not everyone is allowed entry into this domain. To expose it is to risk damage, akin to physical hurt, through a response of others that is devaluing in some way. Some of these responses may be shaming and humiliating; some may involve mockery and ridicule. Other responses may not appear to an observer to be hurtful—for example, an absence of response or one that is inadvertently devaluing. Hobson and I pointed out that harm is inadvertently inflicted on vulnerable people by the use of orthodox therapeutic practices current at that time (Meares & Hobson, 1977). We built our story around a particularly pertinent statement of William James's: "Thoughts connected as we feel them to be connected are *what we mean* by personal selves. The worst a psychology can do is so to interpret the nature of these selves as to rob them of their *worth*" (James, 1892, pp. 153–154, italics in original).

The effect of trauma on the development of self is a second main therapeutic focus of CM, in addition to the theme of self. Two forces can be seen as dominating the therapeutic conversation, one positive and the other negative. The first is toward well-being, health, and the sense of selfhood. The second is traumatic and destructive, intruding into or overthrowing the emergent self, its effect coming through the repeated triggering of systems of memory, both conscious and unconscious, relating to relational trauma.

The task confronting us in order to develop CM as a scientific theory of treatment included, firstly, the need to define self and to understand how it develops and, secondly, to explore and differentiate the features of systems of traumatic memory. These two main themes are discussed in the following sections.

The development of CM was impeded by the "tyranny of distance." By the beginning of the 1970s I had returned to Australia. Hobson also returned to his roots, taking up a readership at Manchester University. Progress now followed two different courses.

In the north of England an abbreviated form of CM was used in relatively brief therapies involving, at first, depression and later, psychosomatic illness and chronic clinic attendees. This form of therapy was manualized as psychodynamic interpersonal therapy. Hobson's colleagues—David Goldberg, Else Guthrie, David Shapiro, and Frank Margison—were the leading figures in this initiative. A series of outcome measures validated the effectiveness of this approach (Barkham et al., 1996; Guthrie, Creed, Dawson, & Tomenson, 1991; Guthrie et al., 1999, 2001;

Hamilton et al., 2000; Shapiro & Firth, 1987; Shapiro et al., 1995). These studies can be seen as evidence of the effectiveness of a version of CM that is complementary to our own.

Definition of the Self System

Since it is proposed that failure of cohesion of self is the central deficit in BPD, it is necessary, in building an approach to this deficit that has a scientific basis, to begin with a definition of this experience. No adequate definition, however, was available to us in the psychological sciences. The two figures most associated with the concept of self in the 20th century, Jung and Kohut, found themselves unable to define it. Toward the end of his life, Jung likened his quest for its nature to "a circumambulation of unknown factors" (1953, p. 1165). Kohut noted that he had never defined self, that it was "unknowable" (Kohut, 1977, p. 311).

Although there can be no all-encompassing definition of *self*, we need to have a meaning for this word that has pragmatic truth, is useful, and enables us to chart the development of it and to follow its waxings and wanings in the therapeutic situation. A useful definition is one that can be operationally defined.

John Hughlings Jackson (1835–1911), called the father of British neurology, was the first person in English language medical literature to use the word *self* and also, most importantly, to build a neural model of its nature and origins. He approached this enterprise by pointing out that a scientific study of mental illness must begin with what is meant by *mind* or *self*. His definition of this construct is useful in that it is clear. First, self is identified by a reflective awareness of inner events, the capacity for introspection. He called this state "object consciousness." It is a capacity analogous to seeing an object in the material world. Introspection, then, becomes a marker of self. The appearance of autobiographical memory (Nelson, 1992), and an awareness of the concept of secrecy (Meares & Orlay, 1988) in child development around the age of 4, signals the emergence of self.

Although introspection, literally meaning "looking within," as if with the eyes of the mind, identifies self, it is not self per se. *Self* is a continuing, and therefore cohesive, background experience, an ongoing matrix of mind. Jackson called this matrix "subject consciousness." The second feature of this definition of self is that it is "double": "Subject consciousness" always goes with "object consciousness." Each is half of the other. Subject consciousness, he said, is symbolized by the pronoun *I*.

Jackson's skeletal model of self (Meares, 2012, Chapters 4 & 6) needs elaboration in order to be more clinically useful. William James adds flesh to the bare bones of Jackson's outline. James had corresponded with Jackson, met him, and quoted him in his major work of 1890. James too has a concept of self that is double, called the "duplex self," "partly known and partly knower, partly object and partly subject." He called the "knower" the I, as Jackson had done (James, 1892, p. 176). (The Jacksonian "I," however, is more complex [Meares, 2012]). James also spoke of the characteristic ongoingiyess of self, introducing the term "stream of consciousness."

James added a number of features to the core description of self. Of great significance is the feeling associated with the movements of inner life that involve the sense of aliveness, of vitality. This sense is allied to a feeling of well-being, a background tone of positive affect of which we are not always consciously aware. James found within it the qualities of "warmth and intimacy."

Using James's description, we can identify at least twelve main characteristic of self, as noted in Table 2.1. The list is not exhaustive. Each of these features can be operationally defined in linguistic terms.

The Jackson–James definition is by no means perfect. First, it does not encompass the idea set out in the "Essential Principles" section that self is always part of a form of relatedness. This point is briefly addressed in the following section.

A second difficulty of the Jackson–James definition is that it does not distinguish self from the current concept of identity. Neither, it might be said, does DSM-IV. The distinction, however, is necessary. In simplest terms, the distinction between *identity* and *self* can be seen as the difference between the individual's public reality and private experience. In ordinary healthy living, self and identity are seamlessly connected. Janus-like, they metaphorically face in opposite direc-

---

TABLE 2.1. Main Characteristics of the Jamesian Self

1. Duality (i.e., reflective awareness)	8. Spatiality
2. Movement (sense of vitality)	9. Content beyond immediate present
3. Positive feeling (warmth & intimacy)	(i.e., of the possible, the imagined,
4. Nonlinearity	the remembered)
5. Coherence	10. Ownership
6. Continuity	11. Boundedness
7. Temporality	12. Agency

---

tions. Identity concerns the individual's relationship with his or her world and involves a sense of place within family, profession, religion, and other social groups. Identity is composed of roles, personal attributes, and conceptions of who one is in relation to others. Self, as William James described it, is categorically different. It is that flux of images, sensations, feelings, memories, imaginings, and so forth, which James likened to a stream. Here the focus is inward. The cardinal feature of self is a reflective awareness of inner events. The reflective process, James wrote, enables us "to think of ourselves as thinkers" (1890, I, p. 296). It brings with it a conception of "innerness" from which we derive a realization that certain experiences are uniquely our own.

The self aspect of the self–identity complex might be the more fundamental. The philosopher Owen Flanagan, for example, states that "the senses of identity, direction, agency and life plan are all grounded in the memorable connections of the stream" (Flanagan, 1992, pp. 166–167).

Development of Self: The Metaphor of Play

The principal aim of treatment of BPD is to facilitate the emergence of self. *It is assumed that the way in which self develops in normal development is the way in which it will develop during therapy.* This is not to say, of course, that the developmental activities are replicated. Therapy is not a case of re-mothering. Rather, *the same principles that are operative in bringing about the appearance of self during childhood are applied during therapy.*

The essential aspects of the activity of the therapist during therapy are derived by following the postulate of Vygotsky (van der Veer & Valsiner, 1988), which he took from Janet and Baldwin: Those functions that we in adult life sense as inner had their first forms in the outer world as activities. The first form of the experience of selfhood, then, is an activity going on between two people. The Conversational Model is based on the idea that this activity is a particular form of conversation.

The main characteristics of self, are:

1. Doubleness or duality
2. Positive feeling
3. Nonlinear movement
4. Cohesion

How do these features of self appear in their first forms during childhood? The answer is that they are activated during particular kinds of play during which the mother (or other caregiver) plays as if she were a double, or alter ego, of the child. *The first kind of duality of consciousness, then, is one in which the mothering figure is the other pole of this dualism.*

The evolution of the development of self is shown most saliently in two particular forms of play. The first is the protoconversation, which is established by 2–3 months, (Trevarthen, 1974), and the second is symbolic play, which arises at about the same time as verbal language, in the second year of life. Both are performed in a state of positive feeling and in both the movements of the activity are nonlinear.

Something of the mother's characteristic behavior during the protoconversation is illustrated by a story recounted in #10 of Chapter 6. This is a game played by mother and child. It is a to-and-fro interplay between them, face to face, in which the language used is largely preverbal, and the conversation is conducted by means of the vocal inflections and tones and by facial expressions. In addition, of course, the mother uses simple verbal utterances. The reciprocity of this interplay resembles, in reduced form, that of mature conversation.

In this game, the mother (the word *mother* is used as a shorthand for all caregivers who play the game) makes responses that correspond to, but do not replicate, her baby's expression. Rather, she represents that expression; her response is a *re-semblance*. Winnicott (1971) noted that the mother's face is like a mirror for her baby. The contours of her voice and her facial expression show the "shape" of the baby's experience at that moment.

The mother's response, however, is not "mirroring." It shows *more* than what the baby has expressed. She amplifies it, as indicated in #10 of Chapter 6. At the same time her response is finely linked, or coupled, to the baby's experience. It shows a high degree of connectedness between them.

The "shaping" response of the mother during symbolic play is different from her behavior when the baby is distressed (again exemplified in #10 of Chapter 6). In both cases, she uses empathy, but her behavior is distinctly different, and the outcome is different. *The protoconversation is generative of well-being.* It may begin in a neutral state or with faint interest in something in the surroundings that the child displays. *The iterations of the play bring forth a state of pleasure that neither partner could have produced alone.* This state escalates during each cycle of engagement between mother and child, during which it can be shown that the mother's response, at each step in the cycle, is somewhat larger than her baby's expression (Penman, Meares, Baker, & Milgrom-Friedman, 1983). The protoconversation, then, not only begins in a state of mild positive affect but is also evocative of pleasure.

The outcome of a suitable response to distress, such as anxiety, is a somewhat different feeling-state: It is one of security. Both kinds of responsiveness facilitate the emergence of self. When, however, the mother neglects to respond often enough to the nondistressing activities of the child, the developmental trajectory toward the emergence of self is impeded. This trajectory includes symbolic play (Bornstein & Tamis Le Monda, 1997).

The three main activities of the mother during the protoconversation— "coupling," "amplification," and "representation"—are the elements of a self-organizing system. *Self* can be conceived as a single self-organizing system made of two parts: the subject and another. Iteration between these parts results in the emergence of a new kind of consciousness (Meares, 2000a) that has the form of doubleness—that is, reflective awareness of inner events. It has the qualities of cohesiveness, positive feeling, and fluid, play-like nonlinearity, a state that reflects the form of relatedness out of which it arose.

DOUBLING AND FELLOW FEELING

Doubling is a very approximate term to apply to the mother's behavior during the protoconversation, because it does not convey the essential affective component of her responsiveness. Nevertheless, it is useful in allowing us to chart the evolution of this behavior in development from its earliest point, when the mother plays a conversational game with her baby. She pretends that her newborn can understand her and reply to her. She, however, makes the reply, like a double, taking the part of the baby. This is a state of *sembling*, a prologue to her later *re-sembling* in the protoconversation. *Sembling* means "seeming"; it has an alternative meaning of pretending. By the end of the first year of life, the child has begun the game of pretend play, for example, via imitation.

Table 2.2 shows the progression of doubling from its first appearance at birth or soon after. Initially the double is external (in the form of the mother), and then progresses toward "internalization," toward the Jamesian "duplex self." The culmination of this process occurs sometime during the ages of 4, 5, or 6, after the child

Table 2.2. A Developmental Schema of "Doubling" in Play	
Birth	*Conversational Play*
	Mother doubles as the child
2–3 months	*Protoconversation*
	Mother as the other who is a double
10–12 months	*Imitation*
	Child now creates the double by means of the body
18 months–4 or 5 years	*Symbolic Play*
	Child creates an abstract or illusory double to whom he or she talks (condensation of experience of the other as double and projection of the child him- or herself)
4–5 years	*Inner Conversation*
	The double is now internal

discovers the experience of the stream of consciousness, and, as it were, a double-ness within. With the discovery of "innerness" comes an awareness that the other also has an innerness that may be different from one's own. Empathy appears.

The felt experience of the other in this emergence, and in therapy, is not that of doubleness. It is better described as "fellow feeling," as suggested by Hobson's somewhat gnomic condensation: "I can only find myself in and between me and my fellows in human conversation" (Hobson, 1985, p. 135). In this statement, *me* refers to who-one-is-in-the-world. It has those features by which one is known. This aspect of the person is usually referred to as *identity* and is to be distinguished from *I* and *myself*. It first appears during the second year of life when social emotions such as shame, guilt, and embarrassment emerge (Lewis, 1992). A sense of *myself* comes later.

A *fellow* is "one of a pair; the mate, marrow; a counterpart, match" (O.E.D). *Marrow* is "the inmost part; the vital part; the essence; the goodness" (O.E.D). These words convey something of the affective tone that "fellow feeling" implies. It is the outcome of a complex interplay between two people, in which there is felt a degree of connectedness or cohesion between them.

FROM DYAD TO TRIAD

The next major developmental scene after the protoconversation is that of symbolic play. It involves a conversation that is structurally similar to the protoconversation in that it can be seen as having right-hemispheric characteristics (see Chapter 3). It is spoken, however, by the child alone, as if the cohesion of the protoconversation has been, in part, "internalized"—as if the experience of "being with" the mother remains as part of the emergent self. The emergence is predicted by the mother's earlier responsiveness to her infant's states of nondistress, in which she institutes a protoconversation from time to time (Bornstein & Tamis Le Monda, 1997).

An example of symbolic play is beautifully described by Piaget (1959). It indicates the main elements of this kind of play. The child is chattering as he plays:

> What he says does not seem to him to be addressed to himself but is enveloped with the feeling of a presence, so that to speak of himself or to speak to his mother appear to him to be the same thing. His activity is thus bathed in an atmosphere of communion or synchronization; one might almost speak of "the life of union," to use the terms of mysticism, and this atmosphere excludes all consciousness of egocentrism. But, on the other hand, one cannot but be struck by the soliloquistic character of these same remarks. The child does not ask questions and expects no answer, neither does he attempt to give any definite information to his mother who is present. He does not ask himself whether she is listening or not. He speaks for himself just as an adult does when he speaks within himself. (p. 243)

This scene, together with that of the protoconversation, provides a metaphor that guides an approach to the development of self in BPD (Meares, 1993a). The sense of cohesion, "an atmosphere of communion" originally experienced in the protoconversation, is now, to a large extent, internalized. This experience—that one is not an isolate, that there remains a "presence," however unconscious, of another who is part of one's existence—is not given to those with BPD who feel a painful and even frightening isolation when alone.

Symbolic play also reflects the partial internalization of "doubleness," of the reflective capacity. The child plays as if alone, apparently oblivious of others, telling a story as he or she plays, using toys or other objects to represent elements of the story. Thought, then, is as if displayed on the living room floor, or wherever the child is playing. Gazing at the movements of "thought" in real space is the forerunner to the inner life of the adult in which images, memories, ideas, and so forth move in mind's eye and are "viewed" in virtual space.

Symbolic play displays other main features of selfhood. It goes on in a state of positive affect, without which it ceases. It also shows the capricious nonlinear form of the stream of consciousness.

The progression from the protoconversation to symbolic play can be seen as a shift from a structure of relatedness that is dyadic to one that is triadic. The change represents a movement between an attentional "cocoon" that contains two persons to one in which there is only a single person within it. This person, however, experiences the situation in a way that resembles the original cocoon experience. In this cocoon state, attention is directed inward, toward its center. Stimuli from the outer world are, to a relative extent, screened out of consciousness. This state is manifest in the first week of life, during feeding. When this is going on, the mother is able to block out, to a greater degree than usual, external noise. This is indicated by a faster habituation to meaningless tones than when her baby is not with her. At the same time, the baby's bodily state suggests enlivenment. Its heart rate rises (Meares & Horvath, 1974). During this early engagement the mother is intensely aware of the finest details of her baby's behavior, some of which will shape her view of what the baby will be like (Meares, Penman, Milgrom-Friedman, & Baker, 1982).

The mother's immersion in her baby's emotional experience continues into the complex "dance" of the protoconversation. In these earliest days, there is nothing more entrancing to the baby than the mother's face. Soon, however, the baby begins to take an interest in things in the environment, which include clothes, parts of bodies, and objects such as toys. This interest is strikingly heightened in the following months. We showed, for example, that in a situation where toys were placed between mother and baby, and when the mother was asked to behave naturally, only 12% of the baby's gaze was directed at the toys at 3 months, but when the baby reached 6 months, gazing at the toys had increased to 60% (Penman, Meares, & Milgrom-Friedman, 1981).

These aspects of the material world toward which the baby increasingly turns while being with the mother become the third part of a triadic relationship. The joint attention toward these things gives them a kind of "meaning." They are the beginning of a zone of creativity that is the basis of self. This creativity becomes clearly manifest in symbolic play, in which the third part has become a story that is being told by means of both objects and language. At the same time, the cocoon now contains only one person. The child's apparent sensory screening—his or her oblivion to those in the environment—indicates an embryonic inner focus. The child's language suggests that there is a feeling of being with another while in this notional cocoon. This "life of union," as Piaget put it, resembles the earlier state.

As the child chatters, telling her story to herself, she speaks as if someone else is there—for example, "Look! She can get up there, can't she!" The child seems to be talking to an illusory other who is both herself and someone else at the same time. This state can be understood as the outcome of a high degree of coherence shown between the baby and the caregiver in earlier stages of development. The kind of inner relatedness implied by the child's behavior during symbolic play is the precursor of more mature forms of "aloneness–togetherness."

The movement from a dyadic to a triadic structure in the therapeutic relationship is an important feature of the Conversational Model. In this kind of conversation, of course, the field of play is no longer in the world but inner, both *in* and *between* the therapeutic partners when there is a state of "fellow feeling" between them. The shared attention is directed at this space, which might be imagined as an invisible cinematic screen upon which both partners project what they are "seeing" of their joint experience. The experience, in the case of the therapist, is imagined. Empathy is used in order to help portray, with the patient, his or her nebulous and unrealized inner life (Meares, 1983). The language in this kind of conversation is technically impersonal in that it is directed toward the "screen" —for example, "It looks like . . . ," "it seems that. . . ." At the same time, the therapist's behavior is also impersonal in the way the mother's is during the protoconversation. Her own concerns are put aside in order to foster immersion in the experience of her baby.

ANALOGICAL RELATEDNESS AND TWO FORMS OF HUMAN LANGUAGE

Symbolic play, which provides one of the models for the kind of conversation that is generative of self, occupies only a small part of the child's day. Most of the time, the child is socially engaged. The two different behaviors and conversations are conducted by different kinds of language. Each reflects a particular kind of thought form that is based in a specific neurophysiology or brain state.

The language of social engagement is, in a broad sense, logical. It is communicative and so has a purpose. Since it is directed toward this purpose of communication and toward objects in the environment, it is linear in a broad and nontechnical sense. This language is adaptive, used for dealing with the outer world. It has long been known that this kind of language, involving "propositional speech" (Jackson, 1958), is dependent upon left-hemispheric function. The language associated with symbolic play is qualitatively different. Vygotsky (1962) has described it as nonlinear, associative, and apparently purposeless. There are good grounds for believing it has a right-hemispheric basis (see chapter 3). The language of symbolic play moves in a nonlogical, capricious way, and is, at times, so condensed that it cannot be understood—which led Vygotsky to conclude that its function is not communicative. Rather, I suggest, this nonlinear form of language is necessary for the representation, and the bringing into being, of self. The child engaged in symbolic play has taken on for him- or herself the representing role of the other. The contrasting qualities of the two language forms are shown in Table 2.3.

The representing that is going on during symbolic play is of a particular kind. Rather like the process of dreaming, the child's personal concerns, aspirations, imaginings, and so forth, are reflected in his or her products. Many of these are of no particular consequence, deriving merely from the day-to-day environment. Others, however, are of larger importance. The representational aspect is not a mere act of copying. It is an act of making an analogical representation.

An *analogue*, in the original meaning of the word (and as noted previously), is a thing that has a proportion or shape similar to another thing. During symbolic play the child is using analogical thought. For example, a drinking vessel lying on its side can become a rabbit burrow or a cave, with the shape of the glass resem-

Table 2.3. The Two Forms of Human Language

Inner Speech (Analogical)	Social Speech (Logical)
1. Nonlinear	1. Linear
2. Nongrammatical	2. Grammatical
3. Analogical, associative	3. Logical
4. Positive affect	4. Variable affect
5. Noncommunicative	5. Communicative
6. Inner-directed	6. Outer-directed
7. Intimate	7. Nonintimate
8. Self-related	8. Identity-related
9. Right-hemispheric	9. Left-hemispheric

bling, in the child's mind, the thing it represents. The small stories being told analogically are the atoms out of which that larger organism, the individual's own
symbolic "narrative of self," is eventually created. This process goes on, in a more
interior way, throughout life. In the earlier form of representing activity, the protoconversation, it is the mother who creates the analogue. She shows in her face
and in the contours of her voice, the shape of her baby's immediate experience.
What she exhibits is the baby's first analogue. The relationship between mother
and child at this point can be conceived as analogical. In symbolic play this analogical relatedness is partly internalized. It is a principal aim of the therapist in the
Conversational Model to find, in the bits and pieces of the other's experience, as
it is selected and recounted, a shape, an analogical resemblance, which gives it
coherence. An analogue is the primordial form of the symbol. Analogical linking
is the means toward the development of symbolic thought, which is so deficient
in BPD. *Analogical relatedness is the principal therapeutic agent in the treatment of BPD
by the Conversational Model.*

The kind of speech used in symbolic play disappears in the outer world between the ages of 4–6 because it is internalized and becomes "inner speech." In
adult life, the two main forms of language are found in pure form only in rare
circumstances. Inner speech is the basis of some forms of poetry. The linear form
of language, lacking symbolic qualities, is found in legal and political documents.

When an inner life is discovered at about the ages of 4–6, these two language
forms become coordinated and mingled. Most conversations now consist of social
speech in which is embedded the elements of the other—of inner speech. Increasing amounts of this latter language are associated with intimacy and also with that
form of dual consciousness we are calling *self*. Conversely, inner speech is lacking
in those whose development has been disrupted. The language of these individuals is linear, seeming to reflect a "stimulus entrapment" (Meares, 1993a, 1997). It
seems as if they are neurophysiologically unable to "turn off" the effect of stimuli
(Meares, Melkonian, Gordon, & Williams, 2005) such that the conversation has
the form of a "chronicle" (Meares, 1998).

This kind of conversation, which consists of a catalogue of external events as
they have impacted upon the subject, is characteristic of those deprived of that
form of relatedness that underpins the experience of self. In this state of relative
alienation, they are forced to orient toward the world rather than toward those
experiences that might become the basis of inner life.

TRAUMA: THE SECOND THERAPEUTIC FOCUS

The experience of self as it appears in the therapeutic conversation is, from time to time, overthrown by another form of consciousness that is more limited, adualistic, and of traumatic origin. This repetitive irruption blocks further development in the sphere of self. A second therapeutic aim is to identify these intrusions of traumatic memory in order to integrate them into the ordinary ongoing dualistic consciousness.

It is important to note that integration of this kind is only possible if the process of self is established. This establishment of the process of self, therefore, must be the primary aim of therapy. It will depend to a large extent on the therapist's imaginative and sensitive capacity to make, in a fluid and natural way, empathic representations of the patient's nebulous, half-glimpsed, but emergent inner states.

The traumatic impacts upon the self system, inflicted in the past, may affect any one or several of the various features of self—for example, the sense of agency, ownership, or boundedness. Perhaps, however, the most important impact is upon the central feeling of self, that positive tone that William James (1890) likened to "warmth and intimacy." This feeling gives "value," providing the individual with his or her sense of personal worth (Meares, 1999c). Damage to this central core by what might be called "attacks upon value" are among the more debilitating of cumulative traumata. They take various forms, including shaming, ridiculing, and simple invalidation. Devaluation is an aspect not only of emotional abuse but also of sexual and physical abuse.

Traumatic memory is a form of psychic life that is different from dualistic consciousness. It is anxiety-ridden and is underpinned by an alienated form of relationship. It is recorded in a memory system that is somewhere down a hierarchy of consciousness (Meares, 1995). This can be explained in terms of dissociation, in the following way.

Traumatic memory is an aspect of a personal and interpersonal system that is essentially dissociated. Dissociation is a controversial subject. Current evidence, however, suggests that it has two main and related forms, which I call primary and secondary dissociation (see Meares, 2012, Chapter 7, for a detailed discussion). *Primary dissociation* has the central characteristic of disconnection between elements of brain–mind functioning that usually operate together. *Secondary dis-*

sociation increases the disconnectedness of a particular constellation of brain–mind function from the remainder of consciousness, creating a "compartmentalization" of psychic life. The primary form of dissociation, a state of "fragmentation," is one of raised arousal. Secondary dissociation is associated with lowered arousal; the individual "zones out." The basic defect in BPD, as proposed in the dissociation model, is one of ongoing, subtle, primary dissociation—a fundamental disconnectedness that is not only intrapsychic but also interpersonal. This defect creates a vulnerability to the states of compartmentalization, to "splitting," and to secondary dissociation.

The theories of John Hughlings Jackson provide a framework by means of which primary dissociation can be understood. He put forward a view of the organization of the brain that predicts its manner of disintegration. He believed that the brain's organization is decreed by evolutionary history, proposing for it three notional "layers" that give rise to a hierarchy of consciousness. The idea of layers, or tiers, of evolutionary structure is a figurative one, since the central nervous system operates in a coordinated manner with all "layers" acting together.

The evolutionary trajectory, Jackson believed, is a consequence of increasing coordination between the elements of brain function, which he conceived as fundamentally sensori-motor. The brain, he thought, is a "sensorimotor co-ordinating machine . . . from top to bottom." The latest evolutionary development, the emergence of a peculiarly human consciousness, which he called "self," comes about not through the addition of a new kind of neural tissue to the brain but as a result of elaboration of existing structures, notably the prefrontal cortex. This elaboration allows greater coordination between areas of brain activity than was previously possible. *"Le moi,"* he said, quoting a French disciple, *"est une co-ordination"* (see Meares, 2012, Chapter 4).

The state of self, or higher-order consciousness, is one in which greater control can be exercised over psychic life. This enhancement has two different and related manifestations. First, the individual is able to gain voluntary access to personal memories in the distant past—that is, to autobiographical memory. Secondly, there is enhanced inhibitory control over earlier evolved aspects of brain function. This inhibitory enhancement not only allows finer emotion modulation but also better selective inattention.

Since some form of memory is part of every form of consciousness, noting the progressive development of memory in an individual life is helpful in illustrating

Jackson's hierarchy of consciousness, as shown in Table 2.4. This idea depends upon the assumption that ontogeny recapitulates phylogeny, at least approximately. Table 2.4 also notes the kind of relatedness that is an aspect of each level of consciousness, together with examples of the possible associated feelings. It is important to note that later higher levels in the hierarchy do not replace earlier or lower levels, but contain them.

Hughlings Jackson considered that an assault on the brain–mind system causes a retreat down the hierarchy of function decreed by evolutionary history. The first functions to be lost are those that evolved and developed most recently. Typically, traumatic memories are stored in the semantic system (Meares, 1995). More severe traumatic disorganization and an immature development of higher-order consciousness contribute to the production of sensory and motor memories.

Certain traumatic memories are beyond reflective awareness and, in this sense, are unconscious. When triggered, they are not known to be memories. Since the memory system that retrieves the original episodes of their occurrence is no longer operative, they cannot be accessed. When what is remembered is semantic, it concerns the perceived facts (the "cognitions," some might say) of the original trauma—for example, that one is deemed hopeless, stupid, ugly, and so forth by the other who is experienced as critical, cruel, controlling, and so forth. The result is a state of consciousness and personal existing that is less coordinated than what we might call "selfhood." What is remembered is relatively disintegrated and also

Table 2.4. Hierarchy of Consciousness

Forms of consciousness and memory	Age of Appearance	Forms of relatedness	Emotions
1. Reflective (autobiographical memory)	Four years	Intimacy, aloneness–togetherness	Reflective (e.g., nostalgia, grief)
2. Semantic (recall of facts)	End of first year	Affiliation	Social (e.g., shame, guilt, embarrassment)
3. Sensorimotor (procedural, perceptual representation)	Early (procedural) Birth (perceptual representation)	Attachment	Reactive (e.g., distress, anger, anxiety, joy)

constricted, since the range of voluntary access to memory is reduced. There is also a reduced capacity to regulate emotional expression (Meares, 1999a, 1999b).

This is the state of primary dissociation. Pierre Janet, the principal descriptor of dissociation, understood its origin in a way that was consistent with Jacksonian theory. His psychological insights, however, went beyond Jackson's neurological schema. He found that the assaults causing what Jackson called "dissolution"—that is, a retreat down the hierarchy of consciousness that evolution has ordained—included psychological assaults. He introduced the concept of cumulative traumas, pointing out the significance of a "succession of slight forgotten shocks" (Janet, 1924, p. 275).

INTRUSION OF UNCONSCIOUS TRAUMATIC MEMORY

The intrusion of the unconscious traumatic memory system into the therapeutic conversation is often shown by very slight changes that include a diminishment of self features and a relative loss of inner speech. They include (i) devitalization, (ii) a negative emotional tone, (iii) an outer orientation, (iv) a loss of reflective function, and (v) a linear thinking process. The change in the underlying form of relatedness is reflected in grammatical structure; questions might be asked, for example, so that a subject–object dichotomy becomes salient. At times, the change in the form of relatedness is the most prominent element of the shift. This involves more than a sense of disconnection and subtle alienation. The "facts" of the original traumatic situation dominate and determine the form of relatedness that now appears.

It is important to remember that the patient, who is now in the grip of those feelings relating to the trauma, may begin to tell a story which, although he or she is not aware of it, has the features of the original trauma and also of what happened at the moment when the memory was triggered. The trigger can be external (e.g., something the therapist did or did not say) or internal (e.g., sometimes paradoxically by an emergent feeling of liveliness or creativity) (Brandchaft, Doctors, & Sorter, 2010).

A common reflection of traumatic memory is a "reversal," which comes about in a consciousness that is now fragmented, with its various elements relatively uncoordinated. The constellation of traumatic memory is as if "loose" or unstable, so that the polarity of the original traumatic relatedness may oscillate into a reversal of the usual traumatic "script," sometimes causing the subject, rather than playing out the experience of the victim, to behave as the other, as if inhabited by the original traumatizer (Meares, 1993a, 1993b, 2005).

TRANSFERENCE–COTRANSFERENCE AND THE EXPECTATIONAL FIELD

In the Conversational Model, transference is understood as a reflection of unconscious traumatic memory. Used in this way, the term always refers to pathology and nearly always to negative affective states. A certain kind of idealization, however, may also be part of a transference.

Since what is transferred from the past to the present is a whole scene, a traumatic script, it cannot be encompassed by the characteristics of the current *other* in this script. Transference of those characteristics, projected onto the therapist, is only a partial manifestation of the script. What is transferred is a form of relatedness that includes, of course, both partners' experiences of each other. The relatedness involves a particular mood or feeling, body feelings, postures, and facial expressions. When the traumatic script is activated, the therapist is also involved. The unconscious traumatic memory system creates powerful subliminal signals, building up an "expectational field" (Meares, 2000a, 2000b) that draws the therapist into its net. The sensitive therapist now feels a slight coercion to behave in a particular way that, on processing the matter, leads to the realization that he or she is cast in the role of the original traumatizer and is in danger of acting out the part. The realization affords another means of getting to know the circumstances of the original trauma. (This phenomenon has been understood in terms of *projective identification*.)

The experience of the therapist in the sway of the expectational field is a cotransference, and it is always an aspect of transference whether recognized or not. Indeed, recognizing the cotransference is an important aspect of working with BPD.

The term *countertransference* is sometimes used to refer to what we are calling *cotransference*. In the original usage, countertransference referred to the activation of the therapist's own unconscious traumatic memory system by aspects of the patient's expression and behaviors. This, the correct usage, should be maintained, in our view. It is not to be confused with cotransference. A third way in which the term countertransference is used, again incorrectly, refers to the therapist's more general responses to the patient, which are independent both of cotransference and countertransference. These responses have no generally accepted names. They include a kind of sympathetic of "contagion" (see Chapter 6 for more discussion of this point).

A THERAPEUTIC APPROACH TO TRAUMATIC MEMORY

The therapeutic approach to the intrusion of traumatic memory is addressed in Chapters 6 and 7. However, a few general introductory remarks are appropriate at this point.

The therapist cannot tackle the so-called facts of the script (or the distorted cognitions) while the trauma system continues to operate. His or her remarks are understood in terms of the reality of that distorted system. What is uttered with benign intent may be experienced as criticism or devaluation (Meares & Hobson, 1977). To repeat, the aim of the therapy is integration. The first step is to begin establishing a form of relatedness that is not part of the trauma system, so that the experience can be reflected upon and played around with, so to speak. Achieving this form of relatedness with a patient who has BPD is dependent on the therapist's ability to set up a relationship in which the patient feels understood and valued. *The sense of being understood creates a feeling of cohesion for the patient. Out of such cohesion arises the capacity for reflection.*

Reflection upon the traumatic experience and the movement from a linear form of psychic material into an analogical, associative mode transforms the traumatic experience into something nearer the form of ordinary dualistic consciousness, so that it can "mingle" with ordinary consciousness, rather than remaining sequestered. Pierre Janet (1925) called this process "liquidation" of the trauma.

So, baldly stated, this liquidation seems a straightforward task. In reality, however, it is complex, difficult, and slow. There are powerful impediments to change.

The first impediment is the kind of relatedness that underpins the adualistic traumatic consciousness. Instead of intimacy it is an attachment, a phylogenetically earlier form of relationship. The individual characteristically lives in states of "non-intimate attachment" (Meares & Anderson, 1993). If the traumatic consciousness is to alter, so also must the pathological attachment to which it is linked. Fear of the loss of this attachment is a fundamental obstacle to integration.

Traumatic attachments create a main form of therapeutic impasse. Other impediments come from the satellite systems surrounding the unconscious trau-matic memories. The satellite systems are designed to prevent the reexperiencing of the trauma, and they most commonly involve avoidance or accommodation (Brandchaft et al., 2010; Meares, 2000a, 2005). In the former circumstance the satellite systems require repetitive strategies to ward off the kind of damage that was done to the feeling of self in the past. In the latter case, the individual habitu-ally behaves, particularly under the influence of anxiety, in a way that he or she believes will maintain the attachment to the other. Such systems might determine the shaping of an entire life.

Chapter 3

Some Thoughts About Language

Russell Meares

THE MAIN PRINCIPLE of the Conversational Model is that beneficial change occurs within and as a result of a relationship. This is a relationship of a particular kind. It is, of course, conducted by means of conversation. The conversation is the therapeutic instrument. The language of this conversation is touched upon in this chapter. Some repetition of points from the previous chapter is necessary. Further aspects of the therapist's linguistic behavior are considered in later chapters.

LANGUAGE AND THE BASIC DEFECT OF BPD

In working with those with BPD, the conversation is directed toward a correction of the basic deficit in this condition. This deficit, as I propose it (Meares, 2012), is a failure of the maturation of that form of consciousness we call self. Its principal characteristic is cohesion. With this cohesion comes a reflective awareness of inner events, positive feeling, and enhancement of the bodily aspects of personal existing, such as the secure feeling of boundedness. In BPD, these and other aspects of selfhood are ill developed. The fundamental quality of personal existing—a state of coherence and continuity—is impaired. The therapy must have the purpose of fostering the experience of personal cohesion.

Self always involves a relationship. One resembles the other, not quite as mirrors of each other, but having corresponding forms. There is a reciprocal, ongoing interplay between these two main components of personal existing, each constituting, nourishing, and recreating the other. Facilitation of personal cohesion, a feeling of connectedness, arises in a conversation in which this feeling is engendered through being understood.

Ordinary personal existing is a unity comprising numerous states of mind that are linked to relationships specific to those states of mind. Each state involves a particular conversation. We speak in a slightly different way to a parent, a sibling, a child, a lover, the bus conductor, a doctor, and so forth. There is, however, communality among these ways of relating. Self can be conceived, then, as a unified but dynamic organization of a "community of selves." In BPD, this community is relatively fragmented. Among the fluctuating forms of relatedness are those that cannot be integrated. These states have a traumatic basis.

A HIERARCHY OF LANGUAGE

Therapy begins when the therapist "enters" the conversation offered by a patient suffering from BPD. This conversation is a manifestation of a state of mind. The notion of "entry" implies that the therapist does not stay "outside" this state of mind, but allows it to become part of his or her own state. This fleeting and partial experience, felt as the words of the patient are uttered, is the necessary prelude to a suitable response.

A suitable response is one that engenders the feeling of connectedness. This is not easy in BPD since the sufferer's state of mind is one of subtle incoherence, which is related to an equally subtle disconnectedness from others. This condition tends to make the other respond in a way that is also disconnected. We find, then, that the therapist working with a patient is in a momentary conflict at the point at which the response is about to be made. There is, first, the sense of the experience "entered," and secondly, of the need to engage. The former opposes the latter. Having this contradictory awareness, the therapist necessarily experiences a kind of double consciousness. If this double awareness is not in play, the therapist is likely to make a response which, to an observer, might seem appropriate, but which is off-key in a slight but definite way. The most common fault is for the therapist to respond as if within his or her own form of consciousness, which is likely to be at a more mature level than the consciousness with which he or she aims to connect. (It is necessary to stress here that "more mature" refers to a specific and particular thread in the course of development, namely the emergence of selfhood.)

Language has a hierarchical form that resembles, and is part of, the hierarchy of consciousness, relatedness, and feeling (spoken of in Chapter 2). In simplest terms the layers of this hierarchy are comprised of phonology, lexicon, and syntax. Language develops in this order.

Phonology is the fundamental language of humankind. The sounds of the voice, its various inflections and intonations, create the language used between mother and child and between other caregivers who play the proto-conversation game with the child. At about 18 months, the lexicon, the use of single words, begins. Syntax develops over the next couple of years and is clearly established at 4 years of age.

The person suffering from BPD is conceived to be experiencing various and fluctuating forms of dissociation, from mild and barely detectable by ordinary means to frankly dissociative (i.e., disorganized; primary dissociation), or in a state of relative numbness (secondary dissociation). The therapist's response to these states should be calibrated by the level of the hierarchy of consciousness. The lower down the hierarchy the patient is experiencing him- or herself, the greater the therapist's reliance on the sound of the voice, combined with a limited lexicon that may be used in a barely syntactical way. The sound of the voice may be the principal source of meaning for a patient on this level of experience.

The kind of calibration needed is suggested by the mother's responsiveness to her baby. In terms of level, the mother is always somewhat above the baby's level. She uses words, for example. The fact that her expression is somewhat in advance of her baby's ability leaves room for movement on the part of the infant to a higher state. For the mother to mimic the baby by staying only at the baby's level would be to confine him or her to that limited state of mind.

CHRONICLES AND SCRIPTS

Different types of conversational style reflect particular states of mind. In the "brokenupness" of BPD psychic life, fairly distinct states of mind appear in different kinds of conversation. Among these various styles of conversation two are particularly characteristic of BPD: what I call *chronicles* and *scripts* (Meares, 1998).

The chronicle is typically a catalogue of symptoms and of problems with the family, with work, and so forth (Meares, 1998, 2000a, pp. 122–123). No part of this chronicling comes from an interior world. The individual is as if *stimulus entrapped*—experience is dominated by external events. The emotions that are part of this often-prolonged account are negative and reactive. There is no pleasure in the conversation, which instead conveys a sense of deadness, without any creative aliveness. The language is linear, and there is relatively little metaphorical usage.

The chronicle form of conversation can be seen as a manifestation of a depleted experience of self. A script-like conversation is understood in a somewhat different way. It is the form of language that comes with activation of the unconscious traumatic memory system. Intrusion of this system into an ongoing state of mind brings with it a language of a simpler kind, lower in the hierarchy. It is repetitive and dominated by the negative affect associated with the trauma. The voice may become shrill and harsh. The same body movements—for example, a chopping of the hand—recur with each acting out of the traumatic script. This script may be triggered by something that occurs in the session. The script is often a recital of a recent event; the account is one of the "facts" of this occasion. These so-called facts are not linked to the individual's past but are told as if the trauma, say, devaluation, has been inflicted anew. This stunted story barely changes in its various repetitions.

RIGHT-HEMISPHERIC LANGUAGE

The therapeutic aim is to transform these traumatically based conversations into those more nearly having the structure of narrative. A properly told narrative involves a coordination between the two basic language forms that make up human conversation. The language sometimes called *social speech* is, in the ordinary sense, logical. It is linear, capable of proposition formation, and generally dependent upon left-hemispheric function.

The second kind of language, *inner speech*, is characteristically analogical and emotional. It is demonstrated both by the mother's talk in the protoconversation and by the child's chatter in conversational play. It is presumably dependent upon right-hemispheric function.

The language of succession, the left-hemispheric form, is essentially that of the chronicle. This style of conversation, when dominant, suggests that the individual is relatively deficient in right-hemispheric function. Indeed, we are proposing that this deficiency, or hypofunction, is the main basis of the reduced sense of personal cohesion in BPD.

The two axes of language, the logical-successive and the analogical-simultaneous, are equivalent to Saussure's (1916) axes of the diachronic, which has the time of chronology, and the synchronic, which is the time of the moment. These axes are figuratively disposed as if at right angles to each other. People with BPD seem to be caught in the zone of the diachronic.

These remarks lead to the notion that a principal aim of therapy for BPD is stimulating right-hemispheric function. Using the models of the protoconversation and symbolic play, we infer that this activity necessarily takes place in an atmosphere of safety, one in which the fight–flight system, which is active in BPD, is relatively quiescent.

The right hemisphere may be stimulated when, as it were, it is spoken to in its own language. The conversation then has the form, figuratively speaking, of one right hemisphere conversing with the other.

Function of the right hemisphere is crucial to the development of self. Early in life, the right hemisphere is developing faster than the left. This development is "experience dependent" (Schore, 2003): That is, it develops as a consequence of those aspects of the mother–child relationship involving mutual emotional communications—what I call *analogical relatedness*. The mother's manner of responding in these situations seems to be designed to stimulate and resonate with those capacities for which the right hemisphere is innately set up (see Meares, 2012, Chapter 15).

The nursery-school child has a language very like a person who is functioning mainly by means of the right brain. It is a language of immediate reality. Conversation with the child "is fitted into the world of objects, interpersonal acts, and events, all of which sustain the meaning of what is said" (Trevarthen, 2004, p. 878). The propositional structure of left-hemispheric language does not fit well with this state of mind. The left hemisphere, however, at this stage of development begins a maturational surge, soon becoming larger than the right hemisphere. At about the age of 5, the two halves of the brain become more truly coordinated and the conversation of the child is now also a coordination, comprising the two language forms. The syntactical language of the left hemisphere is the vehicle of another language that is more emotional and figurative, characteristic of right-hemispheric function. The latter aspect of BPD conversation is relatively lacking, consistent with the evidence that BPD is a particularly right hemispheric disorder.

Right-hemispheric language is characterized by the following features. It is:

• Relatively asyntactical: The language does not follow the order typical of more linear-type speech.

- Abbreviated: The language tends to omit the subject of a sentence, including pronouns. Only the predicates remain, as Vygotsky observed in studying the child engaged in symbolic play (e.g., "goes down there" or "down there" or even just "down").
- Emotional: The interactions and inflections of the voice carry emotional expression, with the right hemisphere being particularly sensitive to the "meaning" of musical sound.
- Shaping: The language represents the "shape" of the overall feeling of a presented reality; it has a synthetic function.
- Figurative: In making "shaping" responses the therapist is providing analogies that can be developed into metaphor. The right hemisphere is involved in both an awareness of metaphor and its expression.

COHESION, REFLECTION, AND THE THERAPEUTIC SCREEN

Cohesion is fostered by the use of right-hemispheric responsiveness. An effect of cohesion is the enhancement of the reflective capacity. Reflection is further potentiated by a particular language form that is grammatically impersonal. The thoughts and words tend to be directed to a space between the conversational partners. It is as if they are gazing at an invisible and metaphorical screen, where a jointly created "movie" is being projected, its images only dimly perceived (Meares, 1983).

This kind of language emerges in a spatial reconfiguration of the therapeutic conversation that begins as a two-person arrangement. The shift to the reflective mode tends to set up a new arrangement in which the conversation is not directed at each other but is as if directed toward a third thing, the invisible "screen." A dyadic situation becomes triadic. Examples of this kind of language include phrases such as "It looks like . . . ," "It seems that . . . ," "There is a sense of desolation . . . ," and so forth. That is, the construction is impersonal. In this joint metaphorical gazing, the therapist is an auxiliary "I," working with the subject as "I," to enhance the "view" into his or her world. This joint gazing might be seen as a forerunner to the reflective process of the individual.

Integrating Pronouns

The therapeutic conversation takes a number of forms, each of which reflects a different kind of relatedness. The previous sections suggest that a language that is without pronouns is conducive to the generation of the consciousness of selfhood.

But this is not to say that the therapist's language is always of this kind. The language necessarily shifts to one in which pronouns are used, analogous to the protoconversation when there is a switching back and forth between face-to-face gazing and gazing away. The aim of the therapeutic conversation is not to have a conversation limited merely to right-hemispheric functions but to have one in which there is a coordination of left and right hemispheres. The generative process, however, necessarily begins with the right-hemispheric type of conversation.

The situations in which pronouns are used are several. One is a "reflection upon reflection." That which emerges in reflection is spoken of in a different way, in this way enlarging the experience. Clearly, those conversations involving the more practical aspects of the therapeutic relationship are spoken in the ordinary way, using pronouns.

Pronoun usage implies a clear differentiation between self and not-self. A conversation conducted exclusively in this way is less than conducive to the "picturing" of interior life. Premature introduction of this kind of reflectiveness breaks up a flow of thought and is counterproductive. A typical conversation is conducted in alternating modes of what James likened to "flights" and "perchings," making an analogy between the movement of thought and the flight of a bird. The state of flight is expressive; that of perching is reflective. It is the flight element of thought—its capricious, wandering course—which shows its cohesion. It is, therefore, the more fundamental of the two states when these metaphors are considered in the therapeutic setting.

QUESTIONS

As a general principle, questions are avoided because they set up the kind of relatedness that is the opposite of that toward which the therapist should be working. Questions tend to enhance a sense of disconnection. It is, of course, impossible completely to avoid questions, particularly as they concern the facts of the patient's life. These questions are most suitably asked at a point that is relevant to the conversation.

For the most part, however, the therapeutic conversation is of a personal and emotional kind. Formulaic questions such as "How did that make your feel?" are felt as distant from the patient's experience. They are often irritating. Not infrequently, in the case of those with BPD, they evoke anger.

It is the therapist's job to try to understand the patient's experience, using the capacity for empathic imagination. This is followed by attempts to represent this understanding. It is often speculatively expressed, giving the patient implicit encouragement to modify, elaborate, or correct the representation. The speculative style depends on phonology, or the sound of the voice, to a significant degree.

THE PRESENT MOMENT

Much of the work in therapy involves changing a traumatically based form of consciousness, which is split off from the ordinary sense of being, into another kind of mental life that can be integrated in the stream of self. A cardinal characteristic of self is the capability to create scenes in the "mind's eye" that come from memory or imagination. The movement of the therapeutic conversation, then, is toward this scene-making propensity of mind.

In traumatic consciousness, there is limited evidence of visualization of interior life. Events are described in terms of their facts. The words used have little figurative power, are not evocative of "pictures" of these facts. There is a sense of these events being spoken *about*—and "aboutness" is to be avoided.

In order to change a conversation of aboutness, for example, the patient talking about the parents who were always putting him down, the experience needs to be sensed as if it were in the present rather than the past. The therapist tends to respond to such stories by speaking of them in the present tense. This has the effect of translating these events from those experienced in left-hemispheric mode into the "momentary" and more emotionally alive right-hemispheric zone of experience. (The terms of "right" and "left hemispheric" are used as shorthand, a way of talking about complex operations in which both hemispheres are involved.)

THE FUTURE

Selfhood involves the visualization of future events, which can only be imagined. When the patient begins to use words such as *should*, *ought*, or *could*, suggesting the possibility of actions different from the past, a milestone in the development of self is reached (Meares & Sullivan, 2004). The therapist does not introduce these terms, but when they appear spontaneously they can be a starting point for the creation of a scene that might contribute to changing the traumatic script.

NATURALNESS

The capacity for conversation is one of the abilities with which we have been naturally endowed. This aspect of our biological heritage is enormously complex. In this brief space only some of the most salient features of the therapeutic conversation with someone suffering from BPD have been addressed. Each conversation with each person with this condition is unique. Only a certain and limited selection from such a multiplicity of forms is possible here. There is one feature, however, that should remain in all these various conversations: the therapist's naturalness. The therapist should hone and develop, in a disciplined way, his or her own style. A central aspect of conversation, as it is defined, is that it is "familiar" language. It is in the domain of the familiar that self is generated.

Chapter 4

The Story of a Therapeutic Relationship

Joan Haliburn and Dawn Mears

THE STORY OF BELLA is used here to illustrate some of the difficulties of borderline personality disorder (BPD) and how it might be approached. Bella (pseudonym) has given written and informed consent for her case material to be used in this guidebook. In presenting this material, we have drawn from the audiotaped conversations between Bella and DM in the therapy, and from conversations between JH and DM in the supervision experience.

INTRODUCTION

In presenting this case material, we have taken care to alter any identifying details and important personal information to preserve patient confidentiality. We have tried to capture the atmosphere of the therapeutic experience and to convey it in a manner understandable to novice clinicians.

We describe important aspects of the therapy beginning with the referral—how the therapist experienced the patient while arranging an appointment to see her, and the therapist's expectations even before the first contact. It is to be noted that this reaction is not unusual and is often the result of pessimistic attitudes that accompany a referral where numerous treatment efforts have failed, and where psychodynamic psychotherapy is considered, not uncommonly, as a last resort.

We describe the early stage of psychotherapy in some detail from the referral to the third session. It is important to bear in mind that the future course of psychotherapy depends on the therapist's forming a good therapeutic relationship, holding his or her experience of the relationship, and using that experience to understand the patient. This approach, referred to commonly as *holding* or *containing*, helps to maintain a connection that keeps the patient attending.

We present the case history under three main headings—the early, middle, and late stages—and describe the progress of therapy under several subheadings; however, it has to be remembered that what happens in each stage is not circumscribed to that stage alone. The important aspects of each stage are described as they unfold, in an attempt to capture the variety of experiences the therapeutic dyad may encounter in a long-term therapy with a patient who has BPD.

EARLY STAGE OF THERAPY

The Referral

The Patient and the Source of Referral

Bella is a 37-year-old single woman, referred by her general practitioner, with a long history of chronic dysthymia, panic attacks, suicidal ideation, comorbid benzodiazepine dependence and BPD. She also has a history of several suicide attempts by overdose in the period of a month. This extreme behavior led yet again to admission to the local hospital (where a pervasive sense of helplessness, hopelessness, and frustration was experienced by her caretakers) and accompanied her referral to a private practitioner.

The patient had been known to the local health service for more than 5 years, during which time she had over 30 admissions for suicide attempts by overdose. Bella's previous treatments included a course of dialectical behavior therapy, with medication supervised by her psychiatrist and combined with case management by the local mental health team. She had later received cognitive–behavioral therapy with a psychologist and support from her general practitioner. Bella had become an unwelcome patient on many levels, and at the time was experiencing difficulty accessing sustained and meaningful assistance.

The Nature of the Referral

The practitioner, DM, a mental health nurse, was doing a psychodynamic psychotherapy training course based on CM (Haliburn, Stevenson, & Gerull, 2009). First, DM describes how the referral came to her:

> I attended a professional development seminar and found myself talking about a case to a general practitioner. Shortly thereafter, he was asking me to see a "dif-

ficult borderline" patient. I agreed, though I remember thinking to myself "What have I done? I asked for this."

I had a supervision session with JH, and I was lamenting the lack of a "good" patient to take on as a training case. We rumbled through my referrals one by one, and when we came to Bella, I just passed her off, saying I had not thought about taking on such a severely disordered client as a training case. If all the others had tried and failed, well, I wasn't going to be of much help—or so I thought.

We talked further about Bella, and having had a long experience with borderline patients, and in the supervision of therapists who have such patients, I encouraged DM to consider seeing Bella, saying, "She sounds like a 'perfect' training case—besides, where else will she get intensive psychotherapy?"

The assurance of regular supervision seemed to help DM make up her mind. It was also clear that she desperately needed to see a patient with significant psychopathology, as her training case. However, DM described having two nightmares directly related to this decision, which she talked about in supervision.

DM and I discussed several issues in relation to the appropriateness of the case: Was this psychopathology too much for a trainee to deal with? Would it end up with the trainee feeling disheartened? What was the supervisor's responsibility for the therapist in training? We talked about the rights of the therapist to refuse; the needs of such patients; and the effects they can have on the therapist, even before they present. Most importantly, the regularity of available supervision was impressed on the training therapist. The need to stay abreast of the relevant literature that was available to her was also stressed. Staying informed about the theory of psychopathology and about the model was vitally necessary. DM commented:

> "I felt overwhelmed at the thought of taking on Bella, and powerless to really effect any change, on the one hand; and on the other hand, I wondered what would happen if I did put the model to the test. I had heard that CM is a treatment for those patients earlier considered to be 'unanalyzable,' and I found myself becoming more interested."

The Expectational Field

The patient responded to DM's call. She agreed to an appointment with the expectation of receiving help, but at the same time "knowing" that she would once again be rejected, "like all the others." This rejection had been her habitual experience of caregivers, and she seemed to be experiencing DM in a similar way, even though she had not started therapy yet. There was already transference—

unconscious traumatic memory, i.e., a traumatic form of relatedness was being "transferred" to this new experience of a therapist, from the past to the present.

A form of relatedness is also being transferred to the therapist, who in this case was already feeling uneasy about the patient—making the therapist a perfect host at that time. The cotransference is the therapist's experience of the patient in this expectational field. The therapist is aware that what she is experiencing is a product of the expectational field. The therapist, who was quite dedicated to her work, felt annoyed and frustrated that the patient would already be experiencing her as abandoning. This, combined with the therapist's uncertainty about her competence in such a case, filled her with dread.

The Therapist's Countertransference

DM once again felt reluctant to see Bella in psychotherapy, and was feeling frustrated even thinking about the possibility. She was aware that the patient had been "doctor-shopping" to procure sedatives and tranquilizers, and again felt inadequate and incompetent as to how she would be able to help this woman discontinue a habit that had been in place for an unspecified length of time.

While making arrangements to see the patient, DM, aware of and consciously working with her ambivalence, was also aware of the necessity to keep in mind certain important issues that needed addressing, particularly the patient's recent traumatic experiences of seeking help and of hospitalization.

The countertransference in this case is the sum-total of the effect of the patient on the therapist and the therapist's own relevant personal background, as well as feelings of inadequacy and incompetence.

Session 1: The Assessment

Suicidal Ideation

Nothing could have prepared the therapist for what she was to be confronted with. The patient arrived on time, with a couple of bags packed, which she forcefully placed on the floor beside her. The therapist could not help but notice the force.

Bella: Had another argument with Mum—got nowhere to go.

DM: Nowhere to go? Can't go back home?

Bella: It's no good.

Bella looked "gray." Her speech was slurred (possibly from misuse of medication), her eyes puffy, and her shoulders slumped. She unhesitatingly proceeded to talk about the numerous overdoses she had taken and about her visits to various doctors who had prescribed her medication that she needed. She had "heaps of medication stashed away" which she intended to take over the weekend.

Bella: If that doesn't work, it's easy to hire a gun.

Dissociation

Bella's story tumbled out. During the past 12 months in particular, she often found herself wandering the streets of a city that was some distance away. She would take with her a quantity of tablets in her bags and look for a place to stay, so she could take all the tablets. She would return home, however, and take an overdose there. An ambulance would be called, and she would be whisked away to the hospital each and every time.

There was no space for the therapist to intervene in this session; DM tried several times unsuccessfully to ask a question or say something. Referring to her mother in a rather dismissive manner, the patient continued.

Bella: Mum—she adopted me—at 3 weeks. She adopted my baby like she was her own.

This confused DM but she had to stay with the confusion. Bella proceeded to talk about other unconnected things. There was very little discernible affect while she spoke. Her speech was pressured and in chronicle form—about an array of subjects that bore no continuity with each other. This left little room for any interjection by the therapist, apart from monosyllabic words and sounds to let the patient know she was being listened to.

Bella was constantly outer-oriented, with no sense of inner; her speech was disconnected and difficult to follow; she was stimulus entrapped.

DM recalled: "It felt—as if I wasn't there—it was hard trying to listen to her—to say anything was out of the question—it would involve interrupting her—"

Stimulus Entrapment

This experience of the therapist is to be expected; it is the result of stimulus entrapment. The therapist feels on the outer periphery, disconnected in similar ways as the patient, who is caught up in her own world. The therapist feels excluded but makes an effort to stay with the patient—in spite of which the therapist dissociates (discussed below).

When a patient is stimulus entrapped, it becomes necessary to let the patient know that you are listening, making an attempt to connect, rather than attempting to make meaning. Feelings of boredom must be grappled with, and a listening and responding stance taken up. To see this behavior as resistance would be to misunderstand the patient and to take up an opposite position, such as withdrawing interest or requesting that the patient slow down or repeat him- or herself, which would lead to further alienation.

Arrangements were made for the next appointment, and later that day DM, in recollecting the session, was alarmed by wondering why "I had not responded appropriately to such a suicidal patient." Earlier thoughts surfaced again. Experiences with other such patients in the mental health system were remembered, followed again by an increasing sense of powerlessness and a need to finish the assessment sessions and give the patient the feedback that she, the therapist, "could not help her." Thinking about her disconnection from Bella in that first session, DM became aware that she herself had *dissociated,* which was unusual for her.

Trying to stay with a stimulus-entrapped patient and trying to understand him or her at the same time can result in the therapist becoming bored to the point of dissociating. Staying on the edge of the patient's experience helps the therapist listen without being rendered helpless. DM had been aware, however, that Bella had a case manager whom she (Bella) could call if she needed help.

When a new therapist is in the room with the patient, how does he or she understand what is happening in the therapeutic relationship?

Giving Value to the Patient

Giving value to what the patient says, irrespective of it being disconnected, incoherent, or difficult to understand, will tend to establish a sense of relatedness from which coherence and connection will emerge. The therapist does not look for meaning or make meaning from what the patient says. By tuning in from moment to moment and trying to couple with the patient's words, the therapist experiences the patient and has a subjective sense of how he or she is being experienced as well.

When the therapist is able to respond to what is given and leave his or her own agenda aside, the patient begins to feel understood and to trust that help is being genuinely offered. Bridging this interpersonal gap is so vital for these patients who, for most of their lives, have felt alienated from people and from the world.

Despite the intrusions of traumatic memory and the repetition of unconscious traumatic material, the therapist's responsiveness and nonjudgmental attitude will help in the formation of a safe therapeutic relationship. The therapist will sense the change in the relationship from when they first met. The patient will similarly feel more able to open up. The therapist must also tune in to areas of vitality, to positive aspects of the patient, not just to the problematic areas.

Traumatic Relatedness

DM became aware quite soon of the transference and of her cotransference. Bella tried hard to impress on the therapist her neediness, while still getting angry in anticipation of her needs not being met. The therapist was already aware that she was beginning to see how much pain Bella was in and was often frustrated at herself that she could not make a difference.

Therapist Countertransference

The therapist, notwithstanding her efforts to understand Bella, found herself caught up in negative thoughts, feelings of annoyance, and most often feelings of incompetence. She doubted herself and her ability to help Bella. These feelings were talked about in supervision.

Session 2: Assessment Continued

Using What Is Given

The second session was similar in many respects to the first. Bella was preoccupied with the tablets she had in her possession, her suicidal ideation, and with events particularly involving her family.

Bella: It's useless—take everything that's there—there's plenty more—there's other ways too—no one can stop me.
DM: It's hard, I can see.
Bella: What's the use—at least there's. . . .

There was a sense of urgency that made DM anxious, but which she was able to contain. Containing one's own anxiety helps contain the patient's anxiety and allows the therapist to be more attuned. The therapist, determined to stay as closely attuned as she possibly could, began to pick up the threads of despair, of feeling unaccepted and rejected by everyone; of feeling alone and of needing to put an end to her dreadful feelings. Staying with the theme of the patient is important.

In the session, it became more evident that Bella could not communicate her distress to anyone, except by threatening to overdose on tablets. The thought of suicide seemed comforting to Bella, it seemed to the therapist. Carrying the tablets with her seemed to provide a kind of soothing function for Bella, like a transitional object.

There was a repetitive quality to Bella's presentation that left no space for the therapist and that was underscored by the presumption that the therapist "would not listen anyway." There was little or no possibility of getting a developmental history from Bella.

It was necessary for DM to draw together the fragments of Bella's story and to try to understand her and allow the therapeutic relationship to develop, within which further exploration could take place. DM alerted Bella that they would have another session 2 days later. At this time she would give her feedback and discuss the possibility of therapy. She also wondered how much of her own ambivalence was coming across to Bella.

It became clear to me (JH) that Bella could easily cause conflict and confusion by her "demanding dependency," which produced a mixture of positive and negative feelings in the therapist. It was important to be aware of, and to understand, the part this dependency played in the developing relationship, particularly in the disjunctions that characterized the early sessions.

That this was a way of functioning that Bella had developed, perhaps from her earliest attachment relationships, needed to be considered; and this was how she related to most people, including the therapist. She was demanding in a rather convoluted way, she was prone to amplifying her difficulties, and she maximized the expression of her needs, in order to make sure the therapist heard her.

A Crisis

That evening there was a message from Bella, saying she had taken an overdose. The therapist called the crisis team immediately. The team member responded: "She's just attention seeking. She's been admitted and discharged six times in a short while. It's typical of you private practitioners—you take on these difficult cases and then need help to fix the problem."

The therapist then phoned the police, who transported Bella to the hospital. The therapist felt shocked at the hostility that had been expressed by the crisis team, and then felt deflated and isolated, wondering how she could manage without the support of crisis services. This pressing issue was discussed in supervision.

The need for the therapist to contact the treating team and, in particular, the treating psychiatrist was discussed, so that she could seek their collaboration. Bella would require attention in times of crises and possibly hospitalization, particularly during the early stages of therapy. If these measures could be assured, Bella would experience the necessary containment in times of extreme difficulty. The therapist also needed to know that she was not alone in Bella's treatment.

Making Contact with the Hospital Team

The therapist contacted Bella's psychiatrist after receiving her permission to do so. It became evident that a conversation with the treating psychiatrist was necessary in order to have the support of the crisis team. This highlights the need for psychotherapists to make contact with other clinicians involved in the patient's care, so that services are not duplicated (as in over-servicing) and that additional help in times of crises would be available.

The psychiatrist called a teleconference, selected a minimum number of key people to be involved, and advised them that psychotherapy would be the focus of treatment. He would admit Bella for 3 weeks of detoxification from prescribed drugs, advise her about the danger of collecting and hoarding medication, and stress the need for her to attend no more than a single general practitioner. If and when admission was required, she would be given a bed in the ward. Bella was to return to therapy on discharge. The therapist would have no contact with Bella during any hospitalization, which would be brief when it happened. Bella would soon return home and to therapy.

The Issue of Medication and the Third-Party Provider

DM recollected:

Medication was to be prescribed by Bella's general practitioner with whom she had a good relationship, but whom she tested on several occasions too. I also felt that it was important that I get her permission to contact her GP [general practitioner] if that was necessary. It was important to treat the medication as part of Bella's life, as important as other aspects of her life. This was very containing for both of us.

By communicating with the prescriber from the beginning, the therapist sees everything about the patient, including medication, as being important, leaving little room for problems later on.

Session 3: Assessment Continued

Anxiety in the Patient and Therapist

Bella was discharged from the hospital after 3 weeks and could hardly wait for her third session. The therapist had promised that she would give her feedback, and together they would decide if therapy was possible, and what form it would take. The therapist's earlier fears were once again surfacing, as she tried to explore with Bella the circumstances of the overdose, but Bella had great difficulty recollecting what had happened 3 weeks ago. She had spent 3 weeks in the hospital and had detoxified from benzodiazepines. She described her experiences in the hospital, once again, in the most negative terms—she did not have a good word for anyone.

Past Experiences, Current Expectations

Bella: They care for no one but themselves. You're the lowest . . . you're a nuisance to them—they wish you were just not there —like a criminal, you deserve to die—so why not? Why not do a better job, and finish it all?

In supervision DM recollected:

I wondered what it would be like to bring therapy with this person to an end. Would it be possible to conclude therapy with such a person? I puzzled within myself why I was thinking about ending even before the therapy had properly begun, and even before I had decided to offer her the therapy.

It was time for the therapist to convey her assessment to Bella and establish an initial formulation of what she had learned from Bella in these sessions. DM had promised to give her feedback, following which they would make a decision together as to whether the therapy would commence. They were then going to discuss the form, frequency, and duration that it would take; how long they would see each other, if indeed the therapist thought she could be of help; and establish a contract to which both she and Bella would need to adhere.

Traumatic Memory

The therapist had hardly gathered her thoughts when the patient said to her: "This is it, you and me, three sessions are up." Bella expected this to end. She expected to be rejected yet again; she had experienced nothing but rejection, in her view.

The therapist was shocked by Bella's statement. She felt devalued. Several thoughts ran through the therapist's mind: Perhaps Bella had not noticed that she had been listening, she had been empathic, and she had tried to respond as best she could and as frequently as she was allowed. Perhaps she had given herself away, subtly or not so subtly, and Bella had become aware of her uncertainty.

The therapist recollected the subtle tones of the sessions: Bella's manner of relating to her, which was at times dismissive—"as if you would care"—and at times ambivalent—"Why am I here? It will be the same old thing that always happens." Most importantly, DM found herself thinking about Bella's history and of her contact with other helping professionals in more recent times. It was as if Bella expected things to be no different from what she had always experienced. DM responded to Bella, "It's difficult—like the same thing will happen again. . . ." DM became aware that Bella was highly sensitive to rejection; she had been primed not to have expectations of anybody. DM pondered in supervision:

> It's amazing, you find yourself thinking about what's happening on so many different levels I never thought possible before. Bella was highly emotional, tearful, often spoke with a raised voice, and also was very effective in raising my anxiety about her safety. I had to keep in mind that Bella could self-harm at any time, but I also had to remember not to become overly anxious, because my anxiety may have made things more difficult for her. It was important to try to understand her and contain her.

The Frame, the Contract, and the Therapeutic Relationship

The therapist, once she had recovered from the initial shock of the response, said to Bella that she had given their sessions some considerable thought and had decided that she would like to be of help to Bella. She suggested that they see each other twice a week, at a particular time, at the therapist's office, for 2 years, after which they could together review the therapy and the contract again.

DM discussed the implications of failing to attend sessions and provided clear information about holidays and breaks. She assured Bella that she would keep her side of the contract. She would let Bella know if she was going to be late or if she could not attend a session, which would only be in case of illness or something unforeseen. She would let her know well in advance if she intended to take holidays. The sessions would be of 50 minutes duration, and she would expect Bella to take responsibility for attending the sessions.

The therapist alerted Bella to the fact that if she required help outside of her office hours, she would need to phone the crisis team, but should she need help during office hours, she could ring her. The therapist would respond if she was free, but if she was seeing someone at the time, she would respond as soon as she could. If in urgent need, Bella would have to ring the crisis team or take herself to the hospital. They discussed the fee, which was acceptable.

The therapist alerted herself to the need for clear but flexible rules and clear boundaries, in order to set up a safe space in which the possibility of trust could develop. DM conveyed to Bella that she would try to help her with her difficulties and hoped that by working together, things would get better for her. It is important to convey to the patient a sense that he or she is a *collaborator* with the therapist, and that they will work *together* on the difficulties presented.

Supervision and Patient Consent

The therapist also asked the patient if she could audiotape their sessions so she could take them to supervision, which was "aimed at helping me to help you." Bella agreed. DM informed Bella that in supervision she would discuss each session with the supervisor, but would play just a small snippet of their conversation—something that she was having difficulty with, or perhaps something that she wanted to discuss that had roused her interest or curiosity.

In supervision, DM added, she would not identify Bella, so the supervisor would have no idea of who she was. The tapes would be erased every few weeks, and while they were in her possession, no one else would have access to them. She needed to dispel any doubts that Bella might have about the confidentiality and safety of the therapeutic and supervisory situations.

DM reminded Bella that supervision was intended to help the therapist help her. Bearing in mind that different patients have different attitudes to the sessions being taped, and to the notion of a supervisor listening in, DM noted that Bella was quite pleased about this suggestion.

A Shared Moment

DM recollected: "It was a most beautiful moment between us, between her and me, as she heard that I wanted to keep working with her, and that she was not being moved on, yet again rejected and abandoned. I suspect she felt valued somewhat, that I would even think of seeing her." The transference–cotransference was indeed quite powerful, as described below.

The Psychodynamic Formulation

In putting together both the information from the three sessions and the history received from the referral source, DM arrived at a provisional framework of understanding what was given to her, and conveyed it in summary to Bella. DM was surprised that she was allowed the space to give Bella this feedback:

> From our conversations, I see you, Bella, as a depressed and anxious person who has lived through a number of traumatic experiences from a very young age. You told me that you were adopted as an infant. You had been sexually assaulted. That created further problems, which possibly had triggered traumatic memories that were difficult to deal with, or to "put a lid on," as was expected of you.
>
> I would say that you became depressed, and had never really come out of that depressed state, while further traumatic events occurred. The baby you had when you were 17 years old [information given in the second session] and having that baby taken from you was truly a big loss for you, I can imagine. Your family saw you as unable to care for yourself; that was their reasoning.
>
> You also seem to have mixed feelings about your mother, I think. It was hard, you said, to get what you really wanted from her.
>
> You had taken medication [antipsychotics, antidepressants, and minor tranquilizers] but not experienced relief from your pain. You have had several treatments, and have not felt better.

Bella did not interrupt the therapist. DM continued:

> You had been experiencing immense pain that was not recognized. You had been extremely distressed and alone and possibly found that pills had "done something for you like nothing else," and so you began doctor-shopping and popping pills.
>
> Your feelings of despair were often too much for the pills to lessen or to

soothe, and many times you might have wanted to go to sleep by taking a whole lot of tablets, which saw you ending up in acute care at the hospital.

This, though it frequently happened, was of no help; in fact, it was possible that you felt more rejected, abandoned, and useless. You were possibly searching for something to make things right.

I think you want to live a happy life, and you have the will to change things. We can together work on the problems and try to improve things. What do you think about the things I've said?

Bella responded with great relief: "You've seen me just three times, and yet you know me so well!"

The therapist felt a great responsibility was being thrust on her by this response. With the patient idealizing her as she did, she felt she had to be cautious and "not make a mistake." She also was aware that the therapy was not going to be easy.

DM would have to cope not only with Bella's threats, but also her manner of alternately idealizing and devaluing her—in the same session. The therapist was aware that she had made a provisional formulation that might need to be modified as the therapy proceeded.

Diagnosis

Bella had been told that she had BPD, and she recognized the gravity of this diagnosis, but experienced considerable guilt that she had been "the cause" of her own problems. The shared understanding communicated earlier helped, and she said so.

A diagnosis is important for some patients, whereas for others it may be less important or even unimportant. If the diagnosis is offered in a way that recognizes the pain that has been experienced and values the person's sense of self, it adds a further dimension to the shared understanding that has been previously offered. However, therapists, depending on their background, may or may not be familiar with diagnostic classifications, but often BPD patients are referred with a diagnosis and are most often, if not always, on medication.

The therapist, by imparting a note of positivity and hope, by sharing an understanding of the patient, and by stressing that the therapeutic venture is one of collaboration, takes an important first step toward creating safety in the psychotherapeutic relationship.

Sessions 4–18: Creating Safety in the Therapeutic Relationship

Empathic Attunement: Listening, Understanding, and Reflecting

Empathic attunement is more than ordinary mirroring or repeating what the patient says, which would be more like parroting. Attunement involves empathic listening, understanding, and reflecting that understanding with emphasis resonating with the patient's emotional tone. It is important to stay empathically attuned, to resonate and respond to both positive and negative aspects of the therapeutic conversation. Responsiveness is more effective in the moment, rather than when the moment is over.

Like working on a tapestry, DM made efforts to set the scene in which she could interact with Bella and allow her to talk about the things that mattered to her. This was going to be hard, as DM was constantly reminded of Bella's history and the difficulties people experienced with her, and the feelings of inadequacy would briefly return. Bella undoubtedly experienced brief periods of dissociation. As a result her story was often fragmented and disconnected. Here is an example of Bella's style of talking about something totally unconnected from the conversation in the moment:

Bella: She's always the center of attention . . . there's no place . . .

DM: (*Trying by nonverbal ways and short verbal utterances to show that she is listening*) She?

Bella: . . . have to please her all the time . . .

DM: (*Still trying to follow*) Have to please her all the time?

It was as if Bella hadn't heard the therapist's questions.

Bella came regularly and on time or much earlier than scheduled. She clearly expressed her faith in the therapist and saw the therapist as her anchor. The therapist continued for some time to feel uneasy about Bella's idealization of her, and clearly felt burdened by the responsibility she felt was being placed on her. She worried if she was ever going to be able to help Bella.

In spite of her fears, the therapist arrived at most sessions prepared to listen to Bella, to try to understand her, and to communicate that understanding to her. She sometimes failed to do so, but she accepted that she was doing her best. It was the early stage of therapy when neither knew the other well. DM could only be "good enough" as she strove to attune to Bella's story. Creating a two-person interaction in the safety of a good therapeutic relationship was most important in DM's view—providing a trusted, secure base (Bowlby, J., 1988)—even though Bella dominated the conversation.

The therapist continued in her attempts to create a space that would provide the safety and security so necessary for the therapy to continue. The therapist's being on time and her efforts to validate and value the patient's communications added a certain predictability that helped Bella, who later expressed her sense of feeling safe. This is important if the patient is going to talk about her personal feelings and experiences.

> Bella: I don't know what I'm going to do on the weekend. Mum doesn't care—if she did, she would not leave me alone. Suppose I'll take a handful of tablets, maybe a bit more. What about the whole lot? There's no point, is there?

This situation was understandably difficult, as each session was dominated by Bella's suicidal ideation and descriptions of how she would overdose. Weekends were particularly challenging. Sundays were difficult for her to get through, being left on her own. DM carefully responded, using nonpersonal pronouns, recognizing the centrality of Bella's experience and conveying to her a tentative understanding of her predicament in the here and now. Painstakingly, DM tried to attune to the cues she picked up—verbal, emotional, and nonverbal.

> DM: It's difficult being left alone, particularly when your mum goes out. Being left alone does something (*in a questioning tone*) . . . thoughts of taking tablets . . . does something.
> Bella: She doesn't care.
> DM: She doesn't care? These feelings have been there for a long time.

DM's attunement seemed to bring about relief, though temporary; Bella would once again become desperate.

Silences

It was particularly difficult after the first few sessions when Bella frequently became silent. DM compared these silences with "trying to wade through mud" or "being stuck in chewing gum." She was aware that Bella became uncomfortable when there was more than a minute's silence, but then she (the therapist) felt quite uncomfortable too, when there was little response to her interjections. Bella seemed to become silent when she felt she had said enough and had not experienced immediate relief. Her frustration tolerance was very poor. DM wondered with Bella what was happening in the silence, but got little response until she decided to say something.

DM: There's silence.

Bella: Uh-hm.

DM: It's difficult?

Bella: Uh-hm.

DM: I wonder if you become silent when you feel you're not being listened to—especially after you have told me so much of what's happening in your life (*tentatively making this link*).

Bella: I'm tired of trying to get people to understand. What's the use?

DM was mindful of her own responses—the way they were put together and spoken were an attempt to match Bella's state of mind, to provide an analogical representation, in which the words chosen were part of Bella's experience, rather than the therapist's usual form of speech.

Bella: I will be better off dead.

DM: When things are difficult, death seems the only solution—there will be no more pain?

Bella: I wonder if I'm going to take an overdose this weekend. I've got so many tablets, a drawer full of them. They are hidden all around the room. [Bella particularly emphasized this point at her Friday sessions.] Mum goes out and leaves me on my own. She goes to church, and I don't like going. I take whatever I can find to overdose, to knock myself out.

Language: Personal pronouns and Attention to Minute Particulars

DM: It gets very lonely [coupling].

Bella: Yes (*in a soft voice*).

DM: When Mum goes out?

Bella: Yes.

DM: Becomes difficult when you're left on your own [amplification].

Bella: I just want to sleep.

DM: You knock yourself out?

Bella: Yeah (*in a tired voice*).

DM: You knock yourself out, rather than put up with the loneliness [representation]?

DM commented:

> The use of impersonal pronouns particularly at the beginning—"*It* gets very lonely" rather than "*You* get very lonely" in my conversation with Bella was helpful. It served to represent what she was feeling and brought her difficulties into the space between us for exploration, with much less possibility of her feeling criticized or judged.
>
> I continued to use words to match what I thought was her inner experience of loneliness and emptiness that prompted her need to reach out for a heap of pills. She "liked" this and responded, further elaborating how empty her life had been, since her early years, while her mother always had a full life, even after her parents had separated and divorced.
>
> These were small steps, but already a language of feeling was emerging alongside a "language" of pill-taking. I genuinely started to experience some empathy for her. Staying with the minute particulars was important.

Gradually there is more freedom in the use of language. Personal pronouns come into use; as the patient's conversation matures, so does the therapist's.

Coupling

By reflecting the essential elements of what she hears Bella say, aligning closely with her words and using these words to continue the flow of thought in the same direction, DM briefly expresses her experience of Bella. She targets what is most personal in her contribution, as in this conversation.

> DM: There's a sense of loneliness, with no one to realize what it feels like. It sounds like there's an emptiness—a sense of nothing—that's . . . difficult to bear? Something seems to happen at those times. [The therapist attempts to couple with Bella's words in the session (what and how she says it) with something similar in a previous session or something she has reported from outside of the session.]
>
> Bella: Yes . . . (in a soft voice and a noticeable shift in non-verbal expression.)
>
> DM: When you knock yourself out with pills, as you said earlier, you don't have to feel the loneliness? There seems to be a connection.

Amplification

DM links the essential elements of what Bella says, often a word that is emotionally charged, along with the associated affect—for example, *loneliness* and *emp-*

tiness—though the patient is unaware of the underlying emotion. Through tone of voice and repetition of the patient's words at times, the therapist seeks to elaborate and almost invite the patient to look at the "feeling" further.

Representation

Similarly, the therapist puts into words what is most immediate and essential about the patient's experience. She uses tone of voice to represent the emotional core of the patient's experience. A slightly questioning tone of voice, a note of tentativeness, and the use of metaphor are ways in which the therapist facilitates the patient's own efforts to represent her experience.

Scaffolding

The therapist explores what is happening currently for the patient and conveys her understanding of what it might be like for her, giving Bella the sense of someone being interested enough to share her feelings and understand her situation.

Attempting to create a space in which Bella could have opportunities to safely talk about herself and her experiences, the therapist provides an understanding and responsiveness—a scaffolding—in the safety of which she can talk about her difficulties and manage her anxiety both in and outside the sessions.

Difficulty Ending Sessions

Bella seemed to have great difficulty ending the sessions, and this was another indication of her difficulty in separating. She would start talking about something new, just close to the end, and linger on with her story.

DM: It's difficult toward the end of our sessions, Bella?

Bella: What do you mean?

DM: I mean, here we have gone over by 10 minutes and we agreed to meet for 50 minutes.

Bella: Does that matter?

DM: I know you would like to go on, but keeping to time is also a way to help give you some structure. Suppose we alert ourselves about 10 minutes before it's time to finish? Then you won't find yourself trying to tell me a whole lot of things in the last 5 minutes. I do want to listen to you, but also there is someone I see after you.

Bella: There's always someone else in the way.

A sense of traumatic relatedness (transference) was evident from the very start, and the therapist had developed a better understanding of how to deal with these situations. She thought better in the moment and did not offer further comment—but registered not only Bella's words, but also the tone of her voice, which seemed to say, "I'm always left out."

Bella swallowed hard, and though it was initially difficult for her, she adjusted to finishing on time.

Therapist Experience of Cotransference and Countertransference

In a supervision session, DM evaluated her own status in relation to Bella's treatment:

> I found myself feeling alternately hopeless and resigned, but with a stronger feeling to continue to do my best. However, there were times when I felt tempted to react by discharging her from therapy or perhaps be punitive in some other way. It felt like a mouse being played with by a cat.
>
> Talking about these feelings helped, because I did not feel alone and also did not think that I was the only therapist who felt this way. Being reminded, and reminding myself, that traumatic experiences give rise to what seems like unaccountable behavior in some helped me to feel more in control and better able to sustain the therapy.
>
> I also felt an urge to directly refer to the tablets that Bella had been accumulating—to ask her to hand them in, or to advise against doctor-shopping— but decided against these urges because it would derail the therapy even before it started. Instead I tried to understand Bella's need to take overdoses and to explore the circumstances surrounding these overdoses, reflecting my understanding in a way that I felt might communicate to Bella that I was trying to be helpful. If I felt that she was taking medication excessively, I would have done something about it.

There was no way that DM could predict what was going to happen from one session to the next. However, DM had begun to deal with whatever arose, even though she was often taken by surprise. One could have said that Bella was still reacting to past mistreatments, and could not trust that anyone would be there for her, yet she longed to have someone just for herself. The next piece of conversation illustrates what I mean.

> Bella: There is no point hoping that others would be there, so it is better to let go of them; but it is so hard, letting go of them.

DM: (*in a questioning way*) Letting go of them? (*Bella appeared not to hear, and went on talking.*)

Inherent in what seems to be a mere repetition is a representing to the patient of what she has said and an inherent request for an elaboration.

Closeness and Distance

The therapist was bewildered that though Bella idealized her, she could feel no real sense of connection with her. No sooner did she feel connected then a sense of distance would interrupt. Bella was attempting to connect with her, but the past experiences of being let down, even abandoned, resulted in her pulling back from the therapist.

DM wondered if she should bring this pattern to Bella's attention. That seemed a reasonable thing to do, considering that Bella was largely unaware of her modes of relating. To leave it unsaid might create frustration on both parts, as the behavior might just be repeated. It would take quite some time before it reached a level of her awareness—for her to become conscious of this fact.

Working in the relationship, the therapist attempted to link her experience with Bella's possible experience. The success or otherwise of such an intervention could only be gauged by what happens next—and certainly Bella responded to DM in the first part of the intervention, and partly in the second. Perhaps, she could not sustain the connection she was forming with DM out of fear of rejection, although that very connection was what she most wanted. What follows is referred to in the CM as "linking." Linking replaces what is classically known as "interpretation." Once a link is made, the therapist works actively in the relationship—a definite use of pronouns such as "you" and "me" becomes more commonplace. The therapist attempts to raise the patient's awareness of their relationship.

DM: I get the feeling that it's hard to believe that I would want to listen.

Bella: Why would you? Nobody else does.

DM: Nobody else does? That must be hard, when nobody listens. It's understandable that you would expect that I too would not listen. (*A short silence ensued, after which the therapist continued.*) Sometimes, just when I have a sense of being trusted, it's followed immediately by an opposite sense, of not being trusted.

Bella: Do you? (*She then went on to talk about something else.*)

A few sessions later the therapist felt that she could be more direct in bringing to Bella's attention a different version of what she had said previously about their relationship, particularly when there was another instance of closeness followed by withdrawal. This intervention created a noticeable shift in the relationship, experienced both by therapist and patient, as illustrated by what happened in the next session, which inaugurated the middle stage of therapy.

DM: It seemed just now there was a feeling of safety . . .

Bella: Yes . . . yes . . .

DM: . . . but then something happened and I sensed a pulling back . . . like you and I were at a distance again.

MIDDLE STAGE OF THERAPY

Sessions 19 and 20

Listening to Traumatic Disclosures

Bella did not entirely dismiss this intervention, in that she appeared to acknowledge it nonverbally. There was an opening up soon after and in the next two sessions. In the 19th and 20th sessions Bella wept as she talked about her teenage pregnancy and the daughter she gave up immediately after birth. There emerged a new feeling of developing connectedness, as Bella was able to share with DM the most personal aspects of her life. DM began to feel a little less anxious about her efforts to reach Bella.

Though it might be considered that Bella had already disclosed this information to the therapist, in each repetition, something more is disclosed. The therapist must remember not to delve into the trauma before the patient discloses it. Too early and deep an exploration of traumatic material, before the patient has some sense of self, in the safety of the therapeutic relationship, may result in self-harming behavior, suicidal ideation, and generally a worsening of mental state.

The Nature of Dissociation

The therapist's fantasy of being able to get a clear developmental history had to be put aside. Bella's story, told initially in fragments with a variety of emotions, sometimes of a conflicting nature and often too difficult to understand, tumbled out.

At times, the therapist felt confused as she found Bella shifting from present to past, from one person to another, and often drifting away. DM had to remind herself that this is how dissociation feels to the listener—not a clear, coherent story, but one told in bits and pieces, with a feeling of unreality that also affects the therapist. She also wondered, was this the effect of taking more medication than she needed? One could never be certain, except to take note of physical indicators which would warrant some action.

The therapist had to be patient, and instead of asking questions, which would only be disruptive, she decided to allow the patient to take the lead. DM followed Bella, interjecting whenever there was an opportunity to be empathic, to convey her understanding, and to allow her to see that she was being listened to.

This approach was often difficult to maintain without getting caught up in the content of what had happened and what was happening. It was important to keep in tune with Bella's experience, to maintain an interest, and to come from a place of *not knowing*, and to be aware of how Bella related with the therapist, rather than simply what she said. The *therapist's subjective experience* was the most important here.

Feeling Tones and the Nonverbal Process

It was important for DM to remain aware of her feelings and reactions to what she was hearing. Attending to the process was of vital importance. The feeling tones of language and the nonverbal aspects of the interaction, when attended to, seemed to complete the interaction in a conversational loop. It took the form of communication from patient to therapist and back to patient again, conveying a sense of being understood.

Staying on the edge of the dissociated experience helped the therapist be with the patient, whereas entering further into the experience might have resulted in the therapist's own dissociating and therefore becoming unavailable. (The therapist knew that she had already had that experience in the first session.)

Disclosure of Trauma and a Reversal

Bella: (*Speaking in a childlike voice that was very different from the adult who previously sat across from me*) You had to do what was expected—you couldn't not (*looking frightened, restless and rubbing her skin*).

DM: You couldn't—that's frightening.

Bella: Yes, but no one cared. At school too, no one cared, no matter what happened. They bullied you if you didn't wear the right clothes—not that I didn't have any nice clothes. My uniform used to touch my ankles—everyone was taking their hems up—and me!

DM: You felt different . . . then you were bullied . . . it would have been really difficult.

Bella: You never messed with Mum.

DM: You never . . . ?

Bella: You never knew what she would do! You just knew (*a look of pain*) . . . something . . . something . . . bad would happen. It's too much—**now go to your room!** Alone . . . (*dissociating*).

DM: I can see that feeling of being alone . . . you are here now . . . we are here now . . . together in my office. (*Bella seemed to connect once again, which was the therapist's intention.*)

In supervision DM noted:

Bella seemed to dissociate, as I tried to empathically connect with her. She also seemed as if inhabited by her mother [a reversal], whom she had been talking about, and for a moment I felt like a child, when her voice tone changed: **"Now go to your room!"** Staying with her was important, and I was determined not to dissociate as I had done in the early stage.

The soothing sounds I made reinforced my presence along with giving Bella eye contact—it helped her not to dissociate further, and she was able to integrate and finish the session. There were several similar sessions, but each time she was less dissociated than the previous time, and better able to settle.

Grief and Loss

It was becoming clear that Bella had wanted to keep her daughter, but her mother had already decided that the child should be sent away to her grandmother, who then lived in the country. Bella was consoled by the fact that she and her mother would make regular visits to see the baby, whom she named *Cassie*.

Bella had been close to her grandmother, who had lived with her and her mother until Bella was 10 years old, so Bella knew that Cassie would be well taken care of. However, Bella longed for Cassie to know her (Bella) as her mother—which, she was told, was a "stupid idea." Cassie lived with her grandmother until her death, when Cassie was 6 years old, and then moved from the country to live with Bella and her mother.

Bella expressed her sense of loss for the first time as she described her mother's devotion to Cassie, and how she (Bella) often felt left out.

As she grew older, Bella said, Cassie was pampered and given large amounts of money and holidays away, something that Bella had never enjoyed with her mother. It was unclear whether Bella felt angry with both her mother and grandmother, and when this was put to her, she replied in a positive voice: "She [her grandmother] was the most beautiful person. She was always there—the only person, the only person—while Mum was busy and working away for days at a time. She moved to the country because of her allergies. I really missed her."

The therapist, impressed by her positive relationship with her grandmother, commented on it. The following conversation clearly illustrates the transference–cotransference in both patient and therapist, particularly the therapist's reaction to the patient's statement.

Continuing Idealization of Therapist

Bella: You are good for me too—you don't cancel or take long holidays. You return my calls within reasonable time too.

DM: (*Not responding to further idealizing*) I can understand you better as you talk about your early life. It must have been difficult when your grandmother left.

Bella: We often went down to see her. She was the best. She died unexpectedly when I was 23. I started to have panic attacks and took a lot of benzodiazepines after that—they were not of much use anyway.

DM reminded herself that Cassie came to live with them after the death of her grandmother and that this changed Bella's relationship with her mother.

The therapist unexpectedly received several calls from the team asking how Bella was, because they had not seen her for a few months, whereas previously she had been a familiar figure in the acute ward or in the accident and emergency wing of the local hospital.

Clarification, Elaboration, and Amplification

It gradually became possible for the therapist to communicate her understanding of Bella in more definite terms; it also became possible for DM to seek clarification from Bella and to elaborate and attempt to amplify her experience so as to help her affect become more available to her.

DM: Let me see if I have it correctly: You were 23 when your grandmother died?

Bella: Yes, but I had hardly seen her—for a while Mum was not talking to her.

DM: You could not see her on your own?

Bella: You would never see the end of it—if I did.

DM: Never?

Bella: I wanted so much to see her.

DM: It sounds like you missed her—you wanted to see your grandmother—but you did not want to displease your mother. That must have been hard.

Bella: Yes. (*She changed the topic at this point.*)

In attempting to amplify her statements, the therapist intended to bring to Bella's attention some of the affects that lay unexpressed. Most importantly the therapist began to handle Bella's idealization of her, and responded appropriately. (We are reminded about the many ways in which the therapist is changed by the patient.)

Metaphor

Twenty weeks into the therapy, Bella shared with the therapist that she loved to listen to the music of *The Phantom of the Opera* and would listen to it several times each day. She wondered with her about the story, and they talked about the music. Bella connected with the story of the Phantom who was disfigured, yet longed to be loved and noticed by a beautiful woman, but was rejected and abandoned by her as he competed with a young, handsome man for her attention.

The therapist recognized the metaphor and used it to enable Bella to connect with her feelings, creating a new experience. It became clear that the family situation, wherein she was forced to compete with her daughter for her adoptive mother's attention—a triangulated relationship—bore some similarity to that in *Phantom*. The use of the patient's metaphor helped open up several areas of current difficulty that were processed as the therapist attempted to understand and give meaning to them.

Sessions 21–50

Pathological Accommodation

As her story unfolded, it became apparent that after Bella's grandmother left to live in the country, Bella often "hung around" her mother when she was home. This "clinging" behavior made her mother extremely frustrated, and soon Bella felt rejected. Bella then became helpful around the house, hoping that her mother would notice and change her attitude—which she occasionally did in a rather off-handed way, according to Bella.

Her mother seemed to get more annoyed as Bella continued to spend more time at home instead of seeing her friends. The more her mother criticized her, the more Bella "hung around." However, she found it more and more difficult to accommodate to her mother, in contrast to her childhood behavior when her mother was away working and Bella had to stay with friends. She tried to please her friends, most of whom attended a state school, while she went to a private school for which she was often ridiculed. When fear is an integral part of the parent-child relationship, the child accommodates as a way of adapting to the different situations he or she finds him/herself in with regard to the parent. This for Bella became a way of being with people for quite a long time—a way of ensuring that she was pleasing to them.

Fear of Abandonment

Bella constantly felt on the brink of abandonment by her mother. It seemed that she had to conform in order to maintain the connection to her mother; at the same time it also became clear that there was an angry side to her too, and "perhaps," thought DM, "the overdoses communicated that anger, which could not be directly expressed." The function and the meaning of the tablet-taking behavior were becoming clearer. The anger, once named and resonated with, became a moment of aliveness in the therapy.

The Experience of Shame and Guilt

Bella: I'm pathetic, needing my mother, always worried about her leaving me.

DM: Every child needs its mother—and you have always worried about her leaving you.

Bella: Always.

DM: Can we talk about that a little more?

Bella: I told you. I'm pathetic—no one else is like me—Mum hates me—I'm pathetic.

There were hints of her shameful feelings earlier on, but these words seemed to betray not only her shame but also considerable guilt. Guilt, however, is more readily talked about, whereas shame, which is a complex self-conscious affect, often remains hidden and thereby hinders progress. Shame tends to block expression and obscure everything that is important and that needs exploration.

DM: Pathetic? It's like it's shameful to need someone, particularly your mother.

Bella: But you're called *pathetic* because you want too much. I used to do so much for Mum, so she would see that I was good—but she didn't. I feel so guilty talking about her this way.

DM: I can see how guilty you feel, like you should never say anything about your mum, or I might get the wrong opinion of her?

Bella: That would be ungrateful.

DM: And you would feel ashamed. I can see how you were made to feel shame. You had to be grateful to mum . . . because . . . ? (*Asked in a questioning way, then she wondered if she had done so too soon.*)

Bella: I could have been worse off. Mum adopted me. (*sobbing quietly*) What would have happened to me, if she hadn't?

DM: That's hard, very hard.

Bella continued to talk about being adopted, and she wondered about her natural parents, of whom she knew nothing. However, she said she was uninterested in finding out because "they didn't want me—there could have been no other reason why they would give me up." She could not be engaged and did not talk about this topic again, even when the therapist asked her toward the end of therapy. She said that it did not really matter to her, adding: "It's not like some people. They go on searching for their biological parents. I don't think I want to do that. I think about it sometimes, but it's not a big issue for me."

Gradually the therapist found Bella to be brighter and more connected. DM too was beginning to feel more optimistic, as she empathically immersed herself in Bella's story, linking issues within the session and between sessions, and working in the therapeutic relationship in the here-and-now. Bella had stopped contacting the mental health and other services by the 26th session.

Text Messages

Bella would often send text messages—either comments on the session or on what was happening outside. The therapist would read them, and nothing would be said about them—the patient made no reference to them either. Then one day

Bella asked the therapist why she did not respond to her text messages. DM replied that she felt Bella was communicating with her about something that was happening outside the therapy hour, and that she would like her to talk about those matters in the session. However, DM added that she attached importance to Bella's text messages and always read them when she could.

Bella: You don't seem to care.

DM: Because I don't reply to your texts?

Bella: And because you're like everyone else.

DM: It's difficult to find time. That's the reason why we agreed that you would contact the crisis team if you were having difficulties. Besides, we need to talk about some of these things that you raise in your texts—they do deserve talking about. I think that's more the reason why I don't reply, and they don't seem to need an answer straight away.

Bella: So you don't mind my texting you?

DM: I would rather you talked about things when we meet—then we can deal with things—but I won't be able to reply to all your text messages.

Any communication from the patient to the therapist must be given importance in the next session. Sometimes the experience of shame may prevent a patient from talking about an issue face to face; sometimes the patient has connected with something after a session, or there has been an event between sessions about which the patient wishes to tell the therapist. There are times when patients e-mail or text and do not expect an answer.

The use of electronic communication is an issue for the individual therapist. It is generally advisable to talk about the preferred method of communication when the frame and contract is set up, so that the therapist is not taken by surprise, or the patient does not indulge in a behavior that is considered unsuitable by the therapist. However, it often comes to our attention that patients commonly communicate by text in their daily lives, and may not hesitate to do the same with the therapist. Whatever the mode of communication, the therapist must not expect him/herself to respond each time. It is preferable to make this clear to the patient, and discuss any communication received between sessions at the very next session. Urgent communications must be responded to in the way that was initially negotiated.

The therapeutic relationship deepened as the patient continued to increasingly idealize the therapist. The therapist focused on the brightness Bella felt when talking about her grandmother—Bella said that talking about her grandmother brought her to life. The therapist observed: "It must have been a difficult time when your grandmother left to live in her own home in the country."

It seemed that Bella was grieving for her grandmother, but she could not stay with the theme. Rather, she talked about her mother who had often gone away on business while she was young. She sometimes did not see her mother for days on end (after her grandmother left) while she would be left to stay with a family friend. The therapist continued to follow what Bella was talking about, taking what was given, and did not pursue an agenda of her own.

A Disjunction Followed by Repair

Bella returned to talking about her grandmother who had died quite unexpectedly when Bella was 23 years old. Her daughter Cassie, 6 years old by then, returned to stay with her mother and herself. This major change marked the beginning of an even more tumultuous relationship with her mother and coincided with the onset of panic attacks and the use of benzodiazepines. This situation was immensely traumatic for Bella to talk about. The therapist felt that perhaps she was not attuned to Bella or had attempted to explore this topic in too much depth, too soon.

> Bella: Grandma would do anything for Mum, but I don't know if Mum took much notice. But I miss Grandma terribly, I wish she was still here—then Cassie could have stayed with her. I wished so often that I could tell Cassie that I am her real mother.
>
> DM: Would she have handled knowing, do you think? (*Silence followed.*)
>
> Bella: (*almost talking to herself*) I really need to take those tablets—get it over and done with.

Once again Bella reverted to talking about her tablets and the need to take an overdose, after at least a few weeks of not mentioning them. The therapist realized that she had not acknowledged Bella's need to have someone of her own. Cassie was her daughter. Bella was very sensitive to what might have felt like a slight.

DM described "feeling controlled and manipulated" at this stage, as Bella repeatedly used the "threat of overdosing" every time she felt misunderstood or not listened to. The therapist began to feel "organized within the relationship as a caretaker—the one who must now be responsible."

Therapist countertransference can be quite strong in such situations. The therapist must be aware of this possibility and deal with his or her feelings, so as not to act on them inadvertently. Talking about these feelings helped; nevertheless, the therapist often felt incompetent and of little help. She said: "It would have been so easy to vent my frustration by discharging her or by being punitive in some way. I feel like a mouse being played with by a cat." Here is an example:

> Bella: I'm going to take an overdose, and it will be their fault. I took an overdose last night and nearly rang the acute team.
>
> DM: Why would you do that? Our sessions will only be useful if they are helping you get better. If you are going to start taking overdoses, what will be the point? I understand how hurt and angry you feel, how let down you feel.

DM remarked that she felt a flash of anger and impatience that Bella was indeed not getting better. Though she was aware of her reaction, the therapist had difficulty containing her annoyance. The session ended in silence, and DM realized that she had threatened Bella at a time when she was feeling powerless and alone, and then she had tried to fix it, by her understanding and reassurance. The therapist is also human. There are times working with patients who have severe BPD when a whole host of feelings overwhelms the therapist. Novice therapists are sometimes not able to control their feelings as well as they can when they are experienced.

The Reality of the Therapist's Countertransference

It was helpful for the therapist to be aware of her countertransference and her own role in her developing anger and frustration, as she strove to "be there" for Bella. She was able to work through her own feelings of guilt at not being able to change the patient sooner than she expected. The following comments made by DM help us to understand how issues in the therapist's life add to the difficulties experienced with the patient and are also responsible for the countertransference.

> In some sections of the mental health field, where short-term therapies are the rule, long-term psychodynamic psychotherapy is often viewed with skepticism and even sometimes suspicion. I feel afraid that the therapy would worsen the patient, and that support practitioners would have to pick up the pieces.

This was an important reason for her fear – how she would be seen or talked about by her peers. "Bella was not being a good patient," she said.

The co-transference refers to the therapist's ordinary and expected reactions to the patient's communications and behavior.

The next day there was a phone message from Bella: "You are going to dump me like all the others. I might as well take an overdose."

DM felt both angry and responsible, but realized that she needed to calm herself before returning the call. Bella phoned again and wanted to know why her call had not been returned. (The therapist had hitherto been very reliable in answering calls during office hours.) DM responded to Bella's second call and said: "I'm very sorry that I didn't call you back yesterday. You sounded so unhappy and distressed, and I needed to think about what I could say to you that would help. Can we talk about it in the next session?"

Sessions 51–75

Traumatic Repetition and Fears of Abandonment

Bella was still very unsure that the therapist would be there for her and that the therapy would continue. Her suicidal preoccupation continued, as DM experienced her like an anxious child, clinging to her lest she go away.

DM realized that she needed to listen to Bella's talk of self-harm without undue anxiety on her part, so that it would be possible to gauge her intent to do so before the end of the session. It became evident that to rush into a risk assessment too early would only create anxiety and therefore a failure to provide containment on her part. She then began to understand the part that self-harm played in Bella's life. It was as if there would be no care or concern for Bella's welfare if she stopped talking of overdosing on tablets.

A Separation

The first real break in therapy occurred at about the 60th session. The therapist prepared Bella in advance that she would be away for 2 weeks. Bella did not take kindly to this break. She became anxious and sought to remind the therapist that she always had enough tablets to overdose if she needed. The therapist, realizing how important this contact had been for Bella, was able to control her own anxiety and help Bella by putting in place a trusted therapist whom Bella could contact if she felt the need. Bella managed by herself until the therapist returned. She did not hide her sense of relief when she saw her at the next appointment.

Processing the Trauma: An Improved Sense of Self

DM took care not to process Bella's traumas too early in the therapy. However, she identified and responded to any sign of intrusion of traumatic memories. Trauma should always be processed in the here-and-now of the relationship, i.e., in the present. As the therapeutic relationship becomes safe, a better sense of self is experienced, and a slightly better sense of cohesion and improved reflective capacity develops. Bella's ability to manage a separation from the therapist was a manifestation of an improved ability to remain cohesive in the therapist's absence. The therapist, with Bella, had built up a "scene" of traumatic memory—she was aware of the happenings, the people, the feelings, and responses involved in Bella's traumatic history.

Changing Language

The therapist, who hitherto used a language that was tentative and rather neutral (e.g., in its use of pronouns, brief interventions, murmurs, sounds, and linking statements), aimed at letting Bella know that she was present, that she was listening, and that she cared. DM now began to open up the sessions to exploration of the material that Bella brought in, amplifying what she said and inviting her to elaborate on what she was experiencing. They talked about the therapist's absence, and that Bella had done very well during that time.

Bella seemed perturbed by the therapist's confidence in her ability to manage without her, and did not attempt to hide this. The therapist wondered if she had gone "overboard" in her praise of Bella. Whatever the reason was, DM sensed Bella's distrust and directly addressed it, as illustrated in the following excerpt.

Linking in Relationship

DM: It seems hard to imagine that I will be here for you (*in a questioning tone of voice*).

Bella: You might find me too hard, a nuisance, like all the others.

DM: It is understandable that you would not trust anyone to be there for you; to feel that I consider you a nuisance, like you said your mother did, but it seems to me there are things happening between you and your mother that often surface before you take an overdose. Do you think we can talk about this?

Bella launched into a series of memories of her relationship with her adoptive parents. She described often feeling *in the way* or *not doing the right thing* or *wanting too much* and always feeling that she *could never please them*. Though she idealized the therapist, her own experience of *being left* was very real (her adoption), and she believed that it would keep happening—she could not trust anyone. She was just beginning to trust the therapist. Working in the relationship and helping Bella to safely tell her story, DM provided a calming and containing influence that allowed the sadness, the anger, and the loneliness to be expressed, and her early memories to be processed.

Intrusion of Traumatic Memories

Bella entertained mixed feelings toward her mother, to whom she had hitherto accommodated for fear of being rejected. She had to be grateful for being adopted and spared from what she said might have been a life of poverty and insecurity. No sooner had she said this than her demeanor changed; she began to feel extremely guilty that she had described her mother in such a "mean" way and attempted to point out some of her mother's good qualities. She began to see herself again as "bad"—traumatic memories had intruded.

> DM: I hear you telling me what it was like for you growing up, but no sooner had you told me how difficult it had been, I also heard you put yourself down, feeling that you are bad for telling me these things.
>
> Bella: Yes . . . I am . . . you must think so too.

It did not seem necessary for the therapist to negate Bella's feelings, as it was possible that Bella had been made to feel bad so often that she had begun to see herself as bad—as bad as seen by the "other." Therefore she must *be* bad. This self-view had to be borne in mind as therapy progressed. Bella had accommodated to others most of her life, and to change that way of being would take time. Furthermore, her adoptive mother was the only person she had in her life. She could not take the risk.

Sessions 76–100

Continuing Environmental Conflict

The home situation continued to be conflicted, as it usually was when Cassie visited. (Bella's mother had provided Cassie with a separate home some distance away when Cassie turned 18 and started attending university). Bella would often take to her bed, rather than stay in their company. But then she felt left out. Her mother referred to her as "antisocial" at these times, and they would argue; Cassie often referred to Bella in disparaging terms as well.

Bella described how her mother and Cassie packed and left home while she was asleep, leaving her alone on Christmas Day, in spite of the fact that the three of them had planned to go away for a few days. She felt completely abandoned. It had become clear that Bella's overdoses were linked to her mother's neglect in caring for her too; but rather than elicit care, the overdoses seemed to antagonize her mother and distance her even more.

A Disjunction

DM: I wonder if your mother distances herself when you take an overdose.

Bella: No one understands. What does it take to make people understand (*spoken in child-like manner*)?

The therapist tentatively reflected this possibility to her, and later wished she had not. It was too direct. Bella felt once again judged and alienated. It may not have mattered how carefully the therapist used her words—Bella was highly sensitized to feeling criticized. The stability of the earlier sessions seemed to vanish, and Bella was once again talking about her hoard of medication with threats of taking an overdose. Attempts on the therapist's part to repair the disjunction seemed of no avail this time. This was a testing time for the therapist.

Bella: I won't be a nuisance to anyone. I won't be a nuisance to you too.

DM: I can understand how you have come to see yourself as a nuisance—no one took you seriously—you think that I see you as a nuisance too?

A Possible Impasse

Any attempt by the therapist to highlight some positive aspects of Bella was met with disdain and a refusal to accept that there was anything positive about her. Any inkling of positivity on Bella's part seemed to be immediately overshadowed by a negative feeling and self-denigration.

When a patient such as Bella shows signs of improvement in their sense of self, the therapist sometimes attempts excessively to change his or her language, to praise the patient in a way which creates separation anxiety with thoughts of the therapy coming to an end. This may be premature and can result in a disjunction.

Bella and DM seemed to be going around in circles, and Bella's continued exclamations of "I wish I was dead" alarmed the therapist, especially in light of what felt like an impasse. DM described experiencing the same feelings of helplessness that she had experienced in the beginning of her work with Bella. Whenever the patient perceived the therapist as "like all the others," any sense of trust was temporarily disrupted, resulting in Bella distancing herself. This then caused her to feel more alone.

DM recalled feeling helpless and hopeless that she could ever bring about change in Bella. However, talking about her experience helped her approach the next session with less anxiety. Knowing that one has reached an impasse is important, and talking about it with the patient is even more important.

Exploring the Impasse

DM: A few sessions have passed in which we seem to almost argue with one another. We seem to be going around in circles. Do you feel that happens?

Bella: I don't know what you mean.

DM: I seem to say something, which makes you feel that I am unhelpful, then you threaten to take tablets.

Bella: Yes, I know I do.

DM: Whenever I hear you say something positive about yourself, it is as if you go into negative mode almost right away; it's as if you are not allowed to give yourself any positives. It's as if I cannot say anything positive about you either.

Bella: How could I? How could I? How could you? After everything that has happened.

In supervision DM noted that it took two more sessions before Bella and she could agree on what was happening and move on.

Sessions 101–124: Transformation of Traumatic Relatedness

Cumulative Trauma and Sexual Abuse

Bella disclosed that she had been sexually abused by her adoptive father when she was 7 years old and in elementary school. She talked about having to keep it a secret for fear that something terrible would happen to the family if she spoke. She was not supposed to tell her grandmother either.

She remembered feeling very anxious after experiencing the sexual abuse; she soon became depressed and never felt the same again. During one of her many hospitalizations she remembered being asked how long she had been depressed and she had said since the age of 14. However her mother corrected her and said that she had been depressed since she was 7 years old. Bella also became aware, though much later, that her mother was investigated for "child neglect" after the abuse was disclosed. This was another source of Bella's anxiety—that she might be taken away from her adoptive mother. There were many reasons why Bella had to be compliant.

Further Grief and Loss

Bella had received treatment for depression from several practitioners, and with each failed attempt at treatment, she reported feeling worse. She then began to talk about her daughter.

> Bella: I wanted something of my very own to love and care about, and I had my daughter. I should have got myself another kitten.

There was an emerging awareness that the desire to have a child was a way of compensating for her loneliness and emptiness. However, Bella could not keep her daughter as her mother had other plans, and Cassie was sent to live with her grandmother. Bella had to resign herself to the possibility that Cassie would replace Bella in Bella's grandmother's affections (this never happened). When Cassie eventually came to live with Bella and her mother when she was 6 years old, it was clear to Bella that Cassie had a much closer relationship with her mother than she ever had with Bella. This was a source of much grief for Bella. It was at this time that Bella reported she experienced panic attacks for the first time.

She had moved away from talking about her father. She dissociated briefly and went on to talk about the daughter she now had but could not claim—she talked about the present.

Then there was a movement back to the past as she described being referred to a counselor to help her with her alcohol consumption and overuse of medication. The counselor, she said, became increasingly frustrated with her and finally ended their sessions, saying that Bella was not trying to help herself. Bella said she missed not being able to talk to her every week and felt bitter that she had been given up so abruptly, adding, "If I had overdosed, it would have been her fault."

The therapist was aware that Bella was disrupted by these early traumatic memories, and she (DM) often felt triangulated when Bella talked about her previous helpers. Still, DM felt that this was the time to listen and not probe or ask questions. She conveyed her understanding to Bella as she sobbed. Bella was able to respond to DM's containing influence, and there was no evidence of her decompensating, in spite of her traumatic memories coming to the fore. It was extremely difficult for the therapist who nonetheless managed her quite well.

Elaboration of Early Experiences

Sometime later Bella started to talk about her adoptive father once again.

Bella: He and Mum split when I was 12 months old; he used to have access to me, and when I was older he would take me for a day each weekend. He sexually abused me, and I was not to tell anyone. He said I would be taken away, and would never see my mother or my grandmother again. I don't know when this started, but one day I ran away and took the train back to Mum's place. The train was stopped before I got there, and I was taken off it and returned to him. He knew people in the railways, and he could get them to do things like that. I must have been 7 or 8 because that was when my friend's older sister was having a baby.

DM: You ran away and were taken back—that made it harder for you.

Bella: He used to be so nice, bought me nice things. I told Mum what he was doing and she did not believe at first, then she said the same—I could be taken away if we said anything. But I could not go back. I refused—nothing would make me go back. Then Mum told dad that she knew about the abuse and that I was not coming back. If he made me, she said she would make a complaint to the police. I have not seen him since.

Validation

Many sessions were spent processing these and other memories that had the potential of triggering fears of loss and abandonment. The therapist validated Bella's sense of outrage at her father, and also her dilemma of protecting her mother or protecting herself. She was threatened no matter which way she turned.

Bella: What could she do? She did the best she could. The welfare people would have been on her back, and I might have been taken from her.

DM: And there was nothing you could do either. You were threatened if you told anyone about the abuse by your father. You could be sent away, your mother would have been in trouble—you could not let either happen.

What If None of This Happened?

What surprised the therapist was that Bella suddenly began to question her memories.

Bella: What if none of this happened to me? Am I making this up?

DM: [On careful scrutiny of these questions, the therapist felt that Bella was asking her something more than what appeared to be on the surface.] I'm wondering if you want to know whether I believe you.

Bella: Do you?

DM: I sense your pain and how difficult it was for you. Things happened that made life hard for you. It's understandable that you worry whether I believe you—you were not believed at first by your mother, you said.

By her manner the therapist answered Bella's question without actually saying *yes* or *no*. Bella did not seem to require an answer. The therapeutic relationship at this stage was being transformed, and the therapist felt the difference. Bella also recollected that her father threatened her if she did not change her story.

Bella: It did not happen—it did not happen—he said that over and over again.

DM: It's difficult, when your own reality is questioned. You were obviously afraid, by the sound of it.

Sessions 125–150: Toward Integration

Developing Self-Awareness and Reflective Capacity

From a rather restricted way of relating, from fragmentation, and from an essentially outer orientation that belied her state of alienation, Bella's communications became more associative. She was developing an improved capacity for self-reflection, with a language that was more and more capable of elaboration.

Validating her experience made it possible for Bella to talk about her early relationships without fear of being criticized or ridiculed. She gradually began to take some responsibility for herself. She had begun to develop the capacity to put words to, and elaborate on, her inner feeling states and to reflect on her circumstances. More and more, both patient and therapist were experiencing a freedom in communication that was never there before.

Being of "Two Minds"

Bella: I'm of two minds as to what to do. On the one hand, if I think about leaving home, I feel guilty and irresponsible toward my mother, who is old and I know will miss me. On the other hand, I can be myself if I go, live by my own rules instead of my mother's. It's her house. What do you think I should do?

DM: [DM felt an urge to answer Bella's question, but held back and asked herself if it could be talked about further. Answering her question could be repeating the infantilizing behavior of her mother; while not answering her could be perceived by Bella as withholding.] Before I answer that question, Bella, could we look at the dilemma you have just talked about?

Bella: What dilemma?

DM: On the one hand, you feel guilty to move because your mother is old and will miss you; and on the other, you want your own place, and you want to live by your own rules—the dilemma.

Bella: You're no help. Mum always told me what was best for me—for my own good, she always said.

DM: I'm not so sure that you need me to tell you what to do. I feel I would have been doing what your Mum always did—and also I remember you said that you hated it.

Bella: You're right. I would not have liked it, if you told me to move out.

Bella presented this dilemma several times, and each time, her difficulty was understood and validated. It was amplified in terms of her need to be grateful to her mother—a need that she felt quite acutely for a long time—along with another emerging need to take care of herself and to make her own rules and be her own person. Her developing autonomy was acknowledged, but yet, it did not seem right to encourage her at this point in time. She had to work through the ambivalence she felt toward her mother. She could emotionally separate from her once she had done that.

Further Traumatic Disclosures

It seemed that each time DM felt that Bella was making gains, another new piece of information would become available, which tended to disrupt her. The therapist had been particularly careful not to delve into her traumatic history but instead to let it unfold and to help her process it at her own pace.

To intrude would mean to repeat her mother's behavior toward her. At this stage, Bella, though disrupted, could be contained more easily than during the early stage of therapy. She talked about having her first sexual experience at the age of 15 and how she had never told anyone because she felt guilty. She said that she had experienced flashbacks and nightmares, which were quite disruptive at the time and made it difficult for her to sleep at night. She began to regret what had happened but ended up saying, "I had no choice."

Another Overdose

The same evening after Bella had revealed her teen sexual experience in the therapy session, she reported a lapse into familiar behavior.

Bella: I knocked myself out on the weekend.

DM: Tell me about it (*attempting to hide any negative reaction and attune to her*).

Bella: I took an overdose when Mum went out and left me on my own. She was gone for 4 hours, and I had nothing to do. I was bored. I hate my life. I don't care if I die (*sounding like a sad little child who felt helpless and hopeless*).

DM: You don't care if you die; that is a sad way to feel.

Bella: That's not new.

DM: You felt so lonely when your mum left you alone.

Bella: You don't really understand.

DM: It must be really despairing—and you have been trying for so long to get her to care for you.

Bella responded well; however, the therapist had a strong feeling that Bella expected something more, perhaps something different. This subjective sense of the therapist proved correct, as is illustrated in the next session.

The Wish for the Therapist as a Friend

Bella: I see you twice a week—there's no one the rest of the time. I wish we could do something different, like go out, have a coffee or something.

DM: (*Taken aback; remains silent, listening.*)

Bella: There is nothing I can do. I can't watch the television, it's boring. I did nothing all weekend. I sat in my room, hoping that Mum did not hear the packets of tablets rustling. She lies in her room, and I in mine. She asks me how I am, and I just pretend, and say I'm OK.

DM: I can see how lonely you are and how much you need your mother. It would be nice if you and she could do things together. If you and I went out together, having coffee, I don't think I would ever be able to help you again. You came to me for help—to feel better and to function better. Do you see what I mean? I could not be both, Bella.

The therapist stayed with Bella, and rather than suggest to Bella, at this moment, that she should find something to do—an activity, a pastime, a job, or some such thing—DM only noted how lonely she was.

Her mother, being much older than her, often rested during the day. The therapist said that she detected a note in Bella of really wanting to be acknowledged by her mother, of wishing she could spend time with her and perhaps do something with her.

The therapist also explored Bella's wish to have her as a friend, letting her know that as a friend she would cease to be of help to her, and help was what she had asked for. Bella took this well, reiterating how lonely she felt, but she seemed resigned to not having more of a relationship with the therapist, other than to see her twice weekly.

What Happens Next?

The usefulness of the therapist's response to Bella was clarified not only in her immediate response, but also in the changes that ensued. A few sessions later, Bella came in and told the therapist that she had pruned a rosebush in the garden that had been bought by her adoptive mother as a birthday gift for her. She was animated, and the therapist joined her in her delight.

They talked about roses and other plants, hints for gardening, and wondered when the roses would be in bloom. The therapist shared with Bella her love of gardening. Bella said she had neglected the garden for a very long time, and it was all overgrown. She wanted to bring it back to order. She remembered that her mother was fond of gardening and tended it with a lot of care, though she had not done so in recent years. Bella was attending to herself as she tended the garden.

They were now able to talk about the things that Bella was interested in, and how she might find things to do that would make a difference in her life. Bella seemed ready to look beyond her extremely restricted life. The process of integration was becoming apparent.

LATE STAGE OF THERAPY

Sessions 151–175

Flights and Perchings

Consciousness is dynamic, and the therapist was aware that Bella had been unaware of her changing mental states. Now she seemed aware, and said so.

Bella: When you said these things before, I used to get mad and scream at you—
you didn't understand. Now I see the difference. I can see what you mean.

Bella was actually describing the flights of consciousness that used to happen in the earlier stages when she would dismiss the therapist, change the topic, or become angry at something that was said. Now she sees the difference. These are the perchings: when she is able to stop and think about something and then reflect on it, from her own and from another's point of view.

> Bella: Thank you for not giving up on me, even though I know I gave you a hard time.

Cohesion and increasing self-reflectivity are aspects of an improved sense of self. They are the result of a widening of consciousness, a functioning at the higher levels of the hierarchy of consciousness when self and other are differentiated and when language is more of a narrative form, rather than fragmented as in the early stages.

A Gift for the Therapist

> Bella produced a bunch of flowers from behind her and gave it to the therapist.

> DM: Thank you, they are gorgeous. You brought them for me?
> Bella: It's just a simple bunch of flowers to thank you for looking after me.
> DM: You have been through such a hard time. I'm glad we have been able to work on this together.

Connecting with the Outside World

Integration happens both in the therapeutic space and in the outside world. Bella talked about and began to attend a drop-in center for people with mental health difficulties. She reported that she wished she had done this earlier. She was finding the socializing particularly interesting and helpful. She was also beginning to form friendships.

She dealt with breaks in therapy much better than was expected. She was becoming more aware of people in her life, her effect on them, and theirs on her. She also began to explore, once again, the possibility of moving away from her mother's home. However, when the therapist took an active interest in this suggestion, she withdrew.

> Bella: She's not young, you know. I was on my way to the day center when my mother rang and said she was sick, but that I "wasn't to worry." I got to the center and felt very anxious, like I had to get back home soon. So I left early.

DM: Your mum and you both worry about each other?

Bella: Uh-hm. I never really looked at it like that, but—yes!

It was evident that the anxiety at separation was mutual: Bella and her mother were equally anxious about each other. However, Bella seemed prepared to work on this.

Separation Anxiety

Several sessions were spent with Bella talking about her mother. It was clear that from her early years, Bella needed to be close to her mother at the expense of her otherwise developing autonomy.

Her mother had often been away, and after her grandmother had moved, a friend cared for Bella—experiences she clearly remembered as making her very anxious and fearful. She could now talk about these earlier experiences with sadness, but without fragmenting.

Traumatic experiences cannot always be remembered, and it is not unusual for such memories to surface in the late stages. Talk of separating naturally brought up feelings of anxiety that were familiar—that is, they were experienced at an earlier stage to a substantial degree.

Bella was trying to establish her separateness and become autonomous. She was worried about the effect it would have on her mother, who had no idea that she was talking about leaving home. She could not bring herself to talk about it with her mother. She gradually began to identify her thoughts as different from her mother's but still experienced guilt in the process. She once again talked about gratitude for having been adopted. Her ambivalence was quite clear. The therapist knew she could not hurry the process, nor could she offer Bella direct insights into the situation.

Intrusion of Traumatic Memories

Bella talked about her childhood memories. In the repetition of these memories, new affect was becoming available, and new understanding was developing. One day the therapist reflected to her:

DM: Every time you talk about looking after yourself, Bella, it's as if something or someone cuts across your enthusiasm, and you begin to feel guilty about even the idea of leaving your mother.

Bella: I do feel good when I think of living independently, but I don't feel good about leaving Mum on her own. She would have no one.

DM: Those opposite feelings would make it very difficult to make a decision.

The therapist could see that Bella's attempts at independence were being thwarted by her mother, who continued to call Bella to get her to come home early from the day center. Bella more clearly began to identify her own thoughts and feelings and was more in touch with her emotions. She said that she was really enjoying the day center, but was feeling very responsible for her mother who was "all alone at home."

Working Through Anxiety

One day Bella came in looking upset and annoyed at the same time. Barely seated, she said, "I've been going round and round in circles, and I don't know what I'm doing. I feel so depressed. Nothing seems right. I don't care if I am dead or alive."

This line of thinking surprised the therapist on two levels. Bella was actually talking about feelings and thinking about feelings. However, the catastrophic manner of the early sessions seemed to return. In supervision the therapist described her perception of the situation:

> It was as if I had not noticed her difficulties, perhaps to do with separating from her mother. She grossly amplified whatever she said. Was it an unconscious way in which to get noticed rather than ignored? She was once again talking about dying—why now? She was again conveying that sense of urgency that felt as if I should immediately do something.

However the therapist put aside her own ruminations and gave value to what Bella was expressing, saying only, "Come, sit down and tell me about it. You seem upset." As Bella talked in a highly emotional way, she became aware of, and expressed her anger toward, her mother, whom she said had often threatened to "cut" her out of her will, and was doing so again. Bella said she talked about this in groups at the day center, and they validated her anger and her difficulty in making a decision about having a place of her own.

Continuing Mother–Daughter Conflict

It became obvious that there was increasing tension and conflict at home between Bella and her mother, particularly on weekends, when Cassie (Bella's daughter) came home. Bella would start the session on a Monday talking about her interactions with her mother.

89

Bella: She keeps reminding me not to take too many tablets. She keeps telling me, all the time, that I should only take one of this and two of that—and you know that she can't be responsible, now that I am a grown woman. I wish she would leave it to me. She says I'm a grown woman, but she doesn't act like I am one.

DM: Your mum must be aware by now that you have not been overdosing on tablets. It sounds like she finds it hard to let you take care of yourself, like a grown woman should?

Bella: You're exactly right! She cannot let go. But it doesn't make sense. There I was—always trying to get her to take care of me because I always felt that she did not really care.

DM: You are beginning to really think about your relationship with your mother.

Bella: She gave me the best of everything, except her time. She gave Cassie all her time, and when Cassie finished school she sent her to university and bought her an apartment close to the university, which she shares with another girl. I never got to go to university, even though I finished school—but of course I didn't do so well, what with all that happened! I have always been jealous of Cassie. I should not be, I know.

DM: It's hard, when you think about the things you've missed out on. Being jealous of Cassie—anyone would have felt jealous. You wanted to be cared for, like Cassie was being cared for.

This was one of the many examples of Bella's reactions to her mother's intrusiveness and overprotection. The talk in the sessions about overdosing often followed conflicts with her mother, during which she would experience her as quite rejecting and undermining. The therapist and Bella talked about this association quite openly.

Bella reported being more assertive with her mother, at which time her mother would threaten to move into a nursing home, leaving Bella to fend for herself. The therapist would convey her understanding of the situation, acknowledge Bella's despair, and validate her need to have a place of her own, like any adult would want. In the process she would amplify Bella's developing sense of self as an individual deserving of an independent life.

Jealousy

Bella talked more about Cassie.

Bella: Cassie was always the center of attention, I feel so jealous. I had to constantly please her—my mum. Nothing I did was good enough. I can see when

I look back, how much I wanted her to notice me. Sometimes I think she didn't love me. But Cassie gets so much from her.

DM: I hear your sadness. It's like there was no space for you. I see you looking back and wishing that it was different.

Bella: What else could I have done?

DM: It seems to me you're blaming yourself, feeling that you should have done more!

Bella: I should have, but then—

DM: There's a lot of sadness about your need for your mother, but also about the fact that you may lose her soon (*questioning tone*)?

Bella: Yes, it's too late. I must have been so bad, so bad that she couldn't love me. But then she had her own problems too. There was Dad first, then my grandmother, then after a while she was alone too, and after my grandmother died, she was alone but for Cassie.

By linking and amplifying what Bella said, the therapist helped her to process these feelings as she talked about them for the first time. Bella talked more about Cassie and her sadness, but felt that she would be there for Cassie. Cassie too would miss her mother, but added that she would manage. "Cassie is very different from me," Bella said.

Sessions 176–180: Change, Agency, and Independent Living

Bella applied to the Department of Housing and was granted a unit, which she inspected but turned down because she found it to be unsafe. She was experiencing an improved sense of self with a new sense of agency, taking particular note of her need for safety when choosing a place to live. She reasoned that she could live at home until she was assured of a safe alternative.

This was a surprise to the therapist. Shortly afterward, she was offered another apartment, which she accepted and moved into the following week. Her mother, who had suddenly become quite ill, was diagnosed with cancer and was advised that she would be required to move to a nursing home, as she required round-the-clock care.

A Session with Mother and Daughter

The therapist had a session with Bella and her mother, at Bella's request. It was a very productive meeting for both of them. Bella was overjoyed to be leaving home while on good terms with her mother, and also felt good that she was not a burden to her, at a time when her mother needed to be free from stress. Bella's mother was also able to express relief that she did not need to worry about her, though her ambivalence was quite clear to the therapist. A further session with both of them served to sow the seeds of reconciliation between them, for which Bella was grateful. She said: "I could not have talked with my mother on my own—not say the kind of things I was able to say. I mean, I think it cleared the air somewhat. I know I will have to come to terms with the fact that my mother will die soon, but at least I heard her say that she loves me."

A Changed Attitude toward Medication

Bella had stopped talking about tablets—she reminded the therapist of this. She had also stopped talking about overdosing. She was never interrogated by the therapist about doctor-shopping or about stashing away tablets, though the therapist often wondered. Had she questioned Bella in such a way in the early stages it might have derailed the therapy. And Bella could have gotten substances if she really set her mind to it.

It's a fine line between being intrusive in such situations and being irresponsible. The therapist needs to deal with each individual case, bearing in mind that the welfare of the patient is the primary task at hand.

Bella went back to the days when she took far too many tablets and to the beginning of their relationship. She had detoxified in the hospital at the beginning of the therapy. She had several appointments with a drug and alcohol counselor. Bella admitted that she had continued to take a few more tablets than she was supposed to, but had completely stopped seeing any doctors apart from her designated GP. She no longer had any tablets with her except a low-dose sedative.

She added that she had a painful shoulder and went to see her GP, who prescribed some anti-inflammatory drugs. The therapist suddenly found herself thinking, "I wonder if she will talk about overdosing on them"—but she never did.

Bella continued to function well. She had developed an awareness of the risks of taking too many tablets and had gotten rid of the medication that she had stockpiled. She said this to the therapist in a rather animated manner, feeling good about her achievement.

The therapist reflected her achievement and also felt good that she had not rushed to get into the issue of her medication—something that she had thought about, but decided against. The therapist had also become aware that there were times when Bella would drink alcohol and take tablets, but that alcohol was never a problem on its own. Bella's general practitioner had instructed her about the risks of combining alcohol with tranquilizers, and was reviewing Bella on a regular basis.

Separation Anxiety Mingling with Grief and Loss

Bella was able to deal with a house robbery without falling apart, and instead was able to report it to the police. She had been dealing with her mother's illness in a rather mature way, as she continued in therapy. Leaving home brought up issues of grief and loss, and she wondered what would happen when her mother died. She then began to worry about the therapist going away or the sessions concluding. A date had not yet been set for the end of therapy. When issues of ending therapy were referred to indirectly in earlier sessions, Bella would become very anxious, often referring to the therapy as if it was going to last forever.

Doubts and Anxiety at Ending

Bella would ask repeatedly, "What if I am not well enough? How would you know when I am well enough? What if I cannot cope when the therapy is finished?" She was coming to accept the reality of therapy coming to an end. She needed to make sure. The therapist remembered the early stage when she had wondered, "Will I ever be able to finish therapy with someone like this?" DM was preempting the possibility of separation anxiety coming up at the prospect of ending and the pitfalls of not recognizing it at the beginning. It was more complicated for Bella. Her mother was terminally ill, and she would also lose her soon. DM reminded herself that separations, including the final separation, needed to be carefully approached.

In each session the therapist attempted to explore Bella's anxiety, linking it with her earlier needs to stay close and to make sure she was being listened to. She helped Bella make links with her fears of being independent and reiterated that she would, in due course, feel differently. It would become clearer to both of them that she was in a different space, and that new space would indicate that the end was approaching. They would talk about it and make the decision together.

Bella: What will I do if I can't cope, if something goes wrong?

DM: I can understand that from not believing in yourself, you are now beginning to trust yourself to be capable of managing on your own, and that brings up some anxiety. I can understand the fears. But, if you should need to see me again after our therapy is over, you just need to get in contact with me. We may need a session, maybe more, to help you deal with whatever issues have come up, and we can do that. It sometimes happens when people have left therapy.

Bella's anxiety over dealing with life on her own often surfaced and was talked about. It was understandable. Staying close to what was her only source of care at the time was a way she had adapted to overwhelming anxiety. Now she had only the therapist.

Bella talked again about how she had tried to be helpful and good but had never succeeded and felt abandoned. This anxiety repeated itself persistently. It was worked with and gradually Bella felt better equipped to cope on her own. She was able to accept that when therapy was over, help was just a phone call away if she needed it—and not just from the therapist: "I have good friends too, and I can call one of them," she added, recollecting that there were other people she had come to know since she had started attending the day center.

Previous Losses Come to Mind and Are Worked Through

Talking about the death of her grandmother, she remembered that the family tended to ignore her grandmother, who was not very well-liked because she was a religious zealot who kept to herself a lot. Bella remembered what a blow it was to her: "I felt all alone. There was no one who really cared about me. What would happen? Mum became worse than she ever was after Grandma died."

Bella continued to describe the time of her grandmother's death. There was not a single person to take her place. She felt traumatized by the funeral process of viewing her body, and she shouted and screamed at the fact that "they" had made up her face to be almost unrecognizable: "She was someone who never used makeup and was refreshingly sweet and simple," she said. Bella described every-one as looking at her with hostility; in fact, a relative threw a walking stick at her to quiet her. Bella said, "Life was never the same after grandma died. I could think of nothing else but her, and nobody cared."

Bella continued to talk about her grandmother and then moved on to the times when she became severely suicidal and experienced a repeated pattern of over-doses and hospital admissions. It seemed as if Bella did not require very much to be said by the therapist, who served to contain her by her presence and her non-verbal gestures of care.

The loss of her baby surfaced again, and Bella grieved that her mother had taken Cassie from her and had brought her up as her own. She sounded angry.

DM: This has been another loss that you have had to deal with, that was too painful. You perhaps could not think about it, among other things.

Bella: At least Cassie wasn't given up for adoption—for that I am grateful to Mum. I often dream of the day when I can tell her that I am her mother. But I feel so jealous of her too. How can a mother feel jealous of her own daughter?

DM: It might have been different if you were bringing her up, like a mother and daughter. But you also said your mother gave Cassie a lot more time, that she did things with Cassie that she had never had time to do with you. It's understandable that you would feel jealous.

Bella: I see.

In supervision DM recollected:

The thought of leaving therapy brought up for Bella a whole host of issues to do with loss and grief and the constant threat of abandonment. We understood the need for her to go through these painful experiences and come to terms with them. We also focused on talking about the gains she had made, consolidating and integrating her accomplishments. We revisited old issues that needed to be finally worked through. We acknowledged how far Bella had come and how capable she had become.

ENDING

Sessions 181–200: Further Separation Anxiety

The idea of therapy ending had always filled Bella with anxiety, which was understandable. By this stage she had a good understanding of her anxiety about separating. The approaching end also coincided with her mother's diagnosis of cancer and removal from home to supported accommodation. Bella dealt with this very well, and demonstrated a good deal of reflective capacity in doing so. In supervision DM recalled:

I didn't expect so much new material to come up at this stage in our therapy, but it did, and I began to truly understand the importance of our relationship—

Bella's and mine. It had helped her tell me more about herself. She felt safe. While dealing with her anxiety about leaving me, she also remembered her own anxiety about her mother's constant threat of leaving her. Earlier she feared I would give up on her. It made more sense to me now. Together we learned a lot. I certainly learned a lot from this experience—about myself too!

In her developing years it became apparent from Bella's account that her mother tended to denigrate and belittle her, particularly when her father still lived with them. At the same time she would want to know where Bella was at every moment. She would openly express how painful it would be to her if anything happened to Bella. Whenever Bella opposed her mother's views or failed to comply with her wishes, her mother would threaten to cease care of her. Bella had developed an accommodating system to her mother from a very early age. Her mother, however, gave her the best of everything materially.

This information provided a clearer picture of the early mother–child relationship, where obviously two very disparate reactions from her mother would potentially create enormous confusion, disorganization, and abandonment anxiety, contributing to Bella's dissociation. It also explained Bella's need to pathologically accommodate to her mother and also Bella's separation anxiety.

Bella was quite upset when she recalled the confusion and anxiety she felt whenever her mother reacted in opposite ways, and she seemed to need considerable understanding in the therapy as she spoke about it. She also had a supportive network of friends at this stage, and they helped her deal with difficulties.

The Therapist's Sense of Loss

DM noted: "I had become quite fond of Bella, and I felt a sense of loss too, as the therapy was coming to an end."

At this point Bella was living in her own place. She was becoming quite separate from her mother and did not seem to need her mother's input as she previously did. They phoned each other every day and saw each other twice a week. Bella was also free to have contact with Cassie without her mother's interference.

Her mother, who seemed to have a similar style of relating as Bella did, continued to create anxiety for Bella by checking up on her. Bella had started doing her own shopping and had started walking for half an hour to get to the day center. She coped well on her own. She also undertook to drive her mother whenever they went out together, but she often took the local bus when she went to visit friends or to the center.

Would You Miss Me?

Bella: I've been thinking . . . (*long pause*)

DM: Yes . . .

Bella: I've been thinking, but I don't know if I should say it . . . how to say it . . .

DM: You don't know if you should say it, or how to say it—and you were the one who could never stop talking! (*They laughed together, both became quite solemn again.*) You seem quite sad, a different kind of sadness from what I have seen before.

Bella: Would you miss me?

DM: I will miss you, and I will think of you, but I will feel happy too, when I think that you will be happy and doing your own thing.

A New Relationship

In the following session, Bella talked about her interest in a man of similar age she had met through a mutual friend, and later talked about starting a relationship with him. She talked about her mother feeling happy for her too, and that Cassie also liked him. "We did not spend too much of time together yet," she said, "because it would be good to get to know each other better."

Working Through Current Loss, Separation, and Ending

It was almost Christmas, and DM was taking a short break. She wondered how Bella would respond, and in looking back, recognized her own anxiety as she thought about bringing up the date when therapy would end.

Bella: I really hate Christmas. It reminds me of being left.

DM: Last year?

Bella: My mother and Cassie left me asleep on Christmas Eve and drove away for their holidays, even though the three of us had planned to go away. Also, everything closes down; everyone goes away. The center closes for the week, my GP goes away, and you go away too. I know I can leave a message on your message bank, even when you are not there.

DM: Comforts you?

Bella: Yes, even though I know you are not there.

DM: You feel soothed.

Bella: I'm not as bad as I used to be. I will keep the coffee club going through the break, and my boyfriend and I will do our shopping together, share some meals, and go to the club perhaps.

DM: You do things, but are happier when we come back?

Bella: You go away and I have to put up with it. I am not as anxious as I used to be, just a bit sad.

DM: Just sad . . .

DM recollected: "We paused for a moment and made eye contact and nodded. We both acknowledged the sadness of the moment."

The therapist had been thinking about raising the subject of their sessions coming to an end some months hence (a finishing date had been set by mutual arrangement), but she wondered if it might disturb their connection at the present moment. There was also an impending break. The therapist decided to mention it because there was a different sense of relatedness between them that was unlike what was there before. She also thought that Bella was dealing with the issue of separation considerably better.

A Disjunction That Was Not Really a Disjunction

DM: Hearing you talk about your sadness reminds me how far you have come, and that we have a short while left until we finish our sessions.

Bella: (*Looked startled, responded briefly, and changed the subject.*)

DM: You looked shocked when I mentioned the end of our sessions. I thought it would help to talk about things.

Bella: It's not fair. Some people have years and years of therapy.

DM: (*Noting that the tone of the session had changed and that Bella looked rather pensive*) I am sorry. It was not the right time to talk about it.

Bella: I was thinking about it anyway. I would have said before that I would take an overdose. I feel differently now.

DM: We have more time to talk about it when we resume. But of course you know, as we talked about before, you can come back for a session if you need to. You can contact me. I will be pleased to see you and be of further help.

Bella was certainly dealing with things well. Two days later, however, there was a phone call from Bella to say: "My mother is dying, and you are going away. I might as well take an overdose. You are pissing me off, just when you know I need you."

The Therapist's Apology: A New Experience for the Patient

The therapist called her back, acknowledging her sense of loss and also the inappropriateness of bringing up the discussion about the end of therapy. Bella was taken aback that the therapist would apologize to her, and remarked that no one had thought enough of her to ever offer her an apology. This exchange could be described as a "corrective emotional experience" (Alexander & French, 1946).

There had been a change in her mother's condition, and the therapist felt that it would help Bella to have an extra session. It helped considerably, as Bella was able to talk about her sense of loss at the now inevitable prospect of losing her mother. Bella was also able to express her anger toward the therapist and feel comfortable in the fact that there would be no retribution. She was also able to express anger at the loss of her mother, just when she was putting her own life in order. However, she could also add that she was grateful that her mother was not worried about her any more.

Emergent Self-Reflective Capacity

Bella: I'm scared. What if things go back to how they were? What if there's no one to talk to?

DM: You fear you will go back to feeling alone and isolated once again.

Bella: It was really awful in my bedroom at my Mum's place. I was so depressed, popping pills all day. But now I have friends, I have a boyfriend, and I am not dependent on Mum. I don't need pills anymore. [She had stopped taking tablets.]

DM: You've made good friendships—real friendships—and you have every reason to feel hopeful. I can hear you say it, even though you sometimes doubt it.

Bella: I sometimes get bored or feel alone in my flat, and think I might as well move back home. But then I will be alone there too now that Mum is not there. The house will soon be on the market and will be gone too. Then I play with my cat, or do some housework, or someone will ring, and we will make plans to go out and I will be fine again. I know that I will be alright. I am much better off than what I was a couple of years ago.

DM: Your life is much richer. You have your very own rich life!

Bella reached into her bag and brought out a packet of multiple types of creative stationery, and they talked about its beautiful colors and how it could be used. The therapist shared her own love of the same thing and a mutual feeling of genuine warmth emerged between them.

On looking back, DM recognized that she had caused a disjunction by bringing up the ending of therapy at this rather inauspicious time of Christmas; she recognized it was inappropriate to have done so. A therapist's excitement at a patient's changing self may lead a therapist to take risks and become less careful in what he or she says. However, disjunctions at this stage can be repaired with increasing connectedness in the relationship; a stage of genuine play emerges, whereas continuing to be tentative at this stage would result in stalling the therapeutic endeavor.

The therapist is less tentative. There is more narrative in the conversation as the patient experiences more of a sense of cohesion.

The Additional Session

Bella's mother had taken a turn and was hospitalized; Bella called the therapist requesting a session. The therapist felt that the extra session allowed Bella to deal with the possible loss of her mother. It also allowed her to express her concerns, yet reassure herself that she was capable and in a better space. She had been independent of her mother for at least 6 months. DM also felt that the form of their conversation had changed quite considerably, and that she could repair a disjunction far more easily: "It was like apologizing to a friend," said DM. Bella had lost her fragility and she was capable of self-soothing. DM was also more confident; she had waded through mud at times, but she had been there for Bella, and now they were in a clearer and safer space.

Sessions 201–210

Continuing to Deal with Loss

Returning from the Christmas holidays was a significant and emotional time for Bella. January was a month of anniversaries—days when she often decompensated with feelings of aloneness and insignificance: her birthday, her adoption, the death of her grandmother, and more recently, the time when her mother and daughter left her alone for the Christmas holidays, and she had made several suicide attempts.

This time, she talked about her mother's frailty and that she probably had not much time left. She looked back at her mother's life, a very busy, useful, and productive life. She was grieving the impending loss of her mother. She pondered her own memories of being in the hospital and the time she had lost all those years. She talked of visiting doctors and being in the hospital "where I was not wanted."

DM reported that as Bella was talking, she noticed the sun shining on her hair and was reminded of a strange dream she had had the night before, and was almost lost in thinking. She almost lost contact with Bella, who noticed this disconnection and became briefly upset and angry with DM, but went on.

Increased Reflective Capacity and a Friendly Misunderstanding

Bella: Mum has always been so strong and capable, it's strange to see her so weak and needing things to be done for her. They really look after her at the home. I wonder how I will be when I grow old. Where has time gone? I'm sure I'm developing arthritis, my face is becoming so lined, and I have some gray hairs. I'm getting old.

DM: You are wondering what will happen as your mother goes downhill.

Bella: What are you talking about? Haven't you been listening to me?

DM: I am truly sorry. I lost track for a moment and went back to when you were talking about your mother's frailty. I know you were talking about yourself growing old—yes, you were worried about aging, yourself.

Bella: I feel like telling you what to say to me. "Yes, I understand" is not enough. How can you understand? I need you to say more, to help me feel you really understand.

DM: I can see you are upset with me. I was distracted for a moment or two, and then I actually panicked, because I missed something you had said. I really welcome that you stopped me and corrected me.

Bella: (*Becoming calm and more receptive*) This has been a difficult month for me. But, we are having a barbeque this afternoon, and I have things to do. I really enjoy the time I spend with my friends—we laugh a lot.

On thinking about this session, DM was aware that something about the content touched her personally, and the dream she had had the night before preoccupied her a little, and she was somewhat disconnected from Bella, even though momentarily.

A Fresh Approach to the Future

The ensuing sessions were filled with Bella's new life – the coffee club and her friends. She was exploring the possibility of starting a course and returning to work. She felt heard and understood. She experienced a newfound freedom to speak her mind in the sessions. She continued to deal with the fact that her mother was becoming old and frail and would pass away soon. She made plans for her future, with much less of a sense of anxiety, without fear of panic attacks and with a sense of purpose.

The frequency of therapy continued as previously, and the finishing date was talked about again. The last session was decided upon, after which they agreed there would be three reviews, a month apart, and if all went well, then therapy would be concluded.

The therapist experienced a deep sadness as she contemplated the ending of Bella's therapy and as they talked about it more freely. She was able to tell her again when Bella asked, that she would also miss seeing her, but would be comforted by the fact that she knew that Bella was doing well and would continue to grow and change. They were to meet again in a month's time.

FIRST REVIEW

Session 211

Improved Self-Regulation

A session was organized for a month later—the longest that Bella had been without a session. She had coped well and was engaged in pursuing her own plans. She also informed the therapist that she was establishing a relationship with Cassie and that they were getting on quite well. She was also supporting a friend who was not very well and was coping with the knowledge that her mother could die.

> Bella: I missed not seeing you, but not in the way I used to. In fact, I was occupied with so much. Cassie and I did a lot together. She talked about the university— she's enjoying it. I have to be there for her; she's taking what's happening with Mum really badly. She has a very different memory of Mum than I do, and I know why.
>
> DM: I can see an enormous difference. It sounds like you and Cassie have a good friendship too, and yes, you both have very different memories of your relationship with your mum, as we have talked about many times before, but it seems to me that you have been able to deal with it very differently.

Talking about Ending

The form that ending takes differs from therapist to therapist, and from patient to patient. At times, the frequency may stay the same until the last session; at other times, the frequency may be reduced until the date of termination. In some therapies, review sessions are set up for a period of time in order to help the patient separate gradually.

Each space between sessions is a mini-separation. Each break is a separation that tests the patient and at the same time enables the patient to function gradually without the therapist's presence. Every therapy begins with the explicit intention to end.

Flexibility of the Dynamic Frame

The therapist and Bella had previously agreed to have three monthly review sessions and to bring therapy to an end at the third review session. However, the news of her mother was not good, and Bella, though improved, seemed a little fragile. She would need support. There was no certainty how she would handle this difficult period. It was agreed that they would continue to meet weekly for the next month, as it was expected that her mother would not live much longer.

Sessions 212–215

Coping with Impending Loss

Bella's mother was hospitalized with heart failure, and it did not seem that she would recover. Bella continued to work through her feelings around her mother's waning health and possible death, which seemed near, but maintained the gains she had made and continued her independence.

Bella's visits to the hospital brought up once again her many painful experiences of being in the emergency section of the same hospital, where she said she was often mostly unaware of what was happening around her. She became very angry and reexperienced memories of the humiliation she had endured when each time she was discharged a day, or a few days, after she had been admitted with an overdose.

Bella: No one cared. You were treated like an unwanted child. It made me more distrustful. I could not trust anyone after that.

DM: That was a difficult time—you felt unwanted. You are remembering how things had been. [New details emerged for the first time, and the therapist felt that she needed to deal with these memories, which even though they were talked about before, seemed to have a new intensity. As Bella continued to talk about these experiences, she seemed to settle.]

Bella: I did not think I would feel these things so deeply, but as I went into the hospital to visit Mum I began to feel strange, like I wanted to get away rather than go in. I knew I didn't like the idea of going in, but I had to be with Mum. I wanted to call you, but I felt I had to go right away, or else I would miss seeing Mum, and what if anything happened—I would not have forgiven myself. I'm glad I did. If I hadn't, I don't think I would be able to talk about it today.

DM: You needed to talk about it, and you also needed to feel the emotion. The hospital connected you with those past experiences, those really difficult experiences, but most importantly, you coped. You faced your fears.

The Future without Mother

Bella could talk about her future without her mother in it, and though it seemed strange, she said, she did not get as distressed as she did earlier. She looked back at her relationship with her mother with very mixed feelings, but remembered the session when her mother also attended and reassured herself that her mother loved her.

Bella was also able to talk more about her mother's background, which only became available to her through the many conversations they had had while her mother became less active and later was often in hospital. She began to express the feeling that her mother had no malicious intent in the way she treated her. She expressed a feeling of freedom, quite different from the sense of burden she had carried, when she constantly wondered why her mother treated her the way she did. She wished that this realization had come to her much earlier, but checking herself, said, "At least I realized it now, before her death."

As her mother was fading away, Bella was also facing the loss of her therapist. It was a time of real need for the therapist to be available for Bella, who was possibly at her most vulnerable. Noting that Bella was facing another real loss, in supervision DM was really concerned about how Bella would cope with this double loss. At the same time she expressed relief that she was able to be there for her.

Sessions 216–222

The Loss of Mother and Request of Therapist to Attend Funeral

Bella's mother passed away, and Bella called DM to inform her. She requested an earlier appointment. She also asked the therapist if she would come to her mother's funeral, which was going to be the following week. DM said she would give it some thought and that they would talk about it when she came for her appointment.

During that session Bella talked about her mother's death; she was relieved that her mother had passed away quietly and with no pain. She was also grateful, she said, that her best friend had stayed with her and was of immense support to her and to Cassie, who was also staying with her for a few days.

Bella did not bring up the request she had made of the therapist on the telephone, so DM brought up the topic of her mother's funeral. She said to Bella she did not think it would be helpful if she went to the funeral. She also added that she would like to be available for Bella as her therapist, particularly as they were intending to continue therapy for a while more. She also added that she would like to be available as her therapist in the future, if it became necessary. They talked around the issues of boundaries and the frame.

> DM: I would like to be with you in your sadness, but I feel I couldn't be there as a friend, like your best friend. But you have a best friend, and you are there for each other. I wish you to remember that I am your therapist and will always be . . . if you should ever need to see me again, I wish to be of help to you. I could not do that if I became your friend.
>
> Bella: I should not have put you in that position. I remember you told me before—it seems such a long time ago, I almost forgot. I think I understand how it's difficult to be a therapist and a friend at the same time.
>
> DM: You felt a great need at the time. Perhaps you had to ask me. But it's alright, because we can talk more freely now than we did before.
>
> Bella: Yes, how true!

Renegotiating the End of Therapy

> Bella: Could we see each other for a while longer?
>
> DM: Yes, I was going to suggest that, Bella.
>
> Bella: I don't think I will need to see you for too much longer, but I know you will be the judge of that. I managed for a whole month when we had a break in therapy to see how I would manage on my own. I managed very well. What do you think?
>
> DM: Of course, you managed very well, and I think you will continue to do well after therapy is over. We can set the dates for a few weekly sessions and then two monthly reviews as we initially decided and then finish. What do you think?

Together the therapist and Bella agreed on a date which both felt would be a reasonable time to finish, reiterating that the door was always open if she needed to return.

Recognizing Self-Capacities

Bella: Thank you for being here for me. I do not know how I would have gone through all this if you were not here. It seems odd that Mum is no more. It's more than odd that I have to meet with Mum's solicitor. He said that Mum rewrote her will only recently. She asked me to get her solicitor's help in selling the house, as Cassie and I would not need it. We have our own lives, she said, and we could get his advice as to how to invest the money. Cassie and I have an appointment to talk to the solicitor.

DM: It's good to know that I've been able to help you and that you are getting through this really difficult time. It seems that Mum has taken care of things before she died. Soon you will be planning the next stage of your life.

Four further sessions were spent in looking back and talking about Bella's mother and about Cassie. Bella thought she would leave her with the knowledge for now that they were sisters. She would not disrupt her by introducing the reality of her actually being Cassie's mother. It seemed that she had given it a lot of thought and had in fact made up her mind that the right moment would come, and she would know it.

Bella had been doing some volunteer work and attending the day center, which she enjoyed, but she expressed a wish to do something more meaningful.

Bella: I keep thinking of Mum all the time. It's like she's everywhere. It was worse after we visited her house—Cassie and me and my best friend. I could not sleep at all, and then it seemed a little better. When I went shopping, I kept remembering the times we went shopping together; I kept remembering her favorite recipes. I couldn't stop thinking about her. In the house, it was strange not to see her there. Cassie was very upset, but we were able to comfort each other, and my best friend was with us too.

DM: You are grieving the loss of your mother. It happens for a while, that you are constantly reminded of her. It may seem that it will never stop sometimes, but with time, you will see, it tends to get better. I think you are dealing with things well, and most importantly you are talking about your mother with Cassie and with your best friend, and you're talking about things with me too.

Bella seemed reassured by the therapist and talked further. The therapist explained further what the process of grief is generally like, so she could allow herself to grieve and not think she was abnormal. They were even able to talk about her earlier losses and put them in perspective as they continued to talk about other related concerns. Earlier losses that had no chance of expression are talked about and worked through in the context of the prospect of losing the therapist and in the context of a current loss as in the death of Bella's mother.

> Bella: When Cassie and me talk about university, I regret having wasted my time in school. I know I can do more, and Cassie says so too. I know I would need to give myself some time to think about it—it's too soon after Mum has just passed away.
>
> DM: You're thinking about your future, and you have some positive ideas there. Yes, you can, once you have dealt with things that are immediate. There is no reason why you cannot attempt to do what you put your mind to.

They talked about the possibilities of work and the jobs Bella felt she would like to do, and also her capacity to work, seeing that she had been out of contact with people and the workforce almost completely. They agreed to talk about this further. She was put in contact with an agency that helped to assess her capacity to work. Her case manager was very helpful to Bella in organizing this next step. Bella had developed a good relationship with her case manager, whom she used to contact on a weekly basis by telephone, until she no longer felt a need to do so. But recently Bella felt that she needed to tell her case manager about her mother's passing and therefore recontacted her. Bella seemed reassured that she was on her way to independence and seemed to accept it with a new sense of vigor and determination.

SECOND REVIEW

Session 223

Growth Amid Grief

Another month later Bella appeared very well.

> Bella: It's hard to believe that Mum is not around. Even harder to believe is that I really miss her (*tearfully*). I wonder if she would have been proud of me if she was alive.
>
> DM: You have come a long way. I see you wonder how your mum would have felt about you. I think she would have been very proud of you.
>
> Bella: But you would say that! I'm sorry—I think you are right. I have a feeling she would have been proud of me, if she was still alive. She was a hard worker

for such a long time, and I think she imagined me doing something like her—a businesswoman—though she never said so. She never said I could do anything. How was I to know?

DM: Yes, you were not to know. It seemed like you and she only made contact really when things were bad. Now you are determined to make a life for yourself, and I am very proud of you!

Looking to the Future

Bella seemed moved by the therapist's response and continued to talk about the future. She talked about her assessment for fitness to work and her meeting afterward with the psychologist who was going to discuss employment with her. She would then put her in contact with several employers, in response to the availability of part-time jobs. Bella talked about interview skills that she had learned, and she was looking forward to her first interview, which she and the psychologist decided would be arranged 3 months from the date of her mother's passing, if she felt she could manage it. However, she would continue to attend the agency on a weekly basis until she was ready.

She also talked about the solicitor who was very helpful in advising her about her mother's house. She was surprised that she was more trusting than she had ever been before. However, she reminded the therapist that she "could not be too trusting." She was looking forward to getting a job and working.

THIRD REVIEW

Session 224

The Importance of Trust

Bella continued to talk about the loss of her mother. She said, however, that she was sleeping better and was generally more occupied with things in her life. She thought about her mother less often but still felt sad that she was gone.

Bella was experiencing some difficulty with Cassie, but indicated that she could handle the situation. It was their last session, she tearfully reminded the therapist. She had started work 2 days prior to this appointment and liked what she was doing. She was looking forward to the day when she "could live a normal life"; her relationship with her boyfriend was stronger, and she also shared with the therapist that she felt she could trust him, as he also had been very helpful to her.

DM: I see how important you find it, to be able to trust.

Bella: I know it was very hard—how do you know what will happen? I always expected the worst. When I look back, yes, there were times when I should have been more trusting, but I'm sure there were times when I'm glad I didn't trust people—certain people—they were not interested in me. When I remember those times in the hospital, now I know I must have been a pain to everyone. But yet I wish things were different.

DM: It was hard indeed!

Bella: It's better now. My best friend is getting better too. We talk about these things. She has had a hard life too and is still in therapy. We talk about it and we help one another. I trust her as a friend now, whereas I could never trust friends before.

DM: It's good to see you looking so capable and so confident.

Bella: I think that being able to trust you helped me to trust other people—not altogether though. I am grateful to you, for your help. You must have believed in me, that I could get better. I will miss you.

DM: I will miss you too, but I will be happy to know that you can now look after yourself—you will look after yourself. I did say that if you have a need to come back and see me, you only need to call me.

It was with some sadness that they said their final good-bye. Upon reflection, DM had this to say:

When we had our final session, I felt very satisfied that we had accomplished the goals of therapy to foster a sense of self and to integrate the traumatic experiences that had hitherto been dissociated.

I personally felt a sense of confidence in my ability to hold and contain difficult cases. I keep returning to the model as a point of reference, reading and remembering key points, such as the role of empathic attunement, listening to disjunctions and disruptions in the conversation, paying attention to the process while being aware of my own internal processes, choosing and shaping my responses carefully.

I keep remembering my role as the facilitator of a play-space [Meares, R., 2005], containing my own thoughts and feelings and allowing the patient to choose the direction of therapy. We were able to come to a collaborative experience of what Robert Hobson [1985] called "alone-togetherness."

As a mental health nurse, I have now seen very many similarly disordered patients like Bella, and working in the Conversational Model has been, for me, a fruitful experience.

Chapter 5

General Issues in Working with Patients with Borderline Personality Disorder

Nick Bendit and Anthony Korner

IN THE CHAPTERS SO FAR, the theoretical underpinnings and the actual applications of the Conversational Model (CM) in a case study have been described. This chapter outlines general practical issues in the psychotherapy of patients with borderline personality disorder (BPD). In doing so, it must be remembered that certain aspects are particular to the model—that is, ways of understanding and ways of responding that are described in subsequent chapters—and others are nonspecific and applicable to other models of psychodynamic psychotherapy.

It is helpful to bear these principles in mind when working psychotherapeutically with patients with BPD, for whom a characteristic instability of mood, identity, and behavior often presents on a background of chronic interpersonal turmoil and a chronic inner sense of dysphoria (emotional pain). The main therapeutic aim here is to create a safe, stable, working environment and to maximize available resources outside of psychotherapy that could help complement and contribute to improvement.

Many patients with BPD engage in psychotherapy with private practitioners, whereas many others receive help from community mental health services. Many receive a combination of ongoing help from both the private and public services. This chapter addresses issues that are useful to any mental health practitioner working with these patients, whether in the public or the private setting. An attempt has been made to make these principles as clear and simple as possible, so as to be useful even to those mental health practitioners who see only the occasional patient with BPD.

THE BEGINNING OF THERAPY

This section discusses how to manage the referral process and the first few assessment sessions. Important issues having to do with assessment, such as information gathering and developing a joint understanding of the problems to be addressed, and how therapy will do that, are described. Furthermore, an approach to developing a safe and manageable structure within which psychotherapy can work is outlined. Finally, some of the broader issues that often arise early in therapy, such as confusion around diagnostic issues and management of stigma, are discussed.

The Referral

Patients arrive at the first session via various routes. Some are self-referred, whereas others are referred by health professionals. Each referral provides specific information about the patient, although the manner of referral may sometimes convey more important data than the letter of referral. For example, there might be a considerable degree of urgency for the patient to be seen immediately, usually indicating a high level of anxiety about the patient. This anxiety may be generated by the patient, the referrer, or often by both patient and referrer. Other less obvious communications about the patient will also start to shape the therapeutic relationship even before the patient is seen, creating expectations on both sides. The therapist should understand that these referral characteristics are often a manifestation of the patient's trauma system. For example, a patient who expects to be rejected may be referred in an offhand manner, possibly altering the way the therapist responds to the referral, such that an experience of rejection is more likely when the patient and therapist actually meet. In the case of Bella (Chapter 4) the therapist felt "overwhelmed and powerless to effect change" after receiving the referral. This response gives a clue (even before the therapist has met Bella!) that Bella may have an unconscious traumatic system of feeling overwhelmed and powerless to effect change. These illustrations demonstrate the need for the therapist to adopt a practice of reflection on the manner and circumstances of each referral.

In practical terms, after the referral is received, the patient needs clear information about the therapist's availability and the time of the first session. To prevent potential misunderstanding, this information is best followed up by letter or written on a card, confirming the appointment time. This action takes into account the possibility that these patients may be highly anxious on the telephone and may feel too ashamed to call and recheck the appointment time. Feedback to the referral source that an initial session has been scheduled is often helpful; similar feedback if the patient fails to attend the session will also be helpful. It is good practice to establish a communicative link with the referrer.

Early Information Gathering: The First Session

The first session or two are best conceived of, and described to, the patient as "assessment session(s)." This assessment involves an evaluation of the patient's problems and needs, as well as a certain amount of information gathering that is somewhat different from later therapy sessions. However, unlike in the usual psychiatric assessment, the fundamental stance of understanding the patient's inner world of feelings and thoughts is privileged in CM over collecting facts and finding out further detail, even though these are important. For example, it is important to find out in the assessment sessions if there have been past instances of attempted suicide and deliberate self-harm. However, focusing on understanding the thoughts and feelings that led to these behaviors and how these relate to the patient's overall difficulties and the circumstances leading to the self-harm, is more important than finding out the details of how much medication was taken in an overdose, or how many cuts occurred in a self-destructive episode. This approach allows the experience of being understood by the therapist and develops an emotional connection between the patient and therapist. This connection is further enhanced by taking an interest in the patient's strengths and interests, as well as recognizing the experience of trauma and suffering, even at this early stage of therapy. The focus on personal experience implicitly conveys the message that what the patient feels and thinks is the core of the therapy. Many patients with BPD have never had the experience that what is inside of them matters to anybody else. This is the first step in building a sense of personal worth and value.

Joint Understanding

This initial process is not only one of gathering information but is also the establishment of a conversation that will involve a back-and-forth flow between the therapist and the patient wherein the form and "feel" of this flow will convey as much as the specific content. The patient tries to describe his or her difficulties, past and present, and the therapist attempts to take an interest in what is being offered, without being overly inquisitive or intrusive. As more of the patient's life is described, the therapist tries, tentatively, to put together a picture that is based on the matters that the patient expresses. Some of this picture may be offered as something that has been understood from the patient, in such a way that the patient can elaborate or modify what the therapist has said. A two-way communication, with a focus on the patient's inner world, is established. Depending on the anxiety of the patient, or other states of distress, these early offerings from the therapist may need to be brief and simple. Nevertheless a conversation is established with an ongoing potential for modification, elaboration, and development. In this way, a collaborative understanding is built. When such understanding is not achieved at this point, some initial agreement may be possible regarding the pieces that are difficult to understand or picture. By the end of the assessment sessions, it may be useful for the therapist to offer a more complete picture—a tentative formulation that links the patient's difficulties with his or her life story, past and present.

Let us consider the case study of Bella, presented in Chapter 4, to illustrate the development of a joint understanding. Bella was adopted into a dysfunctional family; her father was verbally and physically intimidating and sexually abusive. Her mother was slow to intervene and when she finally ended the situation Mum and Bella were both affected by the ensuing changes (although Bella was more affected because she was in an important developmental stage). Mum becomes a single working mother doing shift work and is often absent during the evenings and on weekends. Bella's emotional needs are often neglected, even though she is given good food and care and has her basic physical needs met.

In the initial interviews with Bella it becomes apparent that her distress and multiple suicide attempts were precipitated by interactions with Mum wherein she felt ignored and dismissed.

This experience reminded Bella of being emotionally abandoned, unloved, and uncared for. Mum refused to listen to Bella's experience of being left, Mum felt manipulated and wanted to make her own decision regarding the trip. Bella's response is to take an overdose of medications.

Diagnostic Issues and Stigma

The assessment sessions may also be shaped negatively by previous adverse experiences with mental health services. Two broad areas of difficulty often contribute:

1. Confusion about multiple diagnoses and/or mistaken diagnoses
2. Stigma about the diagnosis of BPD

Patients with BPD may receive many diagnoses, as the problems they present often change dramatically depending on changes in their environments and their relationships. This changeability is confusing both to patients and to those around them. When they are with people who are interested and responsive to their emotional world, individuals with BPD can present in a variety of ways that often reflect some degree of dysphoria and interpersonal dysfunction, without necessarily appearing to be unwell or highly disturbed in an acute sense. At other times, when someone emotionally significant threatens to leave, these individuals are thrown into crisis and appear as angry, demanding, and impossible to talk to. When alone or experiencing alienation or abandonment from a significant person, they are at risk and may act desperately or recklessly to stave off unbearable feelings. Such behaviors commonly include deliberate acts of self-harm, suicide attempts, dissociation, alcohol and drug abuse, violence, and eating disorders. There is often an associated sense of helplessness and despair that "nothing can help."

When behaviors don't succeed in staving off overwhelmingly painful states, transient psychotic states may occur in a high proportion of patients. As a result, these patients may be given multiple Axis I diagnoses (as described in the DSM or ICD diagnostic systems). Furthermore, chronic pain syndromes are common, compounded by a high rate of physical and sexual trauma. Somatization syndromes are also common. It is not uncommon for a single patient with BPD to be diagnosed not only with BPD but also with major depressive disorder, dysthymia, social anxiety disorder, panic disorder, posttraumatic stress disorder (PTSD), an eating disorder, substance or alcohol abuse, and a chronic pain syndrome!

Other aspects of the patient's experience may lead to mistaken psychiatric diagnoses. The emotional instability can be misdiagnosed as bipolar disorder. Feeling occasional relief from unending misery can lead to increased activity, excitement, and inflated plans, which can be mistaken for bipolar II. The fragile sense of self and dissociative experiences may result in the patient hearing sounds and voices (auditory hallucinations), as well as being exquisitely self-conscious to the point of feeling "paranoid," which may lead to the mistaken diagnosis of schizophrenia. Subtler dissociative experiences are common and are frequently missed in initial assessments. Often these experiences are reflected by fragmented presentations wherein there is a sense of missing information and incoherence in the patient's account, which can be misunderstood as "thought disorder," also a characteristic of schizophrenia.

It is often useful to discuss both the utility and the limitations of psychiatric diagnosis as well as seeking to clarify any confusion about multiple diagnoses or previous misdiagnoses. A common understanding of matters of concern may sometimes be more useful than dogmatically insisting on a specific diagnosis. The important point is that a diagnosis needs to be reached on the basis of a collaborative process.

The diagnosis of BPD has gradually become more accepted, partly due to more understanding and research about the disorder, and, perhaps more importantly, as effective treatments have emerged. Yet BPD still remains one of the most stigmatized conditions within mental health, which arguably is itself the most stigmatized area of health care. Two factors that may have contributed to the stigma of BPD are (1) the lack of understanding in the community of what leads to maladaptive behaviors within BPD, and (2) the fact that many of these behaviors have a significantly deleterious impact on others, as well as on the sufferer.

Unfortunately, many of the usual interventions in psychiatry are frustrating or disappointing for patients with BPD. Targeted medication and psychosocial interventions, which may work well in patients without personality disorders, often do not work or have a muted response in this group of patients. These patients usually try to engage many, and varying, health professionals to get some relief from their emotional pain. Commonly, patients with BPD will have tried many psychiatric medications from their general practitioner (GP), community mental health team, hospital, or private psychiatrist. They will often have engaged in short-term psychological treatments, such as supportive therapy or cognitive–behavioral therapy (CBT) from private or public psychologists. Hospital-based social workers and community mental health team case managers may have tried socially supportive interventions. As a result, an expanding group of professional carers have usually tried, and failed, to significantly ameliorate the emotional pain of these patients, leading to frustration and despair.

Frequently the frustration and despair of receiving treatment that has little benefit results in stigma on both sides. Well-meaning and compassionate mental health workers often become "burned out," as they try harder and harder to help.

When their efforts fail, health workers are likely to become resentful or distant to protect themselves from disappointment and any personal sense of failure. This response may then generalize to a rigid attitude about all patients with BPD, often reinforced by pejorative language and interactions among staff members. It is not uncommon to hear case managers in community mental health teams refer to patients with BPD as "impossible," "manipulative," "splitting," or "a waste of time." Often such expressions primarily convey a sense of nihilism and helplessness that is countertherapeutic and interferes with teamwork and cohesion in care in relation to the patient. These circumstances often serve to reinforce and amplify stigma within the community of health professionals.

Negative feelings about mental health professionals may arise in patients as they continue to suffer, and as they repeatedly experience distant or hostile responses from emergency departments, psychiatric units, community mental health teams, GPs, etc. These feelings may concretize and generalize to all professionals and become a kind of reverse stigma, whereby all health professionals are felt to be cruel or uncaring. Internally, patients with BPD are likely to be self-critical and fear that they really do have a condition that makes them "bad" or "wrong." The therapeutic journey may involve helping these patients overcome all of these aspects of stigma: stigma about self and about professional care, as well as stigma from health professionals and the community around them. In the first few sessions, the therapist should be alert to detecting stigma within both the patient and him- or herself and to discuss it.

Contraindications to Long-Term Psychoanalytic Therapy

There are no absolute contraindications to therapy, but certain patient and therapist factors may need to be discussed or thought about further, in order to decide whether psychotherapy is safe and advisable. Patient factors include the following:

- A recent history of patient violence, particularly to mental health workers or previous therapists
- Mandated therapy, such as court orders or to satisfy other agency requirements (e.g., to regain custody of children)
- Dependence on alcohol, benzodiazepines, or illicit substances, such that the patient is unable to come to the therapy session sober
- No consistent housing, such as the patient living "on the streets"

- No significant social support for help in acute crises (no GP, other health providers, friends, or family)
- Organic problems, such as brain damage or serious medical illness
- Schizophrenia or bipolar disorder (note that many patients with BPD have auditory hallucinations and paranoia, which may be misdiagnosed as schizophrenia; similarly, the mood instability of BPD may be misdiagnosed as bipolar disorder)
- Acute safety issues that may be made worse by psychotherapy (e.g., domestic violence where the perpetrator opposes the therapy)

Therapist factors include the following and may necessitate referral:

- Seeing too many patients with BPD
- Poor therapist–patient fit (may become obvious at the end of the assessment sessions, if the patient feels very uncomfortable with the therapist)
- Therapist discomfort (e.g., when the patient is the perpetrator of a traumatic behavior that the therapist has experienced in his or her personal life and cannot comfortably tolerate)

The Psychotherapeutic Frame

The psychotherapeutic frame is a set of agreed-upon principles and conditions that make psychotherapy safe and effective for the patient and for the therapist. Two important principles include:

- Creating a space wherein talking about the patient's experience allows the development of reflection between patient and therapist, and ultimately within the patient.
- Setting appropriate limits that provide boundaries to the "reflective space."
- Some conditions that are commonly set to facilitate these principles are:

  - Regular frequency of sessions (for the patient with BPD this is usually twice per week)
  - Session length (usually between 45 minutes and 1 hour)
  - Length of therapy, how ending will occur (termination), and follow-up after therapy
  - Attendance: stressing that it is very important that the patient come regularly, especially on the days he or she feels too upset to come
  - How holidays, illness, and missed sessions will be handled

- Payment
- Confidentiality, especially mandatory breaches of confidentiality (e.g., sub-poenas; serious risk of harm to self or others, particularly harm to children)
- The importance of the therapist being allowed to talk to other health professionals directly involved in the patient's care (e.g., general practitioner), and how this will be handled (only as much information as is relevant; communication discussed with the patient)
- Therapist supervision and taped sessions (for supervision in CM)
- The unacceptability of dangerous behavior, when this has been a feature of the patient's history (e.g., threats of physical violence, stalking)

These principles are not absolute. The frame needs to be understood as a dynamic process that is subject to ongoing negotiation as circumstances change. It is important to discuss these conditions and modify them to fit the particular needs of the patient and therapist. Negotiations around the frame need to include a discussion of why the frame was changed and for how long, as well as an explicit consideration of practicalities and limits. At the same time, it is important to discuss any underlying meanings in the patient's desire to change the frame. Is something being changed to indirectly deal with a painful emotional experience without talking about it? For example, patients with BPD may decide to reduce the frequency of sessions because of a lapse in trust with the therapist, without feeling safe enough or courageous enough to tell the therapist the reason why.

Setting up and discussing the frame is not always easy. Few patients with BPD realize how crucial an explicit and thoughtful frame is to enable therapy to go ahead when the therapeutic alliance becomes difficult, or when there is a crisis. Equally, therapists often underestimate how a well-constructed collaborative frame can protect them when the expectational field is activated and the therapeutic alliance becomes difficult.

In the case of Bella (Chapter 4) a crisis emerged and Bella went to the hospital before the therapist was able to discuss a suitable frame. The therapist was finally able to do this in the third session, after Bella left the hospital. This set of circumstances illustrates how setting a frame can often be difficult or delayed by the patient's emotional and behavioral turmoil.

Medication

The consensus on medication use is that there is no drug that can be considered a specific treatment for BPD. Furthermore, drug treatments often prove to be ineffective in BPD (National Institute for Health and Clinical Excellence [NICE] guidelines, 2009). However, given the extent of distress experienced by patients with BPD, it is common for a variety of medications to be tried. Patients with BPD may be given medications by their GP, or their psychiatrist, or community mental health team, or during a stay in hospital. The medical psychotherapist is in the position of not only being able to prescribe but also being able to consider the meaning of prescription and medication in conversation with the patient. The significance of the medication for the patient should be considered in the same way as other aspects of the patient's life, not as something "separate." For the nonmedical psychotherapist, the issue of managing the three-way relationship between patient, therapist, and prescriber is important, and is discussed below.

Some suggestions about how to manage the issue of medication treatment during psychotherapy are outlined in the following material.

1. *Medication effectiveness.* The majority of patients with BPD who present for therapy will already be on medication, often on multiple medications. The response to antidepressants, antipsychotics, and mood stabilizers is more unpredictable in these patients, and often muted, compared to the use of these medications in patients without a personality disorder. Guideline recommendations have been somewhat fluid, reflecting the limited evidence available. The current U.K. guideline (NICE, 2009) states that evidence over the last decade suggests that antidepressants probably have very little efficacy in BPD; some mood stabilizers have shown some benefit in limited symptom areas (particularly hostility and aggression); and some antipsychotics may also reduce symptoms, particularly those that involve cognitive–perceptual disturbances. However, the evidence is generally considered weak. Nevertheless, clinicians will find that some patients will get a robust and sustained improvement in sleep, anxiety, impulsivity, or aggression that may make a significant difference in their capacity to engage in therapy. Other patients will get a relatively minor benefit. A significant number will get no benefit and may suffer adverse effects. It is difficult to predict which patients will get a benefit from medication, and which aspect of their difficulties might improve. A trial of medication may be considered where specific symptoms are so severe that:

    • An additional Axis I diagnosis is warranted apart from the diagnosis of BPD.

    • Engagement in psychotherapy is precluded by the level of distress.

    In these circumstances a trial can be undertaken, provided that there is a collaborative agreement about the need. Consideration of progress, response, and the meaning of the medication to the patient would then form part of the ongoing therapy.

119

The level of evidence available does not support any involuntary use of medication on an ongoing basis.

2. *The need for relief of distress.* Most patients with BPD face intolerable emotional suffering and long for relief. Soothing and care have often been absent in their developmental experience, and there is typically a consequent mistrust about therapeutic help through feeling, discussing, and processing painful emotions with another person. Some patients will have more trust in medication, which they see as promising some direct effect on the distressing internal state. Medication may become perceived as a "magic bullet" that might provide relief. This belief system, particularly when therapy gets tough, can influence both the patient and the therapist to look to medication as a way out of a seemingly intractable traumatic system. At the same time, it may be unfair not to consider the possibility of relieving some emotional suffering through medication. Other patients may have had past experiences that make them suspicious of medication as a "substitute" or "counterfeit" for care. The therapist needs to consider whether the desire for medication is being motivated primarily by avoidance of matters of psychotherapeutic significance or whether it may be of value in facilitating participation and understanding in therapy.

3. *Misuse of medication.* In addition to the usual weighing of benefits versus side effects when prescribing medication, the therapist treating the patient with BPD is often presented with a further difficulty. To relieve intolerable suffering, the patient may impulsively take too much, or deliberately overdose without suicidal intent, or attempt suicide through overdose. As a consequence, more lethal medications such as lithium or tricyclic antidepressants are usually inadvisable, but even medications with a safer profile may cause more harm than good in a very impulsive or actively suicidal patient with BPD. Medications with addictive potential, such as benzodiazepines, are particularly likely to be associated with inappropriate use or abuse.

4. *When the psychotherapist is also the prescriber.* The medical psychotherapist needs to feel confident about integrating the roles of therapist and prescriber. The necessary collaboration and discussion can be included in the flow of conversation while the therapist also considers the meaning of the medication and prescription for the patient. The therapist needs to take responsibility for review of progress in relation to symptoms and side effects. Where the patient is already on medication, it is usually most appropriate for the therapist to encourage the patient to continue seeing his or her prescriber. It is important not to undermine any established relationship with a prescriber. Channels of communication with the prescriber should be established.

There are some specific situations where the medical therapist may be understandably cautious about prescribing. In these situations it is sometimes helpful to share responsibility with another physician who will prescribe medication. These situations may include:

- When the patient has a severe personality disorder and extreme behavior
- When the patient has abused prescribed medications in the past
- When the patient has repeatedly overdosed on medication

In these circumstances it is helpful to be as open and explicit as possible about why the medical psychotherapist is asking another doctor to take the prescribing role.

5. *The nonprescribing psychotherapist.* When the patient is taking medication, the two roles of prescriber and psychotherapist are necessarily split. The therapist needs to establish communication with the prescriber and be open about this with the patient. It is preferable that this link be established in the assessment sessions, as it may be harder to obtain permission later in therapy. The psychotherapist carries a responsibility to alert the prescribing doctor to any major changes in the patient's condition that may require pharmacological intervention. When the nonprescribing psychotherapist becomes aware of misuse of prescribed medication, it is important to recognize and address the issue rather than "turn a blind eye." Often addressing the issue involves the therapist helping the patient to discuss this issue with the prescriber directly.

6. *Medication and meaning.* Medication has meaning for patients above and beyond its physiological effect. There are an unlimited number of possible meanings that medication may hold for patients. Two common situations are highlighted here:

- Positive meaning: The expectation of something magical happening when taking medication may underpin the robust placebo response seen in many patients with BPD. Conversely, because hope is attached to taking medication, the patient may feel that hope has been taken away when a medication is taken away by a prescriber, even though there may have been little evidence of its efficacy.

- Negative meaning: There will be negative meanings for some when medication is prescribed. The patient may feel coerced, ignored, or poisoned. Such patients may show a pattern of adverse response to medication trials. Therefore, it is important to discuss the significance of taking medication when it is commenced, changed, increased, or stopped. Where such factors are felt to be significant, discussion between therapist and prescriber (when these are separate roles) may help judicious prescribing.

Case Example: Drug Management Early in Bella's Therapy

Bella was actively abusing medication during the early stages of her therapy and usually arrived at the session looking pale and slurring her words. She was oversedated and had little access to any feelings while in this state. Bella later took an overdose leading to hospitalization; there the treating psychiatrist can see that any attempt at psychotherapy will be futile until she has been through a detoxification program. He told Bella that he would like to help her get the maximum benefit out of the therapy, and he suggested she remain in the hospital for 3 weeks while they help to detoxify and stabilize her on an appropriate regime of medication.

This piece of dialogue illustrates a nonprescribing therapist managing issues around medication and liaison with prescribers.

> Bella: I saw Dr G about my bad arm, and he has prescribed some Valium and Endone to help with the pain. It really surprised me that he gave me the Valium. I didn't think I was allowed to have it because I might overdose on it.
>
> DM: You've been more settled lately, so perhaps he felt he could trust you. But you sound somewhat worried about the fact that he gave you the scripts. Perhaps it's a risk so early in your therapy to have such medications available to you. Perhaps we should remind him of the problems you have had in the past.
>
> Bella: I have stopped getting medication from other doctors, but I still take a few extra pills if I'm on my own.
>
> DM: That's really good! You have been handling that issue really well. Do you think it may be a good idea just to remind Dr G?

Bella offers her mobile phone to DM, and the conversation takes place in front of her. Bella seems to appreciate DM's concern. Dr G says he will order the medications in smaller amounts for short-term management of the injury only.

Crisis Plan

A crisis plan, collaboratively constructed at the end of the assessment sessions, is often invaluable to deal with crises that may occur later in therapy. As with getting permission to talk to other health providers before a crisis emerges, this should be done early in the therapeutic relationship. For the patient with severe suicidal or self-destructive behaviors, a crisis plan may be essential.

The therapist should ask the patient what has worked, or has at least been helpful, in the past when he or she has been in crisis. It is also useful to inquire as to what the patient imagines could prove helpful. However, one has to bear in mind that initially the patient may say, simply, "Nothing." Indeed this is often how it seems to the patient who is frustrated and sometimes hostile about past failures and difficulties with health services and interventions. It may be useful to ask patients about three different domains of help:

1. Things they can do for themselves that are useful
2. Help they might receive from family or friends
3. Help they can access from mental health providers (e.g., therapist, GP, community mental health team, general and psychiatric hospitals)

Asking the patient to be specific is important. The therapist should then try and add some suggestions, seeking feedback from the patient about their usefulness. An important part of the plan is for the therapist to tell the patient some of the extra things the therapist can do in a crisis (e.g., contact family or friends, the GP, or community mental health team), as well as the therapist's availability and contact details in a crisis. It is equally important to be explicit about the limits to therapist availability. With patients for whom out-of-hours crisis contacts are likely, this explicitness will help to make clear the need for people other than the therapist to be involved in care at times. Limits to confidentiality (legal subpoenas; serious risk of harm to self or others that cannot be managed within therapy) should also be discussed. If extra support from the therapist or community supports are not enough in a crisis, the possibility of going to hospital should be discussed, including consideration of the most appropriate hospital service and how it can be accessed.

Once a plan has been established collaboratively, it is useful to write it down and for both patient and therapist to have a copy. The patient's copy is particularly important, as it is often difficult for the patient to think strategically in a crisis, so having written instructions can be life-saving (e.g., providing quick access to the crisis team phone number). If there is a computerized public health record, the plan should be located in an area that is easily accessible digitally, and a warning note should be created to alert a new health-care provider opening the file to the existence of a crisis plan. Although written plans can be helpful and may increase the consistency of care, they cannot cover all eventualities, and clinicians should not be overly rigid in their application. Patients' responses to written documents will also vary, and the therapist should consider how much information in such a document a particular patient will be able to use effectively. The plan should be regularly updated, possibly once or twice a year.

Sometimes the patient will argue that such a crisis plan is not necessary, as he or she will never be in such a bad place again. It is understandable, with the optimism of starting a therapeutic relationship, that the patient wishes, and believes, that crises are a thing of the past. In this situation it is helpful to reassure the patient that it is quite possible that a crisis plan will never be needed—but if it is needed, it can be crucial to get through a bad patch successfully. Then continue with constructing a crisis plan. Other patients will avoid thinking about future crises, because putting fears about the future into words can make those fears seem more concrete and overwhelming. Such fears should be understood, but not allowed to derail this process.

Another important by-product of this process is to develop the idea that the therapist is part of a therapeutic *team*. Patients with BPD often struggle with trusting authority figures and find it easier to place all of their trust in the therapist—which, at best, can be a burden, and at worst, can result in the therapist being placed in an unsustainable and dangerously isolated position at a future time of crisis.

Psychoeducation

Psychoeducation is useful at the end of the assessment sessions to provide the patient with a kind of map, helping the patient to understand the process of psychotherapy and how it will help him or her. Where possible the therapist should use the patient's language and avoid jargon, staying as close as possible to what the patient understands his or her problems to be and allowing the patient to question and modify ideas being discussed.

The first part of this psychoeducation "map" is trying to understand how the patient's growing up in his or her family may have led to the current difficulties. With this understanding, the therapist can educate the patient about how a sense of self can be disrupted, and how that disruption plays out in terms of diagnostic criteria and diagnosis. Most patients find interest and comfort in having the diagnostic criteria explained in terms of frantic attempts to maintain self-cohesion, and the instability of mood, thought, and behavior that result when this sense of cohesion is threatened.

The next part of the map is to describe the form of the therapy. This involves committing to regular therapy of two sessions per week over a minimum of 12 months, as the research data indicate. The intention of the therapy is to develop a conversation whereby feelings, thoughts, and imaginings can be discussed and explored. Although the patient will be encouraged to initiate the topics that interest him or her, the therapist will actively participate in the material. Ultimately, developing a joint understanding of the patient's inner world, as well as understanding and discussing important relationships, will be a core part of the treatment. Developing external strengths, such as enhancing support networks of family and friends, or being able to manage study, work, or parenting more effectively, may be discussed but will not be the primary focus. However such changes do occur, often as a result of the patient developing a stronger sense of him- or herself. It is therefore appropriate to include a degree of optimism about therapy as part of the education process.

Finally, some discussion of the therapeutic journey and prognosis is useful. This could include the following points:

- There is good evidence (research and the therapist's own clinical experience) that BPD can be treated and that improvement can be expected over time.

- Treatment usually takes time, involving significant effort by both patient and therapist, sometimes including a "two steps forward, one step back" type of progression.

- An explanation of trauma systems in practical language is extremely helpful, using examples from the patient's own experience. For example, if a patient lost a parent when he or she was young, the therapist might illustrate the idea of a trauma system by saying

> When I go on holiday, or we have a break in therapy, some powerful and confusing feelings may come up. These feelings may have something to do with my being away, but they may also be strengthened by your experience of your mother dying when you were young. But looking at these feelings together, it may help us understand why things fall apart so quickly when your boyfriend goes away for work.

Similar explanations may be useful for family members or supportive friends, when the patient gives permission for this (discussed further later in this chapter).

BORDERLINE PERSONALITY DISORDER AND THE CONVERSATIONAL MODEL

Case Example: Revisiting Bella

This extract illustrates an effort at helping a relative understand Bella's condition.

Bella's mother came to a session about 6 months into the treatment when Bella was making some noticeable improvements. Her mother was old and frail and had recently begun experiencing panic attacks herself. She seemed a little defensive; there had been some major changes in their home life, including discussions about Bella moving out of the home they had shared for many years.

Mother: I don't think Bella is coping very well with all this change. I'm not sure it's really helping her.

DM: Thank you for coming in today, it is good to meet you. I'm wondering how you are coping with all the changes.

Mother: Well, she is leaving just when I need the help.

DM: It's an unsettling time for both of you, but Bella will still want and need your support. I wonder if I can give you the name of a counselor you can talk to. She can help you to know how best to support Bella and provide you with some support too. You're going to need it.

Mother: I know I'm not going to last forever, and I do want Bella to be right for when I'm not around.

DM: Of course.

Mother: I did my best, you know.

DM: I'm sure you did. Bella has some very good memories, too, about her growing up. Bella is showing some improvement already, so I would say to you not to worry too much. I really want you to get some support for yourself too.

Mother: When I go, it will be just Bella and her daughter, my granddaughter, and this really worries me. I have worn the brunt of the overdoses and the suicide attempts, but when I go it will land on her daughter, and she has her own life to lead.

DM: We have a very good plan in place to help Bella in the future, one that will relieve you of much of the responsibility. The combination of psychotherapy, medication management, the day center, and the crisis management plan in place will mean that she will be much better supported than in the past. Her future looks a lot better now that we have a coordinated team. I am happy to talk to you from time to time, if you are concerned, but I will need to inform Bella of our conversation.

DURING THE TREATMENT PHASE

Psychotherapy with BPD patients presents some challenging problems that are specific to this patient population. In this section, we discuss managing deliberate self-harm, chronic suicidal thoughts, acute suicidal crises, drug and alcohol issues, poor attendance, separations during therapy, and boundary issues. Finally, some auxiliary therapeutic techniques are outlined as well as some suggestions for how to include families in care.

The Therapeutic Stance

There are simple but important principles of how the therapist goes about doing the therapy with a patient who has BPD. These are crucial in CM, but probably underpin all psychodynamic models that have shown effectiveness in working with patients with BPD. These principles include:

- An overarching attitude of curiosity and interest about the patient's inner world.
- Trying to understand the patient's experience, particularly focusing on the emotional aspects, with an attention to small shifts in feeling.
- Trying to tease out the parts of the conversation that have internal value for the patient, rather than things that are external, or valued by others.
- Holding understanding "loosely," so that the therapist's grasp on the patient's reality and experience is tentative, rather than being confident and all knowing.
- Using the patient's own words, staying as close as possible to his or her experience, rather than using jargon or theory-bound ideas.
- Trying to be human in response to the patient's difficulties, rather than responding technically or remaining unfeeling or "neutral." This includes being warm and encouraging. However, it also includes not allowing behaviors that burn out the therapist (e.g., ongoing contempt, rudeness, or verbal attack).
- When there are difficulties between the patient and therapist, either around understanding, ideas, or behavior, the therapist tries to negotiate a position that both the patient and therapist can "live with"—that is, a position that respects *both* the patient's and the therapist's personal realities.
- While the therapist endeavors to build a relationship of trust with the patient, he or she also seeks connection with others involved in care. Therapy is not seen as an exclusive experience. Other mental health practitioners, family, and

friends are encouraged to be part of the support network for the patient going through the therapeutic process.

Deliberate Self-Harm

Although deliberate self-harm can lead to suicide attempts, for the purposes of this section it is defined as deliberate nonlethal attempts to hurt oneself (e.g., by cutting, burning, hitting oneself) or to disconnect from consciousness (by taking relatively small overdoses of sedating tablets). Deliberate self-harm can be impulsive or planned. Either way, it is used to obtain relief from unbearable emotional pain. Such acts may have meaning in relation to self (e.g., of punishing oneself) or in terms of bringing a painful sense of "absence of self" to an end (e.g., terminating depersonalization/derealization wherein oneself, or those around, are experienced as unreal). There may be a communicative element to such acts, although usually one that is unclear to the patient: It is almost always an expression of pain, sometimes of anger, and often a mixture of confused motives. Attributions are often wrongly made by health carers about specific intent, leading to false attributions such as "manipulation" being applied to the patient. The impact on others, nevertheless, is often profound, and clinicians will frequently encounter distress in carers and the patient's significant others.

Most people in the general community and mental health community see self-harm as essentially destructive and irrational, and many are shocked by such behavior. They fail to realize that self-harm is serving a function for patients and is experienced as an effective and rapid means of emotion regulation and self-stabilization, at least in the short term (usually minutes to hours). As patients with BPD have not experienced being able to emotionally stabilize more adaptively or with the help of other people, it is often the only way available for them to avoid a freefall into a terrifying emotional state. These states are often triggered by someone who is emotionally important rejecting them or withdrawing support. However, such emotional cues can be subtle because patients with BPD tend to have marked interpersonal sensitivity based upon a background of mistrust and traumatic experience in developmental relationships. Therefore, the reactions of patients with BPD are often not understood and seem often to have "come out of nowhere" to people around them, who perceive deliberate self-harm as weird, stupid, aggressive, or manipulative, and become angry or helpless in response.

In CM our long-term goal is to help the patient restabilize a failing sense of self by understanding and managing experiences that serve as triggers to self-harm. Therefore, an essential part of therapy is to track episodes of deliberate self-harm, in order to talk through and understand what was felt, and how that led to an emotionally unbearable state. In a sense, although it seems counterintuitive, it is therapeutically valuable to focus the conversation on episodes of deliberate self-harm. However, often both patient and therapist are reluctant to do this. For the patient, being reminded of an episode of terror is usually extremely unpleasant. Quite often the patient is happy to tell the therapist about deliberate acts of self-harm, but much less comfortable talking about the emotional states that led up to them in detail. Other reasons for the patient being reluctant to talk about self-harm may be shame or previous experiences of angry responses from other caregivers. Powerful emotions such as shame are often at play in the patient, and the process of understanding and working through typically needs to occur over considerable periods of time.

For the therapist, hearing about deliberate self-harm is usually frightening and alien, making it difficult for the therapist to maintain the therapeutic stance of curiosity and compassion. There is a risk that the therapist, driven by anxiety, may be likely to rush to a suicide risk assessment, or to start telling the patient not to do it, without understanding what is driving the behavior. This response is alienating to the patient, as deliberate self-harm is often a valued and reliable solution to an unbearable emotional state, which he or she does not know how to do without. As alienation from the therapist is increased, the patient is likely to become more anxious or filled with shame, which could reinforce the need for further self-harm. Bearing in mind that such acts almost always include a communicative element at the level of expression of emotional pain (even though they may also be associated with temporary relief) assists the therapist in maintaining a position of compassion. Indeed, the fact of giving temporary relief in many ways serves to highlight the intensity and severity of a pain worse than the physical pain of self-harm that is experienced internally.

The mainstay of the approach to self-harm in CM is to create an atmosphere of safety, wherein the patient and therapist can explore what has happened, such that the feelings and experiences that were unmanageable can be felt, discussed, and tolerated. Connection between the therapist and the patient is enhanced, providing a new learning experience that can then be drawn upon the next time the patient is facing a similar experience. This is usually an unconscious process, but occasionally occurs with conscious recollection. Later on, deeper understanding of the self-harm act itself may be possible. Sometimes the self-harm act is a kind of body representation of an early traumatic experience, albeit dissociated from awareness. The method, position on the body, and associated feelings may give clues about this, such that the patient becomes aware of how an earlier traumatic experience is relived through self-harm.

If self-harm occurs within a session, the therapist needs to actively contain and control the situation. This will take precedence over the psychotherapy framework. Depending on the circumstances, containment and control may involve such measures as stemming the flow of blood, removing sharp objects, physically restraining the patient, or enlisting external assistance. Once the immediate situation is under control and the patient is calm and able to talk, the therapist should try to identify and understand what precipitated the immediate crisis, looking for some kind of emotional disconnection or disjunction immediately preceding the self-harm action. However, it may not be possible to discuss this until the next session.

The Chronically Suicidal Patient

Chronic suicidal thoughts, urges, and plans are central experiences for many patients with BPD. Some patients will struggle with this state, on and off, all of their adult lives. Most patients will have experienced chronic suicidal thoughts at some stage. Patients are usually relieved to be able to talk about this, as often they have had to hide suicidal thoughts because of shame or overreaction by others, and occasionally hostility from others. Sometimes those around them can tolerate some discussion of this state, but become burned out or distance themselves emotionally over time. In the extract of dialogue between Bella's mother and the therapist (DM) quoted a few pages earlier, Bella's mother says: "I have worn the brunt of the overdoses and the suicide attempts."

In the same sense as with deliberate self-harm, talking about chronic suicidal thoughts is an important and often therapeutically beneficial aspect of psychotherapy. In order to do this, the therapist needs to convey to the patient, both explicitly and implicitly (through the therapist's nonverbal response), that talking about suicidal feelings and thoughts is acceptable and important. The therapist adopts the stance of wanting to know about this dimension of the patient's experience, attempting to understand and build a picture of the underlying contributing factors. Although every patient has a unique experience in relation to suicidal ideation, there are some themes that often emerge with patients with BPD. Recognizing the despair and lack of hope the patient feels is often central. Unlike the acutely suicidal depressed patient, the borderline patient does not feel that something has been lost, but rather that the capacity to experience a rewarding and joyful life has never been there. Chronic suicidal thoughts can be comforting, as the thought of suicide gives the patient an exit strategy for unbearable pain. Some patients report that they are able to go on living only if they know they can kill themselves. Many patients with BPD keep a stash of medication or a much treasured suicide plan, in order to have a sense of control over a life that is felt to be unbearable. Disclosure of such a "secret" requires careful consideration by the therapist: Disclosure tends to imply that the patient wants help in managing the threat posed by such ready availability of a suicide method. Often it is possible to reach an agreement on a method of disposal of the hidden cache.

Understanding and exploring chronic suicidal thoughts can be difficult, as discussed above in relation to deliberate self-harm, as therapists will naturally have an uncomfortable response often involving anxiety, fear, frustration, or helplessness. To deal with this response, the therapist will often have an urge to avoid the topic or to actively do something to stop the patient from feeling this way. Activating a safety plan may reduce the therapist's fear, lecturing the patient may reduce frustration, or focusing on positive aspects of the patient may make the therapist feel better, but these strategies may leave the patient feeling more isolated. Such behaviors give the therapist the impression that he or she is "doing something," reducing the sense of helplessness, while often only reinforcing the patient's suicidal feelings. Safety is conveyed through a willingness to connect with the material that the patient is expressing and not reacting anxiously or prematurely—that is, not shutting down the topic because of rising therapist anxiety. By talking about the suicidal thoughts and not moving quickly to a crisis plan, changing medication, or immediate hospitalization, the therapist conveys the message that this area can be discussed, felt, and tolerated. It is the sense of connection that emerges through an accepting and attuned conversation that will reduce the sense of isolation that is frequently central to chronic suicidal thinking, enabling the patient to have a different experience of these feelings. Over time there is long-term cumulative effect of reducing suicidal thoughts, since suicidal thoughts are often generated by a sense of alienation, disconnection, and aloneness.

For most therapists, the most effective way of dealing with the anxieties and other difficult feelings evoked by the borderline patient with chronic suicidal ideation and deliberate self-harm will be to engage in regular supervision. The supervisor can provide the containment and additional perspective that effectively prevent the therapist from becoming reactive or feeling isolated or helpless.

However, the supervisor needs to be aware that a "parallel process" may also occur. That is, the anxiety and discomfort the patient experiences create a tendency within the therapist to react or give up, which in turn may create a similar tendency within the supervisor, who may feel compelled to activate a crisis plan or advise the therapist to refer the patient to somebody else. These are phenomena that commonly occur within an interpersonal sphere and that we refer to in CM as creating the "expectational field"—that is, the cluster of expectations and tendencies that often come into play in interpersonal interaction and that have a personal background in previous experience (see chapter 2). Supervisors need to be aware of the triadic nature of supervision and the effect of the expectational field on all three parties: patient, therapist, and supervisor.

The Acutely Suicidal Patient

As discussed above, chronic suicidal thoughts are frequently a core experience for the patient with BPD, and to be able to work on this thinking therapeutically, it is important that the therapist does not overreact. This means that there is a higher level of tolerance for talk about suicide within twice-weekly psychotherapy than might commonly be the case in other contexts. Adding brief supportive phone calls or extra sessions is often enough to manage the situation when the therapist or patient is concerned about an increase in suicidal urges.

However, it is equally important to recognize when the patient has moved to a heightened level of suicidal risk, where both patient and therapist realize that safety cannot be maintained by therapeutic work within the session, or even with a temporary increase in contact by the therapist between sessions. While this change may be communicated in different ways, the common factor will be a significant shift in the patient's mental and affective state. Some examples follow:

- The patient states openly that he or she will not be safe or cannot guarantee his or her own safety between now and the next session.

- The patient describes new behaviors that indicate imminent suicide, such as giving away of possessions, tying up loose ends, or revealing actions that are part of a suicidal plan (e.g., accessing the means of committing suicide).
- The session ends with the patient stating he or she will not return, is going to meet a dead loved one, or another similar statement, and the therapist is concerned that this is an indirect way of saying, "I am going to die."
- The therapist experiences a new and worrying reaction, such as a feeling of dread or an image of the patient killing him- or herself. This is particularly worrying if the patient is unable or unwilling to discuss this issue, such that the therapist continues to feel mounting anxiety. Unwillingness to communicate on the part of the patient raises the level of uncertainty and may preclude necessary elements of risk assessment. However, lack of communication is common in patients with BPD, as overwhelming painful internal emotional states may be masked and therefore not expressed verbally or through obvious or intelligible nonverbal communication.

The therapeutic relationship constitutes a powerful protective factor against suicide, particularly when the patient experiences a sense of connection with the therapist. Confiding, trusting relationships are generally protective for people in this regard. However, this factor also means that the person is subject to the vicissitudes of the relationship. Hence shifts in the relationship, particularly for patients with BPD, who have high levels of interpersonal sensitivity, can also trigger overwhelming emotional responses. It is important to assess the degree of alienation the patient is feeling in the therapeutic relationship at this point in time (as well as the more external factors indicated above), and to question whether there has been a disjunction.

In the case of chronic suicidal ideation or nonlethal deliberate self-harm, the clinician will try and stay in the role of therapist and manage within the current framework or temporarily increase support. In the case of acute suicidal ideation, the clinician will generally shift toward the need for protective action, which involves moving away from a purely understanding and containing role within therapy to an action role, mobilizing resources outside the therapeutic relationship. In some ways this shift in role is akin to temporarily becoming a "case manager." However, the therapist attempts to retain connection by explaining that the reason for this shift is to ensure the patient's safety. This response involves the following steps:

1. Assess risk.

2. Refer to previous agreement in crisis management plan.

3. Attempt to collaboratively discuss with the patient which aspects of the crisis plan should be followed, being specific about who will be contacted to help, what will be said, and what steps will be taken from there. If the patient is not willing to discuss this, then the above steps are told to the patient and action is initiated unilaterally. Explain that, although these steps are necessary to ensure safety, the therapy will continue once the patient's safety has been established.

4. If possible, try and formulate a joint understanding of the crisis; this may be possible only later in some acute crises.

5. If community options are not sufficient, discuss hospital options as per the crisis plan. When possible, try to enlist the patient's agreement to enable a voluntary admission. Only rarely is it necessary to organize an involuntary admission under the provisions of the local mental health act. This should be seen as a last resort, as it may challenge the therapeutic alliance, although this risk may be moderated if the patient perceives the action as motivated by the therapist's need to protect the patient.

6. Hospitalization constitutes a break in the frame. Generally, therapy should not continue during the admission. It is appropriate for hospital staff to take over responsibility for patient care. However, maintaining some brief contacts with the patient during this time may help maintain the therapeutic alliance. Hospitalization is best thought of as a short-term intervention to get through a crisis, rather than treatment for the underlying condition. The goal is to resume therapy as soon as is safely possible.

Some situations of acute suicidal risk that present specific challenges include the following:

1. *When the session ends with a suicidal threat.* The therapist may have to take extra time to assess the situation and determine the risk. If it is managed without external involvement, it is still a break in the frame and will need further discussion at the next session.

2. *When the patient communicates his or her intent to die over the telephone.* The therapist needs to ask:

   • Where is the patient *now*?

   • What method is being contemplated?

• Is the patient willing to accept help? If not, the therapist is ethically bound to call emergency services (police and ambulance) and the community mental health team.

There is no infallible system of risk assessment for suicide, and infallibility is not expected by the medical–legal system. However, whenever a therapist makes a decision about suicidal risk, whether the decision is to continue in therapeutic mode or move into case management mode, the following actions need to occur:

• Document clearly that suicide has been discussed.
• Document the decision made, even if it is a decision to continue as usual, and briefly include the reasons for the decision.
• If unsure, particularly when tolerating a high level of risk without further action, consult with a colleague or supervisor as soon as is practicable.

One point needs to be emphasized for all therapists: *There are definite limits to the responsibility that any therapist or clinician can take for a patient's life*. In the field of mental health it is inevitable that some patients will complete suicide. *Not all suicide is preventable.*

In the unfortunate situation of a patient committing suicide, it is important to take the following steps to reduce subsequent morbidity for the patient's family and for the therapist:

1. Contact the family or friends as soon as is reasonably possible to express condolence and sorrow.
2. Discuss the death with other members of the treatment team.
3. Discuss the death with colleagues.
4. Engage in individual supervision.

Poor Attendance/Dropouts

Although patients with BPD have normal interpersonal needs, they often struggle in interpersonal relationships. Psychotherapy involves developing a close relationship with the therapist, which presents challenges for the patient. The full range of human emotions may arise within the therapeutic relationship, although patients with BPD may find themselves confused by unfamiliar feelings and emotions that they struggle to recognize. On the one hand, these patients may experience painful and confusing feelings or the sense of frustration and irritation. On the other hand, tender feelings, appropriate to emotional closeness, may also be experienced as confusing and destabilizing for patients, especially for those who have experienced trauma and abuse. The sense of love, closeness, erotic feelings, or simply vulnerability may all feel unsafe and be difficult to communicate. As a consequence, it is quite common for the patient to deal with this confusion by attending inconsistently, and if feelings become too intense, by dropping out. To help manage poor attendance and minimize dropouts, the following points are often helpful:

- In the assessment sessions, the issue of attendance should be discussed along with the other principles that make therapy safe and effective. It is important to place value on regular attendance. Encouraging commitment to the framework is a cornerstone of therapeutic engagement. It may be useful to point out the obvious, which is that success in therapy depends upon "turning up" consistently. The situation of a patient "not feeling like coming because of distress" should be addressed explicitly by emphasizing that such times may be of particular value in reaching a shared understanding. Many patients with BPD have expectations from their childhood experience that those in authority or carer roles don't want to see them when they are in a bad mood. This leads to similar expectations of the therapist and hence is an area that warrants special attention.

- For some patients, reinforcing the idea of attendance as a responsibility may be achieved by getting them to sign a contract, which explicitly states that attending regularly is their responsibility. A copy is given to patients to take home. The reason for this formality is that many patients with BPD seem to understand and agree to the frame, but are subtly dissociated, as a result of anxiety, and actually not taking much in. A written copy, particularly when the patient is reminded later of what they have agreed to, can protect against this subtle dissociation. It also reinforces the idea that the patient is agreeing to make a kind of "deal," wherein his or her job is to arrive at sessions "come what may," and the therapist's job is to help him or her with whatever emotional experience he or she brings to the sessions. However, some caution needs to be exercised in this regard because some patients will see such contracts as efforts to exert control—in these cases developing a shared verbal understanding may be necessary for a period.

- When there is poor or inconsistent attendance, it must be discussed, no matter how hard it seems or how reluctant the patient is to do this. Reminding the patient of his or her commitment to attending regularly is only part of the discussion. The most important part of the discussion is trying to understand what has happened, and why the patient is dealing with whatever occurred through poor attendance. When the difficulties that underlie poor attendance are understood and discussed, usually it makes it easier for the patient to come more regularly. When there are external problems getting in the way, these should be addressed whenever possible.

• When there is nonattendance, one of the likely explanations is that there has been a disjunction in the therapy. Often when there has been a shift in therapy that is experienced adversely by the patient, the response is one of avoidance. It is incumbent upon the therapist to consider this possibility and to adopt a proactive approach to repair of the disjunction. In CM, the therapist takes responsibility for the disjunction, explicitly recognizes his or her own role in the interaction, expresses regret for any difficulty the patient has experienced, and expresses empathic concern for the patient. Supervision is often helpful in identifying and responding to such events.

• If the patient does not attend for a few sessions, it is important for the therapist to be active in making contact. A single telephone call leaving a voice message is not enough. Many young patients with BPD may not have enough credit (minutes) on their mobile to pick up their voicemails, and therefore will not get the message. If the patient does not pick up the call directly, usually a text message to ring the therapist is more effective, as it does not require credit for the patient to receive the message. If the patient is still unreachable, a follow-up letter or e-mail is necessary. It is the therapist's job to contact the patient, rather than allow the patient to drop out without further contact. Supervision about the case may also help, by generating reflection about what may have precipitated the nonattendance.

Separations: Holidays, Physical Illness, and Other Disruptions to Therapeutic Continuity

Separation from someone who is emotionally meaningful, such as a therapist, child, parent, or lover, creates anxiety in anybody. For patients with BPD, the prospect of separation can be very threatening, and actual separation can be extremely painful, as reflected in the diagnostic criterion "sensitive to abandonment" (DSM-IV-TR; American Psychiatric Association, 2000). This heightened sensitivity is usually due to repeated early experiences of distressing and prolonged separation (either physical or emotional) from caregivers, stored in early memory systems that are not available to awareness. With a fragile sense of self, the patient with BPD relies on an emotionally caring person to be consistently present, to maintain a sense of "going on being" (see Chapter 1 for more detail). When the other person leaves, there are often unbearable feelings, sometimes described by patients as feeling as if they are "falling apart," and may lead to desperate attempts to stabilize their emotions by, for example, self-harming behaviors. This severe response may also occur when the patient does not come to sessions.

To counteract this dynamic, it is important for the therapist to provide a consistent and stable therapeutic relationship, in which understanding and responding to the patient's emotional experience are paramount. When this stability occurs, the patient may become powerfully attached to the therapist, while simultaneously fearing the loss of the relationship. In long-term therapy, there is often a considerable sense of internal disruption for the BPD patient around breaks in therapy. It is not surprising that this dimension of experience becomes more salient for the patient as the relationship develops over time. Breaks in therapy will inevitably occur, with either party taking holidays, experiencing physical illness, having trouble with transport to the session, etc. In some cases—for example, with Bella—unpredictable and painful disruptions in important relationships have become expected, and the patient attempts to prepare and protect him- or herself from the anticipated emotional pain. There will often be an obvious gap between verbal and behavioral expression. For example, the patient may say "I don't care" about an impending break, yet then proceed to take an overdose or cut him- or herself when it occurs.

At the same time, the usual temporary separations that occur in long-term therapy provide an opportunity to become aware of, feel, explore, and manage the feelings that arise. Furthermore, it may be possible to understand previous experiences of "falling apart" and self-destructive behavior, such that a new way of managing future separations with more control may be possible. In other words, the patient develops a capacity to tolerate and reflect upon the impact and feelings of separation experiences, rather than simply reacting to separation in the repetitive way that has been driven by traumatic experience. In normal development there is a process of internalizing interactive experiences until the person has a sense of an "inner world" that becomes self-realizing. Although security in relationship is essential to the development of self, it is also the case that once a basic sense of security is achieved, a process of "self-discovery" goes on between interactive experiences. In an analogous way, in therapy there may ultimately be a shift beyond tolerance of aloneness to the sense of interest in the inner world, which takes on a life of its own, leading to the capacity to be both "alone" and "together" without distress. However, not all patients will be able to achieve this level of development.

Some principles for managing separations within therapy include the following:

1. At the end of the assessment sessions the discussion of the frame should include the provision of a consistent and reliable therapeutic space. Sessions should be, when possible, at the same time on the same day in the same office from one week to the next. Disruptions within individual sessions should be minimized. For example, the therapist should turn off the mobile phone or have the office phone diverted. It is also extremely helpful in the initial sessions to discuss the importance of talking about the experience of separation when it occurs later in therapy, even though the patient may not see its significance at that point.

2. The therapist should attempt to provide the patient with as much warning as possible about anticipated disruptions, such as holidays. For unanticipated disruptions, such as illness, the patient should be contacted as early as possible.

3. Usually there needs to be some mechanism for contact between sessions. For the patient, this may involve communication with the therapist via a third party, such as a secretary. On occasion, the therapist may choose to allow other avenues of communication, such as e-mail or mobile phone contact. For further discussion of this issue, see the following section on boundary issues and limits.

4. When there has been a separation, whether initiated by the therapist or the patient, it is important to discuss the experience and the feelings that have been generated. Quite often the patient will be reluctant to do this, either because he or she feels more comfortable avoiding the feelings that came up, or because he or she feels embarrassed or ashamed at someone else seeing his or her distress.

5. When the therapist is away for an extended period (with some patients, this could be anything longer than a week), the therapist needs to discuss whether the patient would like some extra support during that time. In some cases arrangements may be made for emergency contacts, either with the therapist or with emergency/community mental health teams, depending on the therapist's personal limits and the particular needs of the patient at that time. In other cases the patient may wish to see a temporary replacement therapist while the regular therapist is away. In all

cases there also needs to be a realistic appraisal of the logistics and availability of supports. It is a mistake to make extraordinary arrangements that may prove "undeliverable." It may be important to recognize the limitations and "non-ideal" nature of arrangements, although there is also a "bottom line" message that "help is always available"—which is usually true given that some resources are likely available 24 hours a day, 7 days a week. In all cases the therapist should reflect upon his or her knowledge of local resources and their precise availability.

Boundary Issues and Limits

In order for any psychotherapy to occur, sessions need to be safe for both patient and therapist. Safety is enhanced by explicitly establishing, when the frame is discussed in the initial sessions, the things that should and should not happen. The nature of a "talking therapy" is that emotions and distress are processed verbally, allowing matters to be revisited and modified over time. There are many forms of behavior that interfere with this process because of their essentially "irrevocable" nature. Behaviors such as violent action, sexual contact, theft, and financial exploitation are clearly in this category. It helps the patient to be assured from the outset that such behaviors run counter to the therapeutic process and are therefore not allowed in therapy.

The therapeutic relationship allows powerful feelings and needs and wishes to occur. So, at times of intense need or distress within the psychotherapy relationship, some patients with BPD will attempt to deal with such needs as they did within their childhood families. Many patients with BPD have grown up in families where safety was inconsistent or absent and where rules that are likely to protect children were broken. Because of these early environments, current needs may be dealt with through direct action, without reflection on what the need is about or whether the action is safe or appropriate in the therapeutic relationship. This direct action may involve giving expensive gifts, asking for comforting touch/hugs/sexual contact, or alternatively, storming out, smashing things, or harming oneself within a session. It may be asking the therapist to provide nontherapy support, such as giving a reference for a job, or asking the therapist to directly intervene in a problematic relationship. Psychotherapy, however, involves a commitment to manage almost all needs through talk and conversation. Although sometimes other creative modalities may enter into the framework (e.g., the patient may bring a picture or a poem or keep a journal to which he or she refers in therapy), there is still the maintenance of a conversational frame focused on the patient's world. At times there may be considerable tension, and even conflict, between the patient and therapist over what constitutes appropriate and safe behavior, and tremendous reluctance to discuss and negotiate this area.

However, this issue of boundaries is not a cut-and-dried area. Too rigid an adherence to limits may create an inflexible therapy that unfairly ignores the patient's needs in the present moment. A rigid imposition of "rules" will be experienced by many patients as authoritarian. A lack of limits, on the other hand, is likely, consciously or unconsciously, to lead to exploitative and damaging behaviors that diminish the safety of the therapeutic space. There is usually no absolute correct response. Instead, discussing any request to step outside the usual framework of talking will facilitate understanding what the need is about and how to respond. For example, at times a hug from the therapist may be a wonderfully human response, and at other times, may be part of a worrying recurring pattern to gain comfort and reassurance without discussion and reflection. A particularly difficult area is the patient who has experienced childhood sexual abuse and may have underlying beliefs, often out of conscious awareness, that care is elicited in response to sexual favors. In general, therapists need to understand that the mainstay of the therapeutic relationship is not based on providing actual care and comfort, and it cannot function primarily as a substitute parental relationship. Some practical principles in this area include the following:

- The therapist explicitly discusses, in the early sessions, that this is primarily a talking therapy, and so other interactions outside this frame will be discussed and negotiated before a decision is made about what to do next.
- The therapist tells the patient that he or she (the therapist) will abide by ethical principles that are established for psychotherapists, including confidentiality (within limits discussed previously), nonexploitation of patients (e.g., not receiving expensive gifts or cash beyond the regular fee), nonacceptance of violence, and no sexual contact.
- It is important to be real and responsive when this does not threaten the safety and integrity of the therapeutic work. Rigid adherence to rules, without discussion, negotiation, and reflection, is often counterproductive.
- Limits and boundaries can be different from one patient to the other, and can change within a long-term therapy, depending on circumstances. Each therapist has to determine his or her own personal limits at any given moment, and

this should continue to be a process for reflection throughout a long-term therapy.

- Supervision can be essential when trying to sort out actions and behaviors that stretch therapeutic limits. It can take courage for a therapist to be honest with his or her supervisor, particularly when the therapist has acted in a way that is uncharacteristic or embarrassing.

One specifically difficult area, which commonly occurs, is that of gift-giving: the patient giving the therapist a gift. For many patients gift-giving may have a strong family or cultural basis, and therapist's refusal to accept the gift can be deeply upsetting. There is no correct response, although it is useful to keep the following three principles in mind:

- Gifts usually involve something personal of the patient being offered and should not be lightly or automatically refused.
- Whatever the therapist decides to do, it is important to explore and understand collaboratively why this gift is being given now, the personal significance or meaning of the gift, and the consequences in the therapeutic relationship of accepting or refusing the gift.
- It is unethical to exploit the patient. Gifts of significant monetary value should usually be refused, while simultaneously endeavoring to recognize and appreciate the generosity of the patient.

The use of e-mails and mobile phones has rapidly become a new area of contact outside of sessions between patients and therapists. Older therapists tend to discourage such contact whereas younger therapists have frequently embraced these social technologies. Increasingly, young patients with BPD are surprised when limits are placed on the use of e-mail and mobile phone to contact the therapist. Once again, there is no correct approach, but rather a negotiated and thoughtful agreement that can enhance safety and communication, and that does not become a burden on the therapist. Most therapists will find it difficult to sustain 24-hour availability, and it is also an essential part of the frame that the limits of availability are made clear to the patient.

Many patients with BPD will have a mobile phone but no home phone. They will usually screen calls, such that they will not answer telephone numbers that are unknown to them. At the beginning of therapy it is often helpful to ask them to put the therapist's office number into their mobile phone, so that it does not come up as an unregistered number when the therapist tries to call. Some patients with BPD will have a mobile phone but no credit. Therefore, it is better to leave a text message for the patient, as this is free to pick up, rather than a voicemail message, which requires credit.

Allowing the patient to write e-mails, which can be a kind of journaling, may be therapeutically beneficial. However, there are some potential problems with e-mail, particularly when the patient is using it for emergency communication (and a therapist may not see the e-mail for several days), or when e-mails are prolific or very long, increasing the therapeutic load to an unacceptable level. To counteract these potential problems, the following ideas may be worth discussing with the patient in the beginning of therapy, if the therapist is happy to receive e-mails:

- E-mails are not appropriate when asking for acute help. A telephone call is necessary when the patient wants to get the therapist's immediate help.
- E-mails, providing they are not too long or numerous, will be read by the therapist, but not responded to until the session. During the session they will be discussed. After the session, the e-mail will be entered into the clinical note or kept in a patient file.
- E-mails are not technologically secure, so extremely private or sensitive communications should not be sent by e-mail.

Auxiliary Therapeutic Techniques

Some patients with BPD will wish to express themselves or elaborate on their therapeutic journey through creative means of self-expression such as keeping a journal or diary, writing poetry or stories, creating songs or music, or through painting and drawing. As these creative undertakings may encompass many different aspects of the therapeutic journey, a few common possibilities should be kept in mind:

- Some patients will start some type of creative self-expression for the first time during therapy. This is usually a marker of the development of an internal capacity to reflect on their experience or an increasing sense of self.
- When a patient wishes to share something he or she has created, this is a great opportunity for the therapist to value what is coming from within the patient and to increase the sense of shared understanding.

- In other cases, patients will be too frightened to directly discuss traumatic experiences, particularly those that are filled with shame. It may be easier to communicate to the therapist by reading a piece of writing about what has happened, or even handing it to the therapist to read. This may be a safer step initially, leading to a two-way conversation later.

- A different scenario is the patient who is journaling, or creative in some other modality, but who prefers to keep his or her work private. It is important to not coerce the patient to share, or to intrude upon a private experience.

- Creative self-expression probably enhances recovery, and so the therapist would usually actively encourage this endeavor. Sometimes this may be seen as a kind of "homework" by the patient, although the therapist never takes a coercive position in relation to such activity. It is often useful to suggest that the patient find a quiet place for a few minutes each day, where he or she can reflect on what has been happening emotionally, and then engage in "free writing." This is the kind of writing where the patient doesn't bother about grammar, logic, or appropriateness, but just allows whatever thoughts and feelings come up to "flow" onto the page, without editing. However, therapists should not put pressure on patients who do not have this inclination, as coercive "free writing" is unlikely to build a self-reflective capacity. Empty compliance is likely to be the result.

Case Example: Bella Revisited

Bella began to bring an exercise book in which there were letters to the therapist. Each session she would hand the book to the therapist, DM, and would ask her to read the entries that she made mostly on a daily basis.

The entries were nonreflective and very basic for many months. For example, there would be a sentence to say how awful life is and then a list of medications she had taken or was thinking of taking. Bella had started the book herself and was using it to communicate with herself and her therapist in between sessions.

DM would take a great interest in what was written and encourage more exploration of the thoughts, feelings, and circumstances within the session. Over the months Bella's writing began to change. The sentences were rich with thoughts and feelings and were connected up in the manner of a proper conversation—she had developed a good narrative capacity. DM could see that Bella's inner conversations were changing as the therapy progressed.

144

Including the Family or Friends

For most patients with BPD there is confusion about how much to rely upon and interact with their families. The assessment process will include an evaluation of the range and quality of family and relational supports available to the patient. For some, particularly those who grew up in overtly abusive families, they may have a need to keep distance from their family members, even though they may pine for family support and affection. Others will want distance and closeness with various family members at different times. In CM it is important not to prejudge the value and nature of family contacts, but to help patients sort out what they want from their families and how to achieve this, or how to grieve what they cannot have.

Despite ambivalence and confusion, as described above, some families may have the capacity to provide a major supportive role as the patient goes through the therapeutic process. In general, the presence of at least one supportive person in the patient's world greatly enhances the prospects of a successful therapy. Where possible, the therapist should allow family members to play a role, provided that this is what the patient wishes. Keeping in touch with family members within the limits of confidentiality, can be very helpful. It can also be helpful that close family members have a basic understanding of the framework of therapy and the possible need for them to play a role during times of crisis. Once again, there is no correct stance, so the following points may be worth discussing:

1. If it exists within the local area health service or hospital, a family group is usually an excellent adjunct to individual psychotherapy. This type of group usually involves a series of psychoeducation evenings, where friends and family members are invited to listen to a relevant topic and have some time for questions and group discussion. Topics may include:
   - What is borderline personality disorder?
   - How does it occur?
   - Medications and other biological treatments
   - Psychological and social intervention
   - How to manage crises and difficult behaviors
   - Managing emotions

2. When the patient has a severe disorder that includes several or many suicide attempts, it may be worthwhile to contact the patient's family (if the patient

agrees, and ideally with the patient) early in treatment to introduce oneself and describe the treatment and how it may be helpful. Furthermore, including family members in the crisis plan, if the patient indicates they could be helpful, is important. In some cases they may be a central aspect of the crisis plan.

3. When a family member rings secretly and asks for information, it is important to consult with the patient before disclosing anything about the therapy. If the patient says that it is fine to talk with the family member, it may still be safer for the integrity of the therapeutic relationship to insist upon the patient being present for that conversation.

4. There is some anecdotal evidence suggesting that family therapy sessions may be counterproductive for adult patients with BPD (Gunderson, 2011). These are sessions wherein the therapist tries to conduct therapy with the family members and the patient as a family system in order to promote new ways of relating to each other.

Alcohol and Substance Abuse or Dependence

Alcohol or substance abuse that has not been discussed within therapy is probably one of the commonest causes of poor psychotherapy outcome. This issue is particularly relevant to patients with BPD, for whom alcohol and substance abuse is common. The short-term emotional pain-relieving properties of these chemicals are powerful, so patients with BPD are drawn to impulsive or compulsive use of alcohol and illicit substances. Over-the-counter (OTC) nonprescription tablets, such as antihistamines and opiates (most commonly codeine, in combination with paracetamol/acetaminophen), are also frequent drugs of abuse. Often shame makes it difficult for patients to disclose their true consumption level. Furthermore, disclosure may be withheld if the patient is aware, or believes, that absence of substance or alcohol abuse is a requirement for psychotherapy to proceed.

A detailed approach to the management of substance abuse or dependence is not attempted here. The following principles may be helpful in navigating this difficult area:

• Alcohol or substance *dependence*, when in the moderate-to-severe category, is generally incompatible with psychotherapy. If the patient is dependent, it means that he or she needs alcohol or the substance every day, and therefore will arrive at sessions intoxicated, either overtly or covertly. Psychotherapy is pointless with an intoxicated patient, so referral to a drug and alcohol service for assessment and possible detox is the usual next step. Some of these patients may then seek psychotherapy once they have achieved abstinence or control of the substance dependence.

- Alcohol or substance *abuse* is compatible with psychotherapy. If all patients with BPD who abuse alcohol, substances, or OTC medications were excluded, a large proportion of patients would not get treatment.

- Methadone maintenance is also compatible with psychotherapy, as long as the dose is relatively low, such that the patient is not subtly intoxicated during psychotherapy.

- The therapist should explicitly ask about substance and alcohol use, as well as OTC medications, during the assessment interviews. If usage is occurring at problematic (but not fully dependent) levels, the therapist needs to tell the patient that although this use does not stop therapy, it does need to be monitored in order to decide whether the level of use is manageable within psychotherapy, or requires extra help from a drug and alcohol service. Impulsive binges are usually manageable, whereas heavy and frequent use requires referral.

- A delicate balance is required when considering drug and alcohol use within therapy. The patient with BPD, already fearing rejection and failure, is likely to minimize or hide his or her usage. To counter this tendency and promote honesty, the therapist attempts to understand what the behavior means for the patient and how it helps him or her manage painful feelings (as well as finding out about the amount and extent of use). The value of the behavior to the patient, as well as the difficulties and underlying motivations, are recognized and efforts are made to understand this part of the patient's life in a nonjudgmental way.

- Some patients use alcohol and illicit substances to manage uncomfortable feelings immediately following a psychotherapy session. This is a common pattern that may not be disclosed, but can be detrimental to therapeutic improvement.

- A therapist who suspects drug and alcohol use that has not been disclosed must raise the issue, even though it is challenging for both patient and therapist.

- Occasionally a patient will arrive at a session intoxicated. It is not possible to do psychotherapy in this situation, and so the session should be politely terminated, and the problem discussed at the next session.

ENDING THERAPY: TERMINATION ISSUES

Finishing a therapy involves knowing when to end, preparing for termination, and completing some tasks as termination occurs. These will be discussed briefly in the next section. Subsequently, the chapter closes with some brief comments on self-care, supervision, training, ethical obligations, and teamwork.

Before the End Phase

The end phase of therapy occurs when completion of therapy has become an explicit subject in the therapeutic conversation. Separations (as discussed earlier in this chapter) are usually difficult for patients with BPD, as traumatic memories of childhood losses or absences are triggered. Finishing therapy is the biggest separation in the therapeutic relationship, and therefore will present emotional challenges. Each separation during therapy for holidays or sickness becomes a potential learning experience for how to manage the pain of separation differently from the way it was managed when the patient was growing up. The process of experiencing and talking about separations is an important part of the therapeutic growth necessary to handle termination. If earlier separations in therapy have been processed, termination becomes more manageable, although it may still be associated with significant sadness and distress.

The goal of working toward a completion of therapy should be included in the assessment sessions when the frame is being discussed. This topic is relevant whether or not the frame is explicitly time-limited. Of course, it is important to discuss whether it will be a time-limited therapy to give the patient a clear idea of the period available to work together. On the other hand, if the therapy is not specifically time-limited, it is important to discuss a process of review and to consider how the therapist and patient will know when to finish. Completion indicators may include the patient's goals (e.g., progress in work, relationships, and parenting), behavioral stability (e.g., the absence of self-harming, suicidal, or other destructive behaviors to cope; and the emergence of sustainable, purposive, and creative behaviors), emotional stability (able to self-regulate and cope with emotional intensity without resorting to extreme behaviors), and a flexible sense of self (able to assert in socially acceptable ways and able to manage conflict without decompensation).

For a patient with BPD a time-limited therapy should be a minimum of 1 year. Often, there are pressures within the public health system for therapy to be time-limited to as few as 12 sessions. This kind of help may be necessary in crises but is unlikely to lead to sustainable change. It may be important at the outset to stress that part of the journey will occur in this therapy, and the rest of the journey may occur outside of therapy or within a subsequent therapy. A balance between promoting hope without fueling unrealistic expectations needs to be struck.

During the main body of therapeutic work, termination issues should be discussed when the patient initiates the subject. Bringing up this topic usually indicates that the patient is feeling anxious about what will happen when therapy finishes. The patient's anxiety may predispose him or her to avoid the subject of finishing, and there may be occasions when the therapist has to initiate such a discussion, to allow for necessary reflection on the process.

End Phase: Issues to Consider

To determine if the patient is ready to finish, the following questions can be considered. The answers will assist the therapist in judging the patient's readiness for termination of therapy.

- Are separations being negotiated with ease, or do they tend to reevoke traumatic responses?
- Has the conversation become more reflective (the capacity to be able to tolerate, consider, and discuss painful experiences rather than simply react to them)?
- Is this a "flight into health," whereby the patient is avoiding something difficult by telling the therapist that everything is OK and it is time to finish?
- Is the patient able to appreciate the therapeutic journey and discuss improvements, as well as mourn the upcoming loss of an important relationship?
- Can the patient see a life beyond therapy? Has he or she developed a richer social support system?

During the end phase, the therapeutic relationship has often become more relaxed, with less need to focus on understanding lifelong patterns that have already been substantially worked through. In some cases there may be recognition of the bond that has developed over the period of working together. This bond may contribute to a collaborative approach to the completion of therapy, although the therapist needs to remain aware that ending may prove stressful, and the difficulty of termination should never be underestimated.

Some patients will attempt to avoid thinking about, feeling, or discussing the process of termination usually because the feelings evoked are too painful, or the shame of needing the therapist is being hidden. In this situation, it is the therapist's responsibility to make sure that termination is discussed. Sometimes themes of loss will emerge around other relationships, such as sadness about losing a neighbor, which can be used to prompt discussion about what it might be like to lose this relationship when therapy finishes. Some patients do not turn up for the last few sessions, presumably because of the difficulty of facing loss, sometimes expressed in the question "What is the point?" The therapist needs to balance taking responsibility for ensuring that the subject is talked about with having respect for the particular measures the patient takes to cope with the situation.

It is important to normalize grief. When any important relationship finishes, grief is healthy and normal. To be able to grieve and feel sad during the termination phase, and when therapy is finished, is a mark of health for the patient with BPD. Occasionally, under the weight of these feelings, the patient will temporarily resume self-harming or some other problematic behavior. In most cases this represents a temporary lapse rather than a major decline in function. For the patient who resumes self-harm chronically and cannot regulate in any other way, it is probably premature to finish. It may be helpful to warn patients that feelings of sadness, emptiness, or loss may occur for several months after therapy finishes.

At the beginning of the termination phase it is important to discuss what the process will look like. Will there be a gradual reduction, with sessions moving to fortnightly or even monthly for a few months? Or is it better to continue the current frequency and finish by a specific date? It is probably the patient's preference that will dictate this choice, although the therapist may have limits in terms of flexibility and time. There also needs to be a consideration of possible future contact and whether the therapist will remain available to the patient if more help is required.

We created this checklist of tasks to provide guidance in the last few sessions:

- Discuss what has been achieved in therapy, allowing for input from patient.
- Discuss what still needs to be done. These are the areas/attributes/relationships that the patient wished to change, but the change has not occurred or has occurred only partially. The changes in these areas may be achieved through ongoing life experience or may need further therapeutic involvement in the future.
- If termination is occurring because the therapist is unable to continue but the patient would like to continue psychotherapy, it is the therapist's responsibility to help the patient find a new therapist. This does not mean that the therapist

is responsible for the entire process. Giving names and possible suggestions that are feasible is usually enough.

- Discuss any future contact and communication once regular therapy stops. The therapist may encourage some informal occasional contact in the future, such as a postcard, e-mail, or brief letter, if the therapist and patient are comfortable with this idea.
- Discuss a backup plan for any future difficulties. This may include the possibility of further work in the future with the current therapist, or contacting the current therapist to provide names of mental health workers or other psychotherapists.
- Express appreciation (if genuine) for the patient's courage and commitment during the therapeutic journey.
- Say good-bye. This usually requires a little bit of time and care. Some patients will want to formalize this part of the process with a ritual or a gift. Unless what is suggested strays beyond ethical limits, allowing the patient to structure the good-bye is usually the best approach.

Case Example: Bella Revisited

Let's see how DM and Bella handled this poignant process.

Bella: You're ending the therapy with me just as Mum is sick and dying. Just when I really need someone to talk to, you're kicking me out.

DM: It is really unfortunate that Mum is so unwell. We will work on what we are going to do, as far as ending therapy. I know it is a really bad time, but I want to remind you that no matter when we finish, you can of course come back for a session or two if it is required in the future. You also have friends now. Do you think it's a little different?

Bella: I can't talk to them like I talk to you. What if Mum has another stroke and dies? I know I won't cope with it.

DM: We did decide on 2 years as the length of therapy, but it cannot be set in concrete. We were not to know what would happen. If something major happens, of course I want to be there for you.

Bella: All I need to do is see Dr. G if we have finished therapy, and he will give me a letter to give to you.

DM: Yes, that's right.

This example illustrates how an ending can be negotiated with attention to practical matters such as mechanisms for further contact. It also illustrates the ambivalence that is commonly felt around endings. In all therapies there is likely to be some sense of incompleteness about the closure of therapy.

THERAPIST SELF-CARE

Working with patients with BPD can be rewarding, but it does require stamina and perseverance, as the difficulties these patients face are usually long-standing and emotionally demanding. Furthermore, the instability of mood, behavior, and self-concept requires that the therapist remain stable and emotionally open in the face of emotional storms and difficult behaviors. In order to do this, the therapist needs to set up certain structures, within and without, that are sustainable over the long term. These structures can be divided into five areas: training, supervision, personal psychotherapy, ethical obligations, and balance between work and private life. These areas are necessarily complex and are discussed only briefly in this chapter.

Training

Training provides the foundations for psychotherapy practice. The theoretical component, taught through readings and seminars, consists of the following:

- An understanding of the development of self through infancy, childhood, and beyond.
- Understanding how development can be influenced by trauma, leading to disruptions in the sense of self such as those seen in BPD.
- The theory of CM.
- The practical application of CM.
- How practice can foster the integration of traumatic memory systems and enhance the growth of self.

However, training also needs to encompass the practical "what" and "how" of doing psychotherapy with particular patients. This component involves combining theoretical training with supervision of trainees' work with patients with BPD. This is carried out over a 3-year period, utilizing audio recordings of patient sessions. A minimum of two patients is required, with one patient seen twice weekly for at least 1 year, and the other patient seen twice weekly for at least the remaining 2 years of training.

This guidebook is an attempt to describe the approach and should be used as an adjunctive tool to those in training, although it is in no way considered to be sufficient by itself as training in the model.

Supervision

Supervision is an essential part of training, but extends beyond training to become integral to psychotherapy practice, particularly when treating patients with BPD. Just as the therapist works to foster and sustain the reflective attention of the patient whose experience is frequently disrupted by emotional storms, so supervision works to facilitate and maintain the therapist's capacity to remain reflective, calm, and emotionally open, particularly when the patient–therapist relationship is under pressure. While supervision is important for a number of different reasons, it is this provision of a professionally reflective space that is particularly important when working with a patient population that often evokes powerful feelings within the therapist.

Supervision involves a complex weave of teaching, mentoring, monitoring, formulation, and support. An important aspect of monitoring is keeping an eye on ethical issues. In CM attention is given to both microanalysis (through listening to audiotapes and listening for subtle moment-by-moment changes in emotion and language) and macroanalysis (understanding patterns in relationships, which may involve past, present, and especially "in-therapy" experiences).

As with training, supervision can be provided only by those holding extensive familiarity with CM and having substantial personal experience with patients with BPD. The relationship between therapists and supervisors needs to be sufficiently trusting to allow for the exploration of clinical situations that the therapist may experience as being anything from baffling to embarrassing. When working with patients with BPD, wherein the relationship is shaped in part by implicit traumatic memories, the therapist may find him- or herself feeling surprised, confused, ashamed, disoriented, or panicky. It is the job of the therapist to try and become aware of such feelings, even when subtle or contradictory, and then honestly explore them with the supervisor. It is the job of the supervisor to model an interested and nonjudgmental approach, allowing the therapist to feel safe in exploring difficult emotional responses.

One of the supervisor's most difficult tasks is to carefully navigate the contrasting but occasionally overlapping agendas of the supervisory and psychotherapeutic needs of the trainee. There are times when the interests of providing effective supervision sail close to the trainee's need to understand his or her own process. It is not, however, the supervisor's place to blend these two roles and venture into the therapist's psychological inner world beyond its immediate impact on the clinical problems at hand. Equally, the trainee must negotiate a fine balance between the clinically relevant need for personal disclosure in supervision and disclosures that fall outside of this brief. At times the supervisor or the therapist may need to make the decision to direct an issue that arises in supervision to be dealt with through personal psychotherapy.

Case Example, Bella Revisited

This is an example of the conversation between DM and her supervisor.

DM: It is very hard for me to listen to Bella threatening to take an overdose just because Mum is going out to her meditation class and Bella is lonely. Mum must be nearly 80 years old and as for the impact this must have on her daughter . . . I feel very angry that Bella is threatening me with taking an overdose. The complete selfishness and lack of empathy toward other people repulses me.

Supervisor: It's understandable that you have some very strong feelings. It's a good idea to keep in mind the co-transference and your own countertransference. Having these feelings is not unusual. What is most important is to talk about your feelings, which you are doing here—that's good.

DM: As I said the words *lack of empathy*, I remembered the model and the underlying trauma with which I am working. I can feel some compassion stirring when I think about Bella's past history and the lack of empathy she has experienced. I'm already starting to feel softer, like I can return to the session as a therapist again.

Supervisor: As you get to know your patient by being closely attuned, you begin to appreciate what you are doing, and for whom you are doing it.

Personal Psychotherapy

Personal psychotherapy is helpful for a range of reasons when practicing psychotherapy, such as the following:

- Modeling is one of the most powerful methods of learning, so experiencing personal psychotherapy within CM is an important way of learning what to do (and what not to do).

- Personal psychotherapy allows therapists to experience what it is like from the patient's perspective.
- Personal psychotherapy helps therapists discover their "blind spots," or aspects of themselves in relationships that they automatically enact without reflection. This awareness reduces the risk that these aspects will be played out with patients, or if this does occur, therapists have the capacity to become aware of their actions after reflection and supervision.
- Personal therapy, as described above, can be an adjunct to supervision, allowing the therapist to remain emotionally open and reflective when working with patients with BPD.

Ethical Obligations

Ethical obligations are the set of rules or guidelines for all psychotherapists that have been developed to protect patients' interests within psychotherapy. Each organization is responsible for developing an ethical code of conduct.

In the case of psychotherapists, the ethical obligation of the therapist is firstly to the patient and secondly to the professional organization. The therapist has a responsibility to help the patient, to not do harm, and to uphold the standards of the professional organization. Ethical behavior is essential to create a working relationship of trust and integrity. Awareness and maintenance of appropriate boundaries are essential to sustaining an effective therapeutic relationship. In practice all interventions, including all the contributions the therapist makes to the conversation, carry some risk, particularly with patients who have significant interpersonal sensitivity. Therapists need to think in terms of "managing risk" on an ongoing basis with regard to their ethical behavior, holding an awareness of the professional standards in their organization and in the field.

Codes of ethics are generally presented in the form of prescriptive do's and don'ts. In contrast to these black-and-white renditions, however, are the many instances when determining what is right, or good, can be extremely challenging. Although there should be no exceptions to ethical practice, there are many problems that arise in the form of ethical dilemmas that result from conflicting, yet necessary, values. For example, when working with a patient with BPD in crisis, there are often times when the values of confidentiality and safety come into opposition. At other times the value of care for one's patient and the value of care for oneself may clash. Discussion of ethical dilemmas through supervision, or with peers, is usually the first step in dealing with these tricky situations.

It is the responsibility of psychotherapists to be aware of the ethical process in their practice. In a legal sense the relationship of therapist and patient is a "fiduciary" relationship—that is, a relationship of trust. This means that it is incumbent upon the professional to maintain safety in the relationship and to avoid behaviors that could be damaging to the patient. This process needs to be intrinsic to training, supervision, and continuing education. Psychotherapy associations need to regularly present ethical dilemmas for discussion in seminars, case reviews, and other forums. Psychotherapists should be aligned with a suitable association. A psychotherapist who is professionally isolated is generally considered to be ethically "at risk."

Balance Between Work and Private Life

It will be apparent by now that the work depicted in this guidebook with patients with BPD can be demanding. To sustain enjoyable and effective work, and to prevent burnout, the psychotherapist needs to pay attention to maintaining a balance between work and private life. Each individual psychotherapist has to manage this in his or her own particular way, often adjusting to changing circumstances as his or her life progresses with attendant changes in health, family, and work responsibilities. Basic guidelines include the following:

- *Quantity*. Therapists should not commit to too many patients with BPD. For most therapists, a manageable number will be in the order of one to three at any one time. For those therapists working in a team, a larger number may be sustainable, although more than three severely unstable patients with BPD are probably too much.

- *Professional support*. As mentioned above, supervision, peers, and a psychotherapy association are necessary as a professional safety net. When working with patients with BPD, a network of colleagues and health-care professionals providing reciprocal support protects the therapist from becoming isolated and potentially at risk of unsustainable or dangerous practice.

- *Private social needs*. Psychotherapists need to commit some of their time to maintaining their own private social network. For some, this may be only one or two people. Maintaining a private social network protects therapists from meeting their social needs through their patients.

- *Personal health*. The emotionally demanding nature of working with patients with BPD means that the therapist needs to be reasonably physically well and rested. This means paying attention to getting enough sleep, adequate nutrition, exercise and attending to ill health promptly.

DEVELOPING IMPROVED SYSTEM RESPONSES

In this final section of the chapter we consider the role of advocacy and leadership in developing improved system responses within mental health community teams and inpatient units by exploring (1) team structure and (2) the difficulties within clinical teams.

Team Structure

The optimal management of patients with BPD relies on a responsive and flexible mental health service, often with an array of supports in the early stages of therapy. Although many patients with BPD are managed individually by private psychotherapists, those with the most severe symptomatology and chaotic behaviors will require a team approach. The psychotherapist should be the principal clinician on the patient's team. Given that the psychotherapist is usually the person with the most in-depth knowledge of the patient, he or she is also in the best position to liaise with other services and clinicians when required, so as to ensure the best possible care for the patient. In this sense the therapist may at times be required to take on a leadership role in relation to adjunctive services. Other possible members of the team include:

- A case manager, often within the community mental health team
- A prescribing doctor, who could be a GP, a private psychiatrist, or a community mental health team registrar or consultant
- A crisis support service, usually the community mental health team, but may include nongovernment organizations (e.g., Lifeline), or hospital emergency departments (particularly in rural settings)
- An inpatient mental health unit for crises that cannot be managed within therapy or within outpatient crisis support

Adjunctive programs that may be helpful include:

- Patient advocacy or support groups
- Day programs that may include group therapy or creative therapy
- Family psychoeducation programs

In reality, many urban and most rural areas do not have coordinated teams or available adjunctive programs. It is important for the primary therapist to consider what people and services can be engaged that would fulfill these roles to the best degree possible, given the resources available. Particularly at times of crisis, it will be necessary for the primary therapist to discuss with other members of the treating team what is happening and who should do what.

Specialty tertiary referral programs, offering time-limited long-term psychotherapy for patients with BPD, exist in some mental health services. These are valuable resources, and probably should be reserved for the most behaviorally challenging patients. Such specialized units can offer supervision and training to community mental health workers.

Difficulties within Teams

Working with patients with BPD often creates powerful emotional responses within clinicians. Wanting to protect, nurture, and comfort is often mixed with feeling helpless, frightened, despairing, angry, or guilty. The more powerful these needs and feelings are within the patient, the more powerful the emotional response within the clinician. When the patient is unable to express, or even be aware of, difficult and overwhelming feelings, the discomfort is increased further within the clinician. This may lead to a strong urge within the clinician to do something to reduce what he or she is feeling. Acting on this urge is sometimes referred to as an *enactment*.

Another difficulty may combine with an enactment and result in a significant threat to team cohesion. Patients with BPD often experience different mental health practitioners within teams as "good" or "bad." The "good" practitioner is helpful, comforting, and nurturing, and the patient will often appeal to that person for help. The designated "bad" practitioner is experienced as unhelpful, disinterested, and frustrating. The patient will try and avoid this person at all cost, often appealing to the "good" practitioner to protect him or her from the "bad" practitioner. The greater the anxiety the patient experiences, the stronger this process of splitting is. It is usually most powerful in inpatient units when the patient is typically in crisis, but this splitting can also occur in community mental health teams. *It is important to realize that the patient is not deliberately and consciously trying to "split" mental health practitioners into good and bad. Rather, this is a result of a survival process learned earlier in life and almost always out of the patient's awareness.*

This division into polarized positions within teams often leads to conflict, particularly on inpatient units. When the patient is having frequent and severe crises, this process of splitting is almost inevitable. The way it plays out is usually that one member of the team wants to protect and nurture the patient (fearful of the patient's safety and well-being), whereas another member of the team will want to impose limits and rules (angry with the patient for having "got away with" something). The two sides will tend to become angry with each other, believing that it is the other clinician's attitude that is "the problem."

The management of this splitting process is fundamentally simple, but often extremely difficult. The following process is usually helpful:

1. Determine whether the current tension within the team is a result of splitting, as described above, or whether it is some other tension within the team that is not really connected to the patient with BPD.

2. If it is a result of opposite positions being held around the patient with BPD, then it is important for the team to air all opinions together, usually with the team leader or another senior clinician who is not directly involved taking the role of "chair" in the meeting. Blame and personal invective must be avoided at all costs.

3. If possible, the team members then try and understand what is happening in terms of the patient's unconscious attempts to find care and avoid hurt. The team leader can attempt to bring both polarities and the patient's way of dealing with distress together within a loosely held "formulation" that conveys an empathic appreciation of the patient's position.

4. Sometimes trying to resolve this dynamic within the team does not work, and it may be necessary to have a meeting with the patient and the two proponents of the opposite polarities within the team. What usually happens in these sorts of meetings is that the "good" practitioner becomes less good in the eyes of the patient, and the "bad" practitioner becomes less bad, and a kind of synthesis emerges.

5. Ideally the synthesis can be formulated into an inpatient management plan, to which both of the (previously) antagonistic practitioners and the patient can agree, sign, and take a copy.

6. Throughout this process the idea of feeling, tolerating, and understanding

strong emotions should be modeled in order to create a new experience of reflection, rather than reaction, for the patient. Rushing to do something about painful feelings within the patient or the practitioners (i.e., enactment) is usually unhelpful.

As mentioned before, the above difficulties are more likely when anxiety is high and the patient is in crisis. The following situations are common manifestations of crises on inpatient wards when managing patients with BPD:

- The patient who threatens suicide or deliberately hurts him- or herself
- The patient who is contemptuous or grandiose toward staff members he or she doesn't like
- The patient who is threatening or aggressive
- The patient who develops a crush on, or erotic feelings for, a staff member
- The patient who becomes childlike, trying to get the staff to meet all of his or her unmet parenting needs (sometimes called *regression*)
- The patient who feels powerless or helpless and remains frustratingly passive in his or her self-care

Each patient with BPD is unlikely to have more than one or two of the above manifestations during an admission. Longer inpatient stays are more likely to precipitate the above experiences, as the patient starts to unconsciously enact the problematic patterns in relationships with which he or she was raised. In other words, prior expectations start to shape the behaviors of both patient and staff, whereby staff members find themselves inhabiting positions and taking actions that are uncharacteristic of their usual patient care.

In practical terms, most patients with BPD in a crisis who need to go into the hospital will need at least a few days, and usually up to a week, to rebuild coping strategies. However, when the patient is in the hospital for more than 2 weeks, there is an increasing likelihood of his or her family dynamics starting to play out with the staff and other patients. If an admission exceeds 2 weeks, it is important for the team to discuss the reasons for keeping the patient in the hospital, as the difficulties of admission will often start to outweigh the benefits.

Chapter 6

General Principles of the Conversational Model

Russell Meares

THE THERAPEUTIC FIELD is dominated by two main forces, one positive and the other negative. The first is toward well-being and a state of selfhood. The other is traumatic memory, which intrudes into and sometimes overthrows the form of consciousness characteristic of self. CM focuses on these two main forces.

The opening of a therapeutic conversation between Marguerite and her therapist, Dr. Abel, who have been meeting for about a year, is used at the beginning of this chapter to illustrate several main principles concerning the generation of self. The extract was chosen by the linguist Michael Garbutt (1997) who was making a study of the language of therapists working in this way. This is followed by consideration of a session with another patient in whom unconscious traumatic memory is triggered. In both cases, additional examples are given to better portray the way in which an appropriate response might be made to a particular expression of a patient.

Principle 1: LISTEN

The therapist must listen, in a particular way, to what is offered, however inconsequential it may seem.

Example: Marguerite is a middle-aged woman whose most salient symptom is an intractable depression. It is manifest behaviorally as an inability to cope with anything in her life—to care for her children, her house, even to drive a car. She opens the session speaking in a dull, monotonous voice.

Marguerite: Not much change really.

The therapist can do very little—what should he say? Should he reply with, for example, "It seems you're stuck" or "So, things aren't getting better?" Both seem to follow the sense of what Marguerite has said. But they are only approximations. The therapist, in these examples, would be assuming that he is making an accurate "translation" of the patient's words, using his own. Translations are useful when they are the result of a prior empathic immersion in the patient's expression. They may be off-key, however, when they do not derive from such a process and come from the world of the therapist.

Another therapist, perhaps feeling an unacknowledged frustration with the lack of progress, might say: "But things seemed to be getting better last time." Still another, feeling defeated, might stray far from the opening words and say, "Perhaps we need to look at antidepressants again." What the therapist did say seems banal, yet it is perfect.

Therapist: Not much really (*slight emphasis is given to the word* really).

The therapist has *listened*. He listens not only to the words and what they mean but also to their sounds, to the phonology. He hears the word *really* spoken with a tone sightly different from the other words. Marguerite has not said "Not much change" as a bald statement, in fact. The addition of *really* suggests the possibility of doubt. Perhaps there *has* been some change.

Principle 2: USE WHAT IS GIVEN

The therapist must respond to what is given and not his version of it. (I shall use *he/his* here since the therapist is a male). In the examples given in #1, the hypothetical therapists veered away from what was given in various ways, whereas the actual therapist stayed very close to the material that he is offered, including the words that are used. What is offered may often seem inconsequential, particularly at the beginning of a session, yet it may be the marker of a larger complex of psychic life, represented in miniature form, in an apparent colloquialism or throwaway remark. In CM, the "minute particulars," as Robert Hobson (1985) pointed out, are crucial. Systems of unconscious traumatic memory may show themselves in this half-hidden way, particularly at the beginning of a session. We shall see, in what follows, whether this is the case for the word *really*. On the other hand, the spontaneous asides and apparent conversational pleasantries may have within them the seeds from which can be generated a larger sense of selfhood. In using what is given, the therapist is following the model of the protoconversation, in which the maternal response is "coupled," or closely linked, to the baby's expression.

Principle 3: CHOOSE WHAT IS MOST ALIVE

What is offered by the patient in words or nonverbal communications invites, on most occasions, a number of choices. Often there seems to be little that is lively in an utterance that may be a monotonous recital of recent events, most of which are of a negative kind, involving difficulties and problems with family and work. This is the style of the "chronicle." Any remark that is spontaneous, even throwaway or a casual aside, may be the source of some vitality, may be the germ out of which can be generated a larger area of psychic life that has the visceral feeling of authenticity.

The therapist has little to find that is alive in Marguerite's opening remark. Her voice is dead. The only hint of liveliness is the word *really*, which implies that perhaps there may be some change. His emphasis on the *really* has a faintly speculative tone, which allows her to pick it up should she choose to do so. She might reaffirm that there is no change. Alternatively, she might follow the implication of his intonation.

> Marguerite: Well, except I—I'm getting angry with Sam and I think . . . I guess there is a bit of a change there.

This is, in fact, a significant change. Sam is her husband. As is often the case, she seems to have married a person who recapitulates, in their current relationship, the traumatic elements of the relationship with her parents. He is constantly putting her down, criticizing and devaluing her. She submits to these humiliations since she believes they are reality. To oppose him is a step toward overcoming this traumatic reality. Her response shows that the therapist's simple words have had a positive effect. She tells him, although her expression is tentative and doubtful, that there has been change after all, and not inconsiderable. The voice is now firmer.

163

Principle 4: FIND AND AFFIRM THAT WHICH IS POSITIVE

Therapist: Aha (*voice alive with affirmation*).

What is positive is not always easy to identify. Indeed, in the typical case it may be somewhat hidden. Marguerite's hesitancy and doubtfulness in her form of expression suggest that arguing with one's husband may not necessarily be a good idea. However, this effect is outweighed by the tone of her voice, which is stronger and more animated. It is to this, rather than to the negativity of doubt, that the therapist responds.

Positive expressions are very often veiled and guarded in people with BPD for two main reasons. First, there is an expectation that they will not be "heard" or acknowledged. Second, there is a fear that if the positive expressions are recognized, they will be received as others have been in the past—that is, mocked, criticized, or in some other way devalued. Although that which is positive is spoken of in a way that disguises its significance, perhaps in a monotonous tone or as a throwaway remark, the failure of the other, the therapist, to see through the disguise is likely to be followed by a sudden and negative shift in affect, which may be calamitous. Positivity is at the heart of healthy selfhood. In BPD it has almost been lost, and a state akin to "psychic pain" prevails. When the frail emergence of some positivity is felt to be crushed or damaged by a response, however inadvertent, the effect is severe.

That which is positive may be part of an expression that is also negative, the latter effect being the more powerful. Neuroscientists tell us that the negative always trumps the positive, being about three times stronger. The therapist must not neglect the negative but give priority to the positive. Finding what is positive in the midst of the negative is a skill.

Example: Julia begins the session by talking about an architectural essay that she had read in a newspaper.

Julia: I mean, here we are in a large land, not all of it can be used, but we're cramped . . . into little boxes.

Her therapist, Dr. Boon, senses that the patient is speaking, without being aware of it, of a personal issue, of a prevailing sense of restriction, perhaps even of entrapment. Implicit, however, is the desire to escape. Instead of the negative aspects of her patient's remarks, the therapist responds to that which is implicit.

Therapist: Not to have that freedom to sort of soar up and out.

What transpires in this session is discussed in later sections.

Principle 5: EFFICACY—WHAT HAPPENS NEXT?

The therapist is responding in the best way he or she can. Sometimes the response is effective and sometimes it is not. How does the therapist know if the response has been successful? The answer depends upon an awareness of its aim. The principal objective of the therapist is to foster the generation of that state of mind we are calling *self*. This state of mind arises when a particular quality of relatedness is created, in which some sense of connection is felt between the partners in the conversation. This sense of connection, of course, varies in degree from a feeling that they are both on the same track to a more profound feeling of "at-oneness." This achievement is signaled by the appearance of features of the Jamesian self, detailed in Chapter 2. Among these features is positive feeling. This is shown in both the examples given so far. Marguerite's increased animation showed that the unspectacular but very closely aligned response of the therapist "worked." The response of Julia was larger.

Julia: Oh, yes. It's lovely to be in a spacious place.

She conveys her pleasure not only in her tone of voice but in the implicit sense of personal spatiality created by the therapist's empathic remark.

Principle 6: USING THE LANGUAGE OF THE OTHER

The emergence of a cocreated reality as a "third thing" between the partners in the therapeutic conversation depends upon their development of a way of talking, which, in a subtle way, is unique to these two. The therapist uses his own, natural language and not the formulaic language of someone playing the part of therapist. Speaking in this fashion, he also incorporates those expressions of the patient that capture best the patient's immediate experience. There is a particular focus on those words or phrases that have the potential for development into metaphor.

Example: In the first session with a woman in her 30s, she speaks of her difficulties with the pain of living in a state in which "when I look in the mirror, it's not me I see." Later in the session, when the therapist is explaining the purpose of the therapy, he uses her words, saying that the aim is to find her "me" that was missing in the mirror.

Using the patient's words in a way in which those words seem to have become aspects of a joint currency has a number of beneficial effects related to, and beyond, achieving the sense of cocreation. First, the use of familiar words lets the patient know that the other—in this case, the therapist—is listening with intent to what is said. This will be felt as new and important by those who have suffered the familial background typical of BPD, in which the main figures tended to treat the child in an egocentric way or to neglect the child's reality when it differed from their own. To be listened to, and "heard," is a "corrective emotional experience" (Alexander, 1949, pp. 286–287), the opposite of what is expected of the other. A second effect of using the patient's words is to contribute to the sense that, at that moment, they are partners in a shared reality, in which each has an individual part. They are not fused or merged. On the other hand, neither are they isolated and self-contained personal systems, which is the experience of alienation. A simple response, such as "Not much really," using that patient's words in a particular way, looks easy. But so does the swing of a champion golfer.

Principle 7: THE USE OF THE VOICE AND THE SIGNIFICANCE OF TONE

When Marguerite opens the session with her dull voice, the therapist does not maintain the cheerful mode of expression that may be characteristic of him. It might be thought that such a demeanor would cheer her. It would not. Her sense of isolation would have grown. Instead, his voice is rather subdued, having a low intensity, similar to hers. The tone, however, is somewhat different. It has a certain animation and a sense of calmly waiting.

Following her reply, which shows a movement out of a state of deadness, his voice follows this movement. It is alive with genuine pleasure in her now-found strength. However, with his "Aha" expression he remains aware, as he observes fine changes in Marguerite's face and posture, of its effect. It is too much. It does not accord with the intensity of her feeling. Consequently, his next contribution to their conversation is more subdued, also showing, in milder degree, some of her hesitancy. What he says is attuned to her affective state at that moment.

Therapist: That . . . that seems a good thing.

The capacity to use the tone of one's voice to "stay with" the patient's emotional state is an important aspect of therapeutic practice. Nonverbal vocalizations, such as "uh-hm," can convey a variety of emotions—agreement, wonder, gloom, and so forth—which provide the necessary resonance involved in "analogical representation," to which we shall soon turn. They are "forms of feeling" (Hobson, 1985).

Principle 8: ATTUNEMENT

The *protoconversation* that takes place between mother and baby is a model for much of the therapist's behavior. The structure of this early interplay should not be thought of as simply infantile, something we have left behind. A mature conversational form, like a state of consciousness, contains within it those forms that preceded it in development. As we speak, we are using an experience that is "layered." Contained in this moment of speech are the memories used in its construction, which are working together. They include the most primitive memory system of sensory representation, operative at birth, when the mother's voice can be recognized, and also the most recent, the episodic.

The language of the moment is also layered. It includes the most powerful—the earliest language, the sound of the voice—which is allied to a language of the face. The child begins to build a lexicon in the second year of life. Some time after, words begin to be arranged in a complex order by means of syntax. Language has its greatest effect when this hierarchy of phonology–lexicon–syntax is most fully coordinated, not only within itself but within the form of relatedness, manifest in conversation. This is a shifting and dynamic process. When the therapist says "Aha," the form of relatedness is relatively primitive, of limited complexity. His response necessarily stays at that level. It is attuned to a particular developmental level, in which phonology is dominant. Moreover, the language of his initial response is an early form. It is barely syntactical. There is no verb and no noun. What remains are indices of "value." Despite the sparseness of lexicon and the absence of syntax, the utterance is highly effective. In this case, *less is more*.

As the sense of connection between the partners in the conversation develops, so also does the complexity of consciousness that it both manifests and constitutes. Attunement now becomes a larger matter. It is not confined to simple affective resonance, although this is always an element. In the more developed attunement, imagination is involved. A critical aspect of the therapist's ability to attune his responsiveness to the shifting emotional state of the patient is his sensitive awareness of fluctuations not only in changes of voice, face, and posture but also in the form of language the patient uses. For example, a question is likely to signal a change of state.

Principle 9: A QUASI-MEDITATIVE GAZE

The capacity to discern the changing movements in the conversational text is enhanced by a particular state of mind. It is akin to a certain kind of meditative state, in which one is in a heightened sense of awareness, and in which the gaze is both dispersed and centrally directed, in an undetermined fashion. Such a gaze provides a metaphor for the therapist's way of experiencing, which resembles Freud's (1915) "evenly suspended attention." Two somewhat different forms of consciousness, considered to reflect characteristic aspects of the left- and right-hemispheric function, are brought together, working in coordination. The former is concerned with detail, the latter with the larger picture, its shape. It is a state resembling that of high-level chess players (Bilalic et al., 2011). The novice's eyes flick about, scanning the board, while good players gaze toward the center.

Principle 10: AMPLIFICATION

The therapist's "Aha" is an amplification. It enhances the emergence of positive feeling in Marguerite's voice. Once again, the significance of this response is made evident through consideration of the protoconversation. In this game that the mother plays, not thinking she is doing anything special, she is simply enjoying herself, responding to small indicators of positive feeling displayed by her child, such as interest. She amplifies this mild affect with her voice, with its rising inflection, and her face, which lights up. She often creates interest when the baby is in a neutral state.

This behavior is quite different from her response when the baby is distressed. In this case, her demeanor shows her recognition of the distress. She does not magnify it but takes steps to remedy it. These maternal responses to distress and nondistress situations are models for approaching more complex expressions involving the words of adult life. We return to the issue of distress later.

Amplification is a response to states of positive affect. When we consider the model, or metaphor, of mother–infant interplay, we see that it may refer to an "enlargement" beyond the amplification of a single band in the spectrum of emotional life. Consider the following example.

The scene is a path through a park, just after sunset in early summer. A mother is walking her baby in a stroller. In the sky a plane appears, flying rather flow, engines roaring, lights flashing on its wings. The mother points at it. "Look!" she says, "a plane." The word is drawn out, with a rising inflection. The baby is transfixed, gazing where she points. "Oooh!" she says. The sound she makes is prolonged, rising and falling in an undulant manner. It expresses a range of emotions in this single utterance: awe, wonderment, and a touch of fear. These feelings are very close to those shown on the baby's face. The contour of the mother's voice, its shape, is an analogue of the baby's feeling state. It is a portrayal in sound of his immediate reality.

This is a response larger and more comprehensive than that of Dr. Abel. It not only amplified the interest the baby showed in the strange object in the sky, it also achieved an additional enlargement through her voice, which resonated with emotions that were part of the baby's experience but latent, needing the appropriate response to bring forth these nascent feelings.

An amplification, then, is a response that may, as in the case of Dr. Abel, be confined to a single affective expression. It is often nonverbal. *Wow*, for example, is an important form of amplification when uttered in the right way, at the right time. Amplification also includes a response to positive feelings that are implicit but are not at the forefront of the affective aspects of the patient's expression. Dr. Boon's response to her patient's words, suggesting a stifling in the way she was able to live, was also an amplification. When she spoke of "soaring free," she empathically understood the implicit sense of the positive in these remarks, that they reflected an unspoken imagining of a state of existing that was free of constriction. In this case there is an experienced sense of "fit" that evokes a sudden positivity, verging on euphoria, as her patient says, "Oh, it's lovely. . . . "

The amplification of the mother in the park goes beyond Dr. Abel's amplifications in a second way. The mother uses words, and she uses them in a way that fits the baby's level of consciousness on the developmental hierarchy. She uses only single words. There is no syntax. The baby presumably is beginning to make first sounds of meaning, proto-words such as *Mama*. Her amplification is somewhat higher in the hierarchy, but not too far, like the typical mother in the proto-conversation.

Dr. Abel's initial "Aha" did not fit—it had too many decibels. However, his next remark modifies the amplification, and fit is now achieved, as indicated by what happens next.

The chronic dysphoria that affects people with BPD can be understood as an effect of an environment in which there is no appropriate amplification. In addition, those positive feelings involved in healthy attachments, sometimes called the "tender emotions," have been damaged. It is essential that the therapist develop a skill at detecting glimmers of positivity in the patient's demeanor, and amplify those glimmers in order to give them reality. Ideally, this small beginning becomes the seedling of something larger, as illustrated in the following example, in which the therapist's contributions to the conversation take the form of an extended amplification.

The patient, Vera, is in her 30s. Her history is a terrible one. She was conceived in rape and had to endure, for her entire life, her mother's hatred and continued accusation: "You're just like your father." The mother had married a kindly man when Vera was about 4 years old. However, he died a few years later. Vera's adolescence was troubled. She, like her mother, was raped. In her 20s she developed the stigmata of a BPD. There were overdoses, self-mutilations, hospital admissions, and dissociative episodes. Some of these episodes reached the severity of fugue and involved auditory hallucinosis. Despite the severity of these problems, she managed to stay in a marriage with a kindly older man who may have evoked the positive experiences with her dead stepfather.

After 8 months of treatment with Dr. Cato, Vera has made remarkable progress. However, Dr. Cato has been maintaining her on antipsychotic medication, which she was taking at the time of her referral. Seeing that Vera is now greatly improved, Dr. Cato wants to modify this medication as a means of working toward its cessation. He remarks that he is "anxious" about its potential side effects. Vera, in a cheerful voice and in a teasing way, says, "What, you suffer from anxiety? Is that what you're saying?" Dr Cato laughs, reiterating that he is worried about her developing side effects. She is now also laughing, "I was going to say that's different—a doctor suffering from anxiety and trying to treat it."

They now go into a kind of laughing banter they both enjoy. In a way, they are playing a game. It should be noted, however, that Dr. Cato is active with a double-awareness throughout the exchange. He knows what he is doing. He sees his re-sponsiveness as something like the amplification that the mother's resonance brings into conversational play.

As part of their enjoyment and laughing, Dr. Cato spontaneously tells a brief joke about a doctor in need of medical treatment. After their laughter dies down, Vera says, "He was forgetting he was a doctor himself?"

In what follows, Dr. Cato judges the effect of his unorthodox behavior by "what happens next" (Meares, 2001). There is a pause. She says, "Weird," in a reflective way. This is a word she uses often. It presumably has a personal significance.

There is another pause. Then she says, in a quiet and contemplative voice, "I like this weather we're having." At this point, Dr. Cato's judgment about the effect of his spontaneity is equivocal. On one hand, Vera's attention is directed outward, suggesting that his response was unhelpful and disjunctive; on the other hand, there is a tone of positivity in the remark. The conversation continues:

Vera: I love it when it rains. Mmm. I like the cooler weather, yeah; I don't like the heat.

Dr. Cato: Yes, yes.

Vera: Cold weather.

Dr. Cato: Yes, and playing with the rain. And it's like a child, isn't it? Children like rain.

Vera: Mmm. Yeah, it feels very—also when it's raining—in the car—it feels very secure, like a security thing when I'm in the car.

Dr. Cato: Yeah.

Vera: And the rain's falling.

Dr. Cato: And you're not getting wet.

Vera: Mmm. I've always felt like that, but I don't know why, but that's how it feels.

Dr. Cato: Interesting.

Vera: Mmm. I've always felt like that, but I don't know why, and yeah, I remember when I was . . . um . . . I was in a pram, and I was a baby, and I remember my mother and walking one night, and I could see, you know, the traffic lights changing colors and the cars, and it looked really pretty. I remember that. I remember feeling very secure and warm, sort of snugly sort of thing.

In an individual whose conversation earlier in therapy was stimulus entrapped, replete with somatizing references and in the style of a chronicle, this is a remarkable movement. The beautiful autobiographical memory of the streetlights in the misty rain is the first of its kind to emerge in this therapeutic conversation. Its appearance indicates reflective activity, the identifying feature of the Jamesian self.

Amplification, as noted in Chapter 1, is an essential part of the process, we believe, by which self emerges. Self is seen as a self-organizing system. The main features of a self-organizing system are coupling, amplification, and representation (see Chapter 1). The iterations in the system typically begin with coupling and progress through amplification to representation. The last two phases contain the earlier ones.

In this illustration, Dr. Cato shows a fluidity of response and ability to move with the affective life of the conversation. He follows the positive elements of Vera's teasing, allowing them to take their own course through his continuing coupling (i.e., linking his response very closely to what is said) and amplification.

Since Dr. Cato's "agenda," at this point in the conversation, concerns her medication and his role is medical, it would have been very easy, and understandable, for him simply to brush it aside and to continue with his task. Rather remarkably he is able completely to abandon it and to follow Vera's "agenda." His joke about the doctor is spontaneous but also calculated. It is like an amplification of what she had been doing to him earlier, implicitly giving it approval as a form of conversational play. Further amplifications follow (e.g., "Yes, yes"). Dr. Cato is clearly aware of the consciousness that he is trying to facilitate: one with a nonlinear play-like structure, which is the dynamic shape of self. In order to do so he enters into and facilitates a play-like form of conversation, since the form of a conversation, to repeat the main principle of CM, not only manifests and constitutes a form of relatedness but also manifests and constitutes a state of mind. It must be clear that he was not merely playing around. Every contribution to the conversation was disciplined, coupled to Vera's expressions. Amplification has a main part to play in this story in which self appears for the first time after months of therapy.

Principle 11: STAY AWARE OF ONE'S OWN FEELINGS, THOUGHTS, AND IMAGININGS

In the examples given so far, the therapists have shown a sensitive awareness of their patients' experiences, in the moment, fluidly adjusting their responses in order, as it were, to "meet" each patient's experience (Robert Hobson [1985] quotes Martin Buber's "All real living is meeting" at the beginning of *Forms of Feelings*). However, they were also using a second form of noticing and listening, which is internal. The inner states that are engendered during the therapeutic conversation are frequently called *countertransference*. Since this word has three main meanings, in this text we use different terms for these different aspects of the therapist's experience. The first of these is *contagion*.

Principle 12: PUT ASIDE THE CONTAGION OF PREVAILING NEGATIVE AFFECT

The dysphoric world of BPD and its limitation in terms of imagination, access to memory, and affective coloring have an effect on the therapist. Very frequently, particularly as the session begins, the patient's expressions, in words, voice, face and posture, convey a state of hopelessness, helplessness, and inertia. There are complaints of pain and despair. This mood seeps into the therapist's system, as if by osmosis. It needs to be recognized because there is a danger of the therapist responding, almost by reflex, to an experience that is apprehended not by empathy but by sympathy.

There must be an acknowledgment of the patient's mood, but the main response is made as if the therapist has put aside, in another part of his mind, the prevailing negativity. The acknowledgment can come with a nonverbal communication that "stays with" the mood. We return to the example of Dr. Abel's meeting with Marguerite. His subdued tone acknowledges, by its implicit placement of himself within the reality of his patient, the "grayness" that the words convey. But he does not react to this mood. A reaction tends to arise when the therapist is in some way thrown off course, disturbed, and even, on some occasions in working with those suffering BPD, made psychically disorganized (i.e., dissociated).

The impulse at these times is to fall back into the use of one's "agenda"—what one has learned from previous times—and to neglect the peculiar reality of the other, which involves another agenda. The therapist jumps out of the discomfort felt in the relationship at this time, perhaps going into a withdrawal, or else attempting to establish another kind of relationship in which he senses himself as more competent and in control. His ultimate agenda, after all, is to get the patient better. An obvious jump is to medication. A less obvious way is to assume that what he experiences of the patient's affective state is the same as that of his patient. On hearing the words "Not much change really," Dr. Abel might heave an inward sigh and wonder if her state will ever change, whether the process will ever end. He might say, "It seems you feel pretty hopeless about things"—which is what *he* feels but not precisely what the patient feels. Connection will be lost and the therapeutic process stalled. Dr. Abel, however, does not jump. He "stays with" what is expressed.

Principle 13: "STAYING WITH" COMPARED TO "ABOUTNESS"

The expression "staying with" is an important aspect of therapeutic behavior, applicable in a number of contexts, but particularly involving an affective state. The therapist stays within a particular mood in order to develop a theme of which it is part. In doing so, the therapist does not *point* to the mood and talk *about* it. Talking *about* keeps issues at a distance. In this way, it may become a defensive posture in which the patient and therapist unconsciously collude.

Talking *about* introduces left-hemispheric linearity when the relationship requires right-hemispheric immediacy. This therapeutic behavior, introduced too early, is an intrusion, breaking up an emergent flow of thought. On the other hand, however, reflective activities of the patient are encouraged and fostered. It is necessary, for example, to *point* to shifts in the therapeutic conversation by, as it were, *reviewing* what has happened. The change in these two conversational states might be pictured in terms of William James's analogy between the movement of thought and the flight of a bird, in which flights are interspersed with "perchings." In a perching scene a story is re-created in its sensory aliveness.

Principle 14: USING EMPATHY

Empathy is a crucial therapeutic skill and art. It involves two main processes. The first is listening of the special kind briefly described in the section on attunement. This kind of listening depends upon a dispersed attentiveness in which voice qualities, together with facial expression and posture, are as important as the literal information in the patient's words. This steady psychic "gaze" is followed by imagination, in which the therapist attempts to grasp the nature of this other reality, which is not his own, and may not correspond with how he would feel. After the initial immersion in the patient's experience, the empathic statement sometimes arises in a form as apt as prolonged conscious thought would produce, as if the imaginative process has worked unconsciously,

An example of the empathic process is provided by the conversation between Vera and Dr. Cato. He "stays with" the apparently spontaneous shifts in the direction of her thought, his own thought and responsiveness fluidly adjusting to each movement. His immersion in her experience allows his imagination to bring to mind a scene that reflects something of the nature of what is "behind" or "below" her words, their origin in a nascent self. He responds to the pleasure in her voice when she says "I love it when it rains" with a contribution that is unexpected, although it is directly connected to the rain: "Yes, and playing with the rain. And it's like a child, isn't it? Children like the rain." He intuitively anticipates the story she later tells of the child in the pram on the streets in the misty rain.

Empathy cannot be, and should not be, precise, as if the therapist were supernatural and could read the patient's mind. Even if the therapist's expression fails, it can still be useful. It shows that the patient has a mind, different from the therapist's, which is bounded and "owned." It may also trigger unconscious traumatic memory, which can then be processed.

Principle 15: USING RIGHT-HEMISPHERIC LANGUAGE

We return now to the conversation between Marguerite and her therapist, Dr. Abel. Although they have been speaking for barely a minute, a great deal has already happened. An important aspect of what has transpired so far is the use of what can be called *right-hemispheric language*.

Those scenes during early life that are the likely occasions during which the embryonic self emerges and is fostered seem to be governed by right-brain activity. The protoconversation can be conceived as a conversation between two right hemispheres in which the mother, behaving naturally and without thought about her actions, uses a particular language in talking to her baby. It is abbreviated and barely syntactical, made up only of the main words of meaning. It conveys emotion through the use of the voice and face. It is a language of immediacy, of the present moment. This experience is as if internalized by the child so that when symbolic play makes its appearance at about the same time that language dependent upon words is developing, he or she speaks in a way that suggests right-hemispheric dominance.

Although the right hemisphere is not capable of propositional language, it can produce brief emotional utterances and sometimes language is composed purely of emotion, rhythm, and melody (i.e., song). The abbreviations of right-hemispheric language characteristically involve omission of the subject of the sentence, particularly pronouns. Sentences may be incomplete and broken up, as if thought were going too fast for language to follow, or as if it needs to stay with the moment-to-moment experience that is evolving.

The therapist's first remark is of this kind. "Not much really" is used rather than, for example, "You don't notice any change." Again, the first part of the therapist's second contribution to the conversation is entirely emotional, made by the sound of the voice. His "Aha" conveys enthusiasm and affirmation.

Principle 16: SHAPING VIA ANALOGICAL RELATEDNESS

Right-hemispheric language is characterized not only by its form but most importantly by its function. A principal function of the right hemisphere is to give "shape" to the sensory impressions impinging upon us at any moment. Its role is the creation of coherence. Dr. Abel's next two contributions to the conversation with Margucrite have the form of shaping. I call this kind of responsiveness *analogical relatedness*. As mentioned in an earlier chapter, an analogue, in its original meaning, is something that has proportions or shapes that resemble, but do not copy, the proportions or shape of another thing. The mother's face and voice during the protoconversation are analogues of her baby's experience at that moment.

Returning to the conversation between Marguerite and her therapist, his adjustment after the affective intensity of his "Aha" to a lower key and more tentative expression is effective, as demonstrated by what happens next. Marguerite's voice becomes firmer, and she makes a more extended statement about her personal experience, which is beyond the mere symptomatic, implied in her opening remark.

> Marguerite: Well. (*The word is drawn out, almost making two sounds, conveying doubt. She pauses for a few seconds.*) It's not being objective, but it's a good thing for me because I don't think it helps to be hounded like that (*pause*). Even though I understand his position, and know where he's coming from, but . . . (*pauses for a few seconds, sighs*) Mmmmm . . .

Therapist: (*After waiting a few seconds*) Aha. You . . . you understand how he might be, but still, not good for you and so . . .

Dr. Abel has immersed himself in Marguerite's experience so that he is presumably registering the sensory details of her voice in a way of which he is not consciously aware. The sound of her drawn-out *well* suggests that she is in two minds, in the grip of two realities. She begins to enlarge on this expression in what follows, trying to verbalize it. There is one reality, which is "objective," which says that she cannot cope with the ordinary processes of living, that she is "hopeless" and "useless." This reality is opposed by another that is not given a name, but which is, by implication, her own "subjective" reality.

The word *objective* comes from the lexicon of a higher-order consciousness, in which rationality is dominant. It is the language of "social speech" that comes, as it were, from outside. It is language of the imposed traumatic reality that she experienced during the developmental period. This is the language that said to her such things as, "You stupid child, can't you do anything right!" This reality is maintained by the husband's prevailing denigrating attitude toward her. The "subjective" reality, in contrast, is barely expressible (she sighs) and cannot be adequately portrayed in propositional terms.

It is likely that Marguerite hardly knows what precisely she is saying. What Dr. Abel says in giving it form is making it "real," giving it a kind of "meaning" that she only partly apprehends. His response will be like that of the mother in the protoconversation who portrays in her voice and face the immediate reality of the child.

He too has not fully grasped what she is trying to express. His "Aha" says, by implication, "I think I am beginning to understand." He does not wait, however, until his understanding is clear, so that he is able to make a clever, well-formulated propositional statement of the left-hemispheric kind. This may come later. Instead, he moves with the moment, doing his best to say what he has understood, describing, in highly abbreviated form, the two realities. The language retains its right-hemispheric form. In talking of her subjective reality, he says, "Not good for you and so. . . . " The incompleteness invites her to help him finish his expression.

Once again, what happens next tells him that his contribution, which is made as if he is feeling his way into a particular zone of experience, is successful, has created a sense of connection.

Marguerite: Well, he (*pause*) was like acid eating away at me, ya know, with his sort of demolishing me, really . . . mmm . . . so . . . (*firmer voice*). [The context is more clearly "inner" in its metaphoric usage. The "acid eating away at" her conveys the nature of one aspect of her personal reality. Dr. Abel's next response is surprising and, at first sight, even rather odd.]

Therapist: Yes, an acid eating away at you (*slight pause*) is unreasonable (*spoken with a rising tone of voice, as if in inquiry*).

Marguerite: Yeah, well (*pause*). It's not helpful to the situation at all . . . (*pause*). And even as I say it now, I think, ya know, I've been equally intolerable with my own children and I erupted, ya know, because. . .

[Here she seems to be once again describing her divided feelings. First, there's her "situation" and, second, her understanding of her husband's viewpoint, understood because she has behaved like him.] (*After a few seconds, she begins again. Her voice is now lively and animated.*) Heidi [her daughter] came over and looked at the lunch I was making and then said "I don't want that dog food bread," ya know what I mean—it's perfectly good wholemeal bread. Ya know what I mean, they're lucky to get it. (*She is laughing, enjoying the conversation. Her affect and demeanor are transformed. She is in positive mode.*) I was—and they had—ya know, I make them nice nutritious lunches—they don't have jam and, ya know, stuff like that.

Here she is able to say, implicitly, that even though the children have taken on the devaluing role of their father in relation to her, she can overcome it and, moreover, that she is a competent mother and not the person portrayed in the "objective" traumatic reality.

This remarkable shift, which is the culmination of a small "cascade" of similar shifts, follows the therapist's way of saying *unreasonable*, which managed to contain, within this single word, her double and conflicted reality. The word *unreasonable* depicts the subjective aspect of this reality, but the way it is spoken suggests the possibility that the opposite and objective aspect may also be true.

His representation of her daily lived experience creates the feeling of being understood. A connection is made.

His statement/inquiry is the outcome of an empathic immersion in what she has been telling him. His response is quite unlike that of sympathy, which might be the response of Marguerite's friends, should she reveal to them that her husband is "like acid eating away" at her. They would probably exclaim that this is monstrous, intolerable, and that she should leave him. The sympathetic response will lead nowhere.

Principle 17: TRACKING

Dr. Abel might have chosen to make a different response, picking out the salient metaphor of the acid. The fact that he did not do so attests to his ability to keep in mind a theme that had been developing from the word *really* to *well* to more extended, although implicit, descriptions of her divided inner world. His tracking of the movement of Marguerite's thought enables him to make a response that precisely follows this movement.

As part of this movement she tells of her anger at her husband, which she says is not "objective," a word that relates to that which is rational, which is reasonable. The image of the acid, however, portrays something that is not reasonable, that is inhumane. The therapist captures this doubleness with condensation in a single word. To have focused on the metaphor of the acid alone would have stalled the process, which is leading to a larger coherence of her personal reality. The shaping function must have priority.

Principle 18: THE AGENDA OF THE TEXT

It would seem, from what I have been saying, that the agenda of the therapeutic conversation is set entirely by the patient. The therapist uses what is given and does not work from preconceived ideas about how a particular session will evolve. The outcome, as in this session with Marguerite, may be surprising. The therapist, however, does have an agenda. It is to foster the emergence of self, which has *cohesion* as its fundamental characteristic. Out of cohesion grows the capacity for reflection. This agenda, however, can be accomplished only within a relationship and must be played out, hand in hand, with what we might call the "agenda of the text." Self does not emerge in normal development by instruction, prescribed strategies, and so forth. Cohesion arises in response to an atmosphere of—cohesion.

Principle 19: NOTICE REPETITIONS

The therapist should notice repetitions of words or phrases and, without necessarily making any overt reference to them, ponder their significance. They may be the markers of crucial aspects of psychopathology. Although that which is repeated may seem to be merely a colloquialism, a habitual manner of speech, it should not be overlooked. An example is provided by Marguerite.

As she comes to life, she is now talking in a different way, the words coming more freely. Among them she uses "you know what I mean" twice and "ya know" twice. Repetition may be quite inconsequential. Nevertheless, the therapist should consider the possibility that these interspersions in the conversational flow are not mere "fillers" and random verbal noise. It may be that they relate to the developmental period. What, then, could be their significance?

Marguerite is now in a state unlike the demeanor evident only minutes before, which was dull and lifeless, conveying, perhaps, passivity and helplessness. Could it be that it was in such states that she received parental responsiveness that gave "meaning" to her immature, undifferentiated emotional life? And that when, on the other hand, she was animated and enthusiastic, the appropriate analogical responding was not available, so that what she had expressed on these occasions possessed dubious meaning? That this may have been the case is suggested in the following section.

Principle 20: BEWARE OF ACCOMMODATION: THE ISSUE OF PATHOLOGICAL ATTACHMENT

The possibility that Marguerite may have gained comfort and care as a child mainly when she was sad, helpless, and as if depleted of vitality leads to a larger issue. It concerns a particular manifestation of attachment needs that Bernard Brandchaft has called *pathological accommodation* (Brandchaft et al., 2010). The imperative of the child, fueled by separation anxiety, is to establish a bond with the caregiver. The child will do whatever is required to maintain the bond, even to the extent of sacrificing his or her own reality. The behaviors that must be "emitted" by the child vary. Commonly, they are behaviors that are experienced by the parent as engaging and typically exclude expressions of negative affect. Also commonly, any behavior of the child that is a burden to the parent, such as the exhibition of distress, is excluded. Sometimes, and almost paradoxically, it is the child's vitality—his or her enthusiasm, noise, and leaping around—which is a burden. This may have been the case for Marguerite's parents.

Marguerite's parents were both World War II orphans. After the war, they had been transported from Britain to an institution in Western Australia, where they suffered hardship and abuse. They left this place without the resources of money or training. They formed a bond as fellow survivors and moved to Sydney, where they imagined a better life was possible. They both worked hard, for long hours, in lowly occupations. The child was sometimes left alone in the house.

A reconstruction of Marguerite's early life suggested that, typical of traumatized people, who experience stimuli with enhanced intensity, her parents could not stand noise. It was only when she appeared in a state that reminded them of their time as orphans—sad, bereft, and diminished—that they showed their care for her. The boisterous vitality of childhood would have been irksome, an intrusive irritation, or worse.

This consideration throws some light on the intractability of Marguerite's condition, the history of which includes two prolonged and failed treatments. Although she truly suffered from a low-grade and atypical affective disorder as a consequence of her own traumatic background, this same state is associated with attachment—with safety and solace—for her. It is perpetuated by a separation anxiety that had been magnified by being left alone for long periods at a vulnerable stage of life. A therapy simply focused on the prevailing affect is stymied by the obstacle of pathological attachment. The therapeutic agenda of Dr. Abel was different. Although he acknowledged that which was negative, his aim was to potentiate the emergence of a different state of mind, showing the characteristics of selfhood by means of a relationship of a particular kind, which differs from a pathological attachment. This experience enables her briefly to escape the shackles of pathological accommodation.

Principle 21: COUPLING, AMPLIFICATION, AND REPRESENTATION AS THE ESSENTIALS OF SELF-ORGANIZATION AND ANALOGICAL RELATEDNESS

The therapist responds, now speaking for only the fifth time, resonating with her emergent enlivenment. His voice is filled with positive energy and enthusiasm, which amplifies her positivity.

Therapist: Right—you do good things. [This amplification enhances her liveliness, her voice rising as she continues her story about the children and the food. In telling this story, she exhibits the form of reflective activity characteristic of the Jamesian self.]

Marguerite: Oh, they get top qu—they don't get sweet rubbish, but they get—ya know, they're always complaining that I don't give them that, but what I meant is I (pause) . . . they get the . . . best really in terms of nutrition and what-not, and there she was and I just—and they often say it: "All you give us is dog food," ya know (*laughing*), and I don't know, let it by—past this time I thought: oh crikey, ya know (*pause*) . . . ya know I did the whole guilt bit like "those African kids don't get—kids anywhere, ya know, all over the world, that don't have food and you're lucky to get it and you ought to say thank you and I was . . . (*laughing, as if at the image she paints of herself, as a parody of stereotypic maternal behavior*).

Marguerite speaks as if viewing herself, as if gazing at a stage "mother" who is also herself. This sense of the viewer and the viewed, in the unified experience of mature consciousness, is a cardinal and identifying feature of the "duplex self" (James, 1892, p. 176).

The therapist's part in the emergence of this higher-order consciousness, from unpromising beginnings, is comprised of forms of therapeutic conversation that can be called *coupling, amplification,* and *representation*. These are the main components of a self-organizing system. *Self* can be conceived as the outcome of the process of self-organization in a system made of two parts: self and other. Coupling, amplification, and representation are also the features of analogical relatedness. They are necessary basic components of the therapist's contribution of "forms of feeling" (Hobson, 1985). Their outcome in this case is the emergence of reflective consciousness.

Principle 22: USING METAPHOR

Metaphor is a particular and most important aspect of analogical relatedness. It enables the partners in the conversation to show each other the shape and qualities of their inner experience.

Although the conversation usually begins with a largely "outer" focus—for example, Marguerite getting angry with Sam—as it progresses it must, if evolving satisfactorily, become more "inner." In this progression, inner states and their feeling basis must be portrayed. Since what is inner cannot be seen, some device is needed to show the other what it is like. Metaphor provides the visibility of discourse. Objects and events in the outer world are used as a means of creating a kind of a picture that gives an imagined physicality and sensory representation to a state that is otherwise condemned to remain hidden. For example, Marguerite uses the word *hounded* to describe what it feels like to be the recipient of her husband's devaluation of her. The image of the dog is *transferred* from the outer world and applied to an inner state. The word *metaphor* is derived from a Greek wording meaning "to transfer."

A metaphor is a development of figurative language beyond analogue. Analogue is the use of a thing or event in the outer world to represent another thing also in the outer world. The analogue resembles, but does not copy, the thing itself. In the child's story told during symbolic play, a stick is an analogue for a man; a tiny model of a man is not.

Simile does the work of metaphor where the similarity between the subjects compared concerns one that is inner—for example, her husband's criticism of her was "like acid eating into" Marguerite.

Figurative language is a crucial aspect of the kind of conversation necessary to the generation of self—that is, to analogical relatedness. It can have an amplifying effect, as exemplified by the beginning of the session with Julia, which began with her talking of space.

> Julia: There's more to a living environment than utility. . . . I mean, here we are in a huge land, not all of it can be used, but we're cramped . . . into little boxes.
> Therapist: Not to have that freedom to sort of soar up and out.
> Julia: Oh, yes. It's lovely to be in a spacious place.

What happens next shows that the metaphor of soaring free, which is complementary to "cramped," is successful, creating a sense of connectedness, of "fit." Julia's voice, as she speaks of the "spacious place," conveys her sense of pleasure. There is also a shift from the general to the more personal. The spacious place is the place she is now in, an old building with high ceilings.

The therapist's response illustrates the difference between an analogical response and a literal "matching." A matching with the word *cramped* would have produced something quite different. What the therapist says is an analogue in that it is the corresponding "shape," articulated positively, of the patient's negative statement about a lack of freedom. It enlarges the concept of the spatiality of self, taking the thought beyond what is said, while staying closely coupled to it.

In providing a larger and clearer picture of a certain experience, the metaphor has a major representing function in human speech. It can develop in a series of linkages, concurrent with the evolution of a particular theme important to the sense of self (e.g., of the sense of personal space). Hobson (1985) called this phenomenon the "moving metaphor." It is exemplified by what follows in the conversation between Julia and her therapist (see Principle #30).

Principle 23: POTENTIATING REFLECTION

A change has now come to the conversation between Marguerite and her therapist. A different language and a different form of relatedness are about to emerge. Following her laughing description of herself as a competent mother, the therapist exclaims: "But that's what you really think!"

The language is clearly syntactical, as was his previous statement, which highlighted Marguerite's enlivened demeanor as she described herself as someone contrary to that depicted in the traumatic "script." At this point, it is as if the therapist metaphorically, and sometimes actually, sits back to open up a space in which both partners will "gaze" in order to view more clearly, in greater sensory and emotional aliveness, what has so far transpired between them. The therapist's aim is now to potentiate the reflective capacity that has arisen from the earlier period, in which his objective has been the attainment of cohesion. In order to foster this objective, a therapist might use language such as, "Let's have a look at this." This way of speaking implicitly uses the metaphor of insight as "seeing into the mind."

Together, Marguerite and her therapist contemplate her dilemma of being governed by two competing systems of personal reality.

Principle 24: SCENE SETTING AND THE EMPATHIC SCREEN

In the first part of this conversation between Marguerite and Dr. Abel, before the clear emergence of reflective capacity, the structure of the relationship was as if face to face, like the mother–child dyad in the protoconversation. When the therapist shifts the conversation to the reflective mode, the structure changes. Attention shifts to what I have likened to a metaphoric cinematic screen on which the partners in the conversation attempt to portray a partially glimpsed personal reality. In this process, the therapist's empathic capabilities are exercised. Together, patient and therapist build up a scene, in its visceral aliveness, of a specific occasion and experience. The language tends toward a particular structure. It is directed toward the "screen" with phrases such as "It looks like . . . ," "It seems that

. . . ," and so forth. The language, in this way, is rather like that of symbolic play. Pronouns are characteristically missing. Although in an emotional sense it is highly personal, in a technical sense this structuring of language can be called impersonal.

Scene setting is not attempted at every opportunity available. There are multiple opportunities from which to choose. For example, the occasion might have been used when Marguerite was unable to finish the word *quality* (see Principle #21) and can only utter the first syllable, *qu-*, because the unconscious traumatic memory system tells her that she is not the kind of person who can produce *top-quality* food. She is lesser. However, to have interrupted the development of her thought at this point would have been a disruption, an intrusion into an evolving state of mind. Timing is important. A space may appear in the conversation in which this somewhat different kind of interplay can be comfortably conducted.

Furthermore, very often it is only a fragment of the scene that is, as it were, "set before the eyes" of the conversational pair. It is returned to in different ways from time to time. The process often begins with the depiction of a scene outside the therapeutic relationship. However, it is most important, when possible (usually after the relationship is well established), to identify and use traumatic intrusions into the therapeutic conversation, since the system's working is likely to be unconscious, unguarded, and in this way "raw," more alive than a consciously remembered situation. Therapeutic activity is likely to be more powerfully effective at this point.

In the session with Marguerite, the therapist focuses on what has so far transpired. The conversation elaborates, re-represents, what has been revealed. The nature of scene setting is considered in Principle #31.

Principle 25: CHANGING THE SCRIPT

The conversation between Marguerite and her therapist now moves to a discussion, deriving from "acid eating into her," about her husband's relentless criticism and demolition of her. She is now quite calm and in a more reflective state of mind.

Following this, Dr. Abel says: "What if," pausing as if to give weight to his word, "you told him to stop?" Using very simple language, he is working toward changing the traumatic script, comprising the attributes of self and other, derived from repeated relational traumata as a generic system. As a first step toward changing the traumatic "script," he suggests a change in her behavior, so altering the way the script is played out in the external world.

Marguerite sees herself as useless, incompetent, and helpless, at least when the traumatic reality prevails. In this condition, the "other," who cannot be opposed, "hounds" her with reminders of her deficiencies. An approach to overcoming this state must begin with the subject becoming aware of the destructive system in which she is caught. In various ways, most of the different methods of treating BPD seek to alter the script by bringing it to conscious awareness. This first step must be followed by a change in behavior. If this behavioral change is not evident, no real change can be considered to have occurred. What has happened is merely "cognitive."

Marguerite replies that in the last week or so she has, in fact, told her husband to stop. For a few days she felt wonderful. Free. But then she realized that this newfound way of behaving was a "delusion," that is, it was contrary to what she considered to be objective reality. Consequently, she reverted to the familiar, unpleasant, but apparently safer mode of experiencing herself. We shall return to the complex matter of changing the script in Principle #28. (Marguerite's conversation, "What if . . . ," is briefly discussed in Chapter 8).

Principle 26: IDENTIFYING THE APPEARANCE OF THE TRAUMATIC SYSTEM AND THE NOTION OF TRANSFERENCE

The traumatic memory system is omnipresent, but its influence upon conscious life varies. Its dominance is lost during the opening of the session with Marguerite so that during her enlivened period it is no longer evident, except for the inability to say the word *quality*. Such spontaneous intrusions allow the traumatic memory system to be processed with greater effectiveness than that kind of therapy that is merely *about* what has occurred at another time. The intrusion has the immediacy of the moment. It is essential that the therapist recognize the subtler intrusions in addition to the eruptions, which cannot be missed. Indications of the appearance of the unconscious traumatic memory system are noted in Chapter 2. Here is an example.

The session is with a middle-aged woman, Deborah, who lives alone and who has a traumatic history involving destructive devaluation. She begins in a characteristic way, in a monotonous voice, with complaints of bodily distress, of various pains, of difficulty in sleeping. The therapist shifts the negative mood state by staying with what is given and responding to something she perceives to be potentially positive. She says that the dreams seem to concern something "deep." The patient now exhibits increasing positivity, her voice losing some of its harshness and developing a faintly musical quality. This leads, after some minutes, to her speaking of living an imaginary life as a gypsy, wandering free, enjoying music, and wearing colorful, flowing garments. The scene then shifts to the previous weekend, when, with a friend, she visited a stud of Arab horses. Two of them are close by a fence where she and her friend have stopped to gaze at the view. She says of the horses:

> Deborah: And like the enigma . . . you know, the enigma of music, the beauty of the music, the flowing, the beauty of the music.
>
> Therapist: Ah, the beauty.
>
> Deborah: Oh, yeah . . . um, so yeah, just anything and Joy [her friend], Joy sort of looked at me and she could see I was relishing a couple of things I was saying to her about these horses.
>
> Therapist: You were really relishing them.
>
> Deborah: Oh, yeah, you know because I said to Joy it takes nothing really to . . . to keep me quite (*laughs*), you know, just like . . .
>
> Therapist: Exquisite things . . .
>
> Deborah: Yeah.
>
> Therapist: Beauty.

The features of selfhood begin to emerge in Deborah's conversation following the therapist's remarks about her dreams. In talking of an imaginary life, she displays an essential characteristic of selfhood: that is, the reflective capacity. A further characteristic of selfhood, symbolic thought, is evident in the comparison between the horses and a particular shaping of sound, the music of Elgar. The therapist's responses are very simple. She does not pursue Elgar, which might lead somewhere imaginative but can be taken up at another time. She "stays with" the positive affect conveyed in the word *beauty*. This choice is a good one because it is the positive feelings that are destroyed in BPD. The positive feelings of people with BPD have a frailty that is usually guarded since exposure invites possible harm. This dynamic is implicit in what follows. The textural shift is characteristic.

> Deborah: Yeah and . . . yes, it's . . . yeah. Oh and Chuck rang me on Sunday, Saturday, from Nambucca. He's now passed through and he's in Coffs Harbour. . . . Ah . . . "Would you like to come pack up and live with me?"—blah, blah, shit, shit. That's all, Chuck. I said "Hey." I said, "You've only just arrived. How about you settle in there?" . . . blah, blah. He said, "Hey, how come all of a sudden you're not as hot and keen on the idea as you were earlier this year?" I said, "Chuck we're about January 2009. Oh," I said, "It's now September 2011" (*pause*).

What happened, which the therapist does not yet know, but soon will, is that Deborah was ridiculed, mocked, and in other ways hurt and devalued when she showed the side of her that was tender, joyful, and took pleasure in beauty. When the therapist resonates with the word *beauty* at its first utterance, Deborah's mental state is momentarily disorganized ("Oh, yeah . . . um, so yeah"), but she quickly recovers. When, however, the second resonation is made, the shift into the more disorganized, negative state is complete. The expression of pleasure in beauty reminds her of all those people who had demolished her at those moments of such expression, shattering the feeling. Chuck was one of them. He treated her as if she were simply there to be picked up and dumped at his whim, as if she had no life of her own and was, in effect, worthless.

Some of the indications of the emergence of the unconscious traumatic memory system are apparent in this shift:

- *Change in affect*. The mood becomes more negative. Anger may be displayed, or anxiety, but most commonly emotion is deadened and vitality lost. In the case of Deborah, the change in feeling state was not in the force of her words, but in a loss of their faint musicality, a certain lilt in her voice.
- *A change in bodily feelings*, which might be particularly visceral.
- *A change in bodily posture and facial expression*. This may range from very slight (e.g., eyes downcast) to quite pronounced (e.g., a clenched, thumping fist).
- *A change in linguistic organization* is evident in Deborah's case.
- *A change in the grammar*, indicating a loss of connectedness with the therapist. The patient, for example, might ask the therapist a question, implying a relationship that has a distancing quality in it.

- *A change in grammatical structure* to more linear and less associative language.
- *A change of subject of the conversation to more external matters.* The patient might begin to talk of the problems of other people rather than of him- or herself, or talk "about" his or her own experiences without being "in" the experience.
- *A change of content to that which is negative.*

Principle 26: SCENE SETTING (PART II)

After the pause Deborah stops describing Chuck's phone call, and the therapist begins the process of "scene setting" with what is immediate, what happened in the room, in Deborah's body.

Therapist: I was interested to . . .

Deborah: Yeah . . .

Therapist: . . . ask you . . .

Deborah: Yeah . . .

The therapist speaks rather tentatively, which is a good thing, since Deborah has demonstrated that she is afraid of entering the traumatic experience. Twice before, in previous sessions, the therapist has picked up negative shifts in the conversation, but has been unable to go on with the processing because Deborah's harsh, powerful voice had rolled over the top of her own, signaling anxiety. Wisely, the therapist did not persist. It is necessary, in order to process the trauma adequately, that it is done in an atmosphere of *safety*. The patient must feel confident that the therapist will not break down defenses in order to force upon her an experience with which she is unable to cope. This confidence has grown over some months, so that now the processing is possible. Nevertheless, the therapist's quiet voice, moving slowly, is consistent with maintaining the sense of safety. Even so, Deborah interrupts her, twice, with "Yeah." The therapist goes on:

Therapist: That, um, I wanted know what you were thinking then to . . .

Deborah: —to jump to something else.

Therapist: Oh, you're good.[Here the therapist is giving positive reinforcement to the patient's ability to recognize shifts that are going on within her, which is necessary to therapeutic process.]

Deborah: Why do I?

Therapist: Hmmm (*as if pondering*). It's fascinating. [The therapist is not caught in the trap of explaining, early, what is happening. It is desirable for the patient, in company with the therapist, to make the discovery.]

Deborah: I do. Something bumps in straight away.

Therapist: Something bumps in . . .

Deborah: And, see, that's the problem. That's what stops me from wanting to socialize because my mind will *PHOOMP* and go off. And I can talk about anything and everything, but do I give another person the chance to get to say something? I don't think so!

Therapist: Oh, I think . . . oh, I see. I think, you were telling me about the gypsies, and you, and you being a gypsy, and the skirts . . .

Deborah: And then we talked about the horses.

Therapist: And then, that you were mesmerized by these exquisite horses, you were relishing their beauty, as you said.

Deborah: Ah, gorgeous.

Therapist: And then I saw your face, you kind of . . .

Deborah: Yeah, Chuck.

Therapist: You . . . your face dropped and you talked about . . .

Deborah: Chuck.

Therapist: Chuck.

Deborah: Yeah.

Therapist: Like, you were in this really lovely space.

Deborah: Wasn't I? And then I . . . yeah. So why can't, why can't it always be that nice? So that's why, you know . . .

Therapist: There are these intrusions.

Deborah: Yeah.

The therapist and patient continue fleshing out the experience as it happened between them. It is, of course, never completed. What is done is "good enough." The task should not become laborious.

Principle 27: CHANGING THE EXPECTATIONAL FIELD

In such an episode, the therapist should ponder her own part in it. In this case, it is internally triggered and not precipitated by any behavior on the part of the therapist that resembles the original abuser. However, in what follows it seems likely that the therapist has been drawn into the traumatic system in a different way. This is through her experience as the other in the patient's "reversal"—that is, a traumatic state in which, as it were, Deborah is "inhabited" by the original abuser. At times, Deborah is intimidating. Her voice can become harsh and overwhelming. These occasions are usually fueled by anxiety. As the therapist attempts her explanations of the traumatic experience, she senses, rather faintly, that she is about to be attacked. Sensing this, she has the evidence to hypothesize that this will be an aspect of Deborah's usual experience of others when she is not in a reversal. Such an awareness helps the therapist to contribute imaginatively to a later and more complete scene setting in which she processes the effect of the expectational field that is an aspect of the unconscious traumatic memory system.

Deborah works for a firm selling high-quality wine. Her role is secretarial but includes a range of tasks beyond the merely clerical. She finds that her bosses are very often "ripping shreds off" her. This has also been her experience in previous jobs. The hypothesis arises that this repeated experience is an effect of the expectational field. The scene is now re-created in which she is about to be interviewed by the manager. The particular features are as follows.

- The actual scene is visualized. In this case it is outside the door of the manager's office. Deborah is in a concrete reality, not merely an idea. The details of this reality—the colors, shapes, sounds, and smells—are laid out, as if a picture were being made.
- The feeling is sensed, including the expectation that she will be criticized, diminished—"ripped to shreds."
- The body feeling—for example, the tightness in the gut, the beating heart, the muscular tension
- The bodily posture—for example, slightly hunched, head down.
- Body movements—for example, awkward, not rhythmic, fidgety
- Facial expression—for example, apprehension, or anticipating shame, or frozen
- Voice—for example, hesitancy, incoherence
- Perceptions of the other—for example, his size, his expressionless face

This scene might be played out, in part, in the room with the therapist. This activity is not prescribed but is suggested to the patient who, in this way, has the choice of performing the role or not. If the patient is uncomfortable about the procedure, it can be done in imagination.

Principle 28: CHANGING THE SCRIPT (PART II)—"AS IF IN A MOVIE"

Having re-created an aspect of the traumatic script, the therapist and patient go through it again, playing it out "as if in a movie," as if Deborah were not in the grip of the traumatic script. Deborah stands straight, her face is calm, her walk rhythmic and voice, although quiet, is confident. Once again, the activity is not prescribed. The patient is merely invited to perform the scene, as if in a game, with the therapist joining in, helping to enlarge and make more sensorily alive the portrayal. Otherwise, it can be done in imagination. It is important that the patient feels that he or she is an agent in the production of his or her own actions and experience rather than feeling helpless and under the control of a more powerful figure, the therapist. There is a danger that this experience replicates the traumatic script.

The next time Deborah is called to the manager's office, the meeting is a success. Sometime later she made an appointment with her managers to explain that she had been, in effect, harassed and felt bullied by them. Her demeanor was apparently quite calm. Extraordinarily, they apologized to her.

There are many variations to changing the script. Some emerge spontaneously through the patient's intuition that the commands of traumatic memory *need* to be overcome and *can* be overcome. An example, for one patient, was the power of a hallucinatory voice that said, whenever the patient attempted something new, "Hopeless bitch, can't do anything." This changed, with the tone of the voice remaining much the same, to "Take it on."

Principle 29: TRANSFERENCE–COTRANSFERENCE AND THE EXPECTATIONAL FIELD

As pointed out in Chapter 1, transference phenomenon are regarded in CM as the effect on the participants in the therapeutic conversation of the activation of the traumatic script, during which the patient feels as if he or she were once again in the presence of the original abuser, whose attributes, intentions, and so forth are given to the therapist—transferred from a situation in the past. It is always, however, a traumatic form of relatedness that is activated, not the sense of a single figure, the other. The subject is now the person who was traumatized, in the presence of the original perpetrator. This experience of the patient has an effect on the therapist, which, if it can be accessed, may help the therapist in imagining what the original traumatic relatedness was like. This effect is the "expectational field."

An example of this effect involved a middle-aged woman whose BPD features included inexplicable rages, depression, and binge drinking. In early sessions there are long silences interspersed with somewhat incoherent and disconnected speech. The therapist finds himself irritated by the patient's demeanor. Why can't she say what she means to say? However, on pondering his experience as a cotransference, he comes to the hypothesis that his impatience with her and his critical attitude toward her are reflections of the expectational field. He knows he is not usually critical. Perhaps his critical attitude, although not expressed, is a replay of the relational trauma? Using this idea, the therapist worked toward a very good outcome for his patient.

The situation for the therapist working with Deborah, in which there was a reversal of the traumatic script, was more complex. The therapist came to know something of the experience of the subject, rather than the behavior of the other. Her realization of a faint apprehension that she might be attacked gave her an inkling of the attributes of the subjective pole of the traumatic script.

A further complexity in the use of cotransference as a means of hypothesizing the nature of the traumatic script is provided by what might be called the *negative expectational field*. In this case, the influence is toward an *absence* of actions. It is, therefore, somewhat more difficult to register as an aspect of one's immediate experience. Take the following example:

The patient is Olivia, who is in her 30s. She has been very damaged by an emotionally abusive childhood and a period of living on the streets as an adolescent. Although intelligent, she works only as a part-time cleaner, has no relationships, and rarely goes out, since she has multiple phobias. She begins the session in a dull voice, talking of the "drizzle" on the way to the session. Then in a brighter voice she says. "I had a busy weekend. I went out to tea," and gives a little laugh. The therapist says "Yup," as if waiting for the session to start. Olivia then goes on to describe what happened at afternoon tea.

As the session goes on, the therapist realizes what had happened at the start of the session. In this case the realization was intellectual, unlike the realizations of the previous examples, which were based on a faint emotional state evoked in the therapists. Reconsidering his patient's opening words, the therapist realized that he had been told of a triumph. A person who could barely go out, who avoided cinemas and social gatherings, had gone out to tea, overcoming her phobic inhibitions. He should have responded positively, perhaps with a "Wow!" No response was given. He had repeated the relational traumata in which no value was given to the child's experiences of vitality, of enterprise, of creativity. He had been affected by her expectation that no valuation would be forthcoming.

The negative expectational field is particularly important in BPD since those suffering the condition are likely to have experienced constant devaluation and scant valuation and affirmation of their emergent selfhood. They have had very little experience of analogical relatedness.

Principle 30: WHAT HAPPENS NEXT (PART II)— THE "MEANING" OF A DISJUNCTION

Olivia's story about what happened at the afternoon tea party allows the therapist to form a hypothesis about the nature of the disjunction, which was observable only in a loss of the brightness of her voice that followed his lack of response. It is useful always to hold in mind, as a general principle, the idea that the story a patient tells after a disjunction has occurred may also tell the therapist what has happened in the disjunction.

At the party, Olivia expressed an opinion on a subject about which she knows a great deal. Her best friend flatly contradicted her, giving no value to what Olivia had said. She felt as if she had been hit. In his reconsideration of the opening of the session, the therapist realized that he had done something similar, although on a micro scale, in his failure to respond to her brightness, her laugh, and her "busy" weekend.

Principle 31: VISUALIZATION AND THE NARRATIVE OF SELF

A principal marker of selfhood is evidence of the "mind's eye," when scenes from the past, or in imagination, are as if "viewed" in mental space. In order to foster the emergence of self and to facilitate the transformation of traumatic consciousness into a form that can be integrated into the mature consciousness of self, it is necessary to transmute an account that is *about* trauma—that is, one that is depicted in words that have no picturing value—to one that can be *seen*.

The visualization begins, at times, in a concrete way, with a re-representation of what has just happened: for example, the incident in which Deborah was tripped into the traumatic zone. The therapist begins with what Deborah's face looked like. Later visualizations include the imaginary.

It is often said that traumatic experience must be turned into words so that it can become part of a story. Verbalization, however, is not enough. The recitation of traumatic events is, in our experience, ineffective. Speaking *about* such events in a way that does not arise from their sensory aliveness is akin to "second-hand thought," which comes from other people. Speech can be considered a double process, the first part of which is imagery. This fundamental process is illustrated by the stories of two female adolescents who were helped a great deal by a focus on images that they could barely "explain."

The first case was of a girl of 13 who was admitted to the hospital in a state of quasi-catatonia. She was mute, very thin, and the movements in her body were stiff. She walked like a robot. Since she could not speak, it was suggested that she convey how she felt by means of painting, just using her fingers, if she preferred, rather than brushes. Her first image was merely the outline of her hand (Figure 6.1), as if the only sense of personal reality was bodily. A number of images followed. Several involved a doll with no arms, like an image of a child deprived of the ability to cuddle (Figure 6.2).

FIGURE 6.1. Mute traumatized girl can only paint the outline of her hand.

FIGURE 6.2. The girl, now improved, paints dolls with no arms.

The story, however, did not progress in a straight line, in the manner of a chronicle, with pictures of dolls with arms, for example. Instead, the girl drew strange diagrams that were like anatomical representations of the interior of the female pelvis. The shapes were coherent and fluent (Figure 6.3). At this stage she had improved remarkably. The change was most clearly evident in her body. She moved with considerable grace and rhythm. It emerged that she had been severely sexually abused.

The second patient was a girl in late adolescence who made frightening suicide attempts but who could say very little about what led up to them and what emotional states were associated with them. Her life, as she described it, was "normal." She behaved in the ward in a "normal" way, interacting with other adolescents. When it was suggested that she paint her feelings and sense of who she was, she merely produced patterns. Then one day one piece in the pattern had changed. It

FIGURE 6.3. Painting correlates with great improvement in clinical condition; e.g. now moves rhythmically.

was black, whereas the others were pink. Moreover, again unlike the other pieces, it was attached to another (Figure 6.4). In subsequent paintings, the black piece became elaborated and more complex, taking up most of the painting and incorporating symbolic elements, such as a cross (Figure 6. 5).

The therapist, in working with these patients, made no interpretations and simply provided a quiet commentary, amplifying some aspects of these representations and, now and again, offering wondering speculations about what they expressed, particularly in feeling terms (e.g., "The doll must be sad"). There was never any clear explanation of the "meaning" of these images, yet they showed a progression, paralleled by clinical improvement, which was analogous to the movements of a story.

These were not stories of the usual kind but of a kind that moved from one symbolic representation to another by means of linkages that were analogical rather than logical. In the first case, for example, the images evolved around a theme of the body. These two stories provide a model of how a series of visualiza-

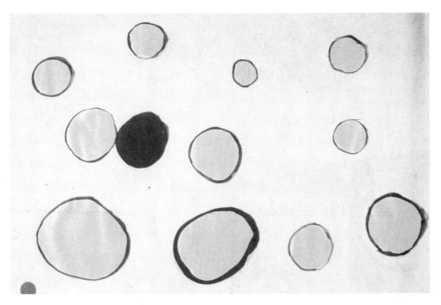

FIGURE 6.4. Suicidal adolescent could paint only patterns, until this picture which showed a different piece.

FIGURE 6.5. The different piece now becomes more complex through symbolic elaboration.

tions of personal experience can turn into what might be call a "narrative of self." In many cases this emergence may not be realized by either partner in the conversation, and no deliberate scene setting is undertaken. Such an emergence may occur over different time scales. The progression may develop over many months or even years. On the other hand, it can happen in a single session when various episodes are recounted that, at first sight, have little connection among them. On reflection they are seen to have a common basis in a particular generative metaphor, Hobson's (1985) "moving metaphor." An example of this latter occurrence is the session with Julia, who spoke of an environment in which "we're cramped . . . into little boxes" (see Principle #22). This image of personal space is linked by the therapist to its obverse, to soaring free, which leads the patient to remark, "Oh, yes. It's lovely to be in a spacious place." This remark is a condensation, referring both to how she feels at this moment and to the place she is in.

Julia now switches to another scene. She is reminded of another room, in a university building that, like the one she is in now, was old and spacious. By means of similar linkages, the narrative moves through a series of scenes: a pathology museum, fetuses in bottles, the emergence of planets, the notion of universal design, a room in a tower where a guru conducts meditation classes. The linkages are shown in Figure 6.6.

The therapist's role in the linking of these episodes is largely, though not entirely, analogical. Much that is analogical is created through the contours of the voice, in brief vocalizations. In those contributions that are not clearly analogical, the therapist stays very close to the experience. For example, the link between episodes 7 and 8 goes as follows:

Julia: I wondered as I came through school and we had all of this hard religious instruction, what then happens to the soul of the aborted fetus or the, um, or one who hasn't made it?

Therapist: Mmm.

Julia: There would have been a soul.

Therapist: Mmm, there would have been.

Julia: Yeah. Anyway, well that's a big one.

Therapist: Yeah.

Julia: Yes so all of this, the windows, the curtains, it's very much the . . . very similar.

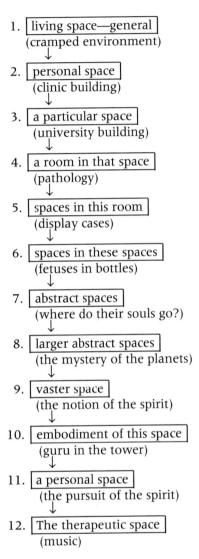

1. living space—general
   (cramped environment)

2. personal space
   (clinic building)

3. a particular space
   (university building)

4. a room in that space
   (pathology)

5. spaces in this room
   (display cases)

6. spaces in these spaces
   (fetuses in bottles)

7. abstract spaces
   (where do their souls go?)

8. larger abstract spaces
   (the mystery of the planets)

9. vaster space
   (the notion of the spirit)

10. embodiment of this space
    (guru in the tower)

11. a personal space
    (the pursuit of the spirit)

12. The therapeutic space
    (music)

FIGURE 6.6. This schema displays successive episodes in the therapeutic conversation between Julia and her therapist. Each episode occurs in a space. The episodes are analogically linked by the metaphor of space.

Therapist: It's kind of unnerving, isn't it, to wonder what happened to those babies' souls, I guess, 'cause they're so helpless, aren't they?

Julia: Yeah, so it would not be of their making. Um, there must be, um, I'd imagine they'd be . . . Oh, then but if I'm right about the, um, everything, the whole concept being thought out way beyond where we're at. . . . Remember when I said about the planets kind of spilling out of the . . . and it's all in, in, uh (*pause*) . . . it's all been planned? So that, that would have been planned for too, wouldn't it? The soul of the . . . uh . . .

As Julia begins to talk of the fate of the soul as a "big one," she shifts the topic to "all of this, the windows, the curtains," as if anxiety or embarrassment has arisen, and she changes the subject to the immediate surroundings. The therapist "stays with" the feeling, which maintains the theme while implicitly acknowledging the anxiety with the word *unnerving*. This leads to the next episode, the mystery of the planets.

During this session, the patient's experience of personal space has been processed in a natural and conversational way. The starting point of "entrapment" shifts, so that in episodes 10 and 11, a view of the future is presented in which there is the possibility of "soaring free."

How this has come about is implicitly explained in the final shift at episode 12, which is a return to the therapeutic space. Julia talks of the pleasure of listening to music with a companion who, like her, values the music. This is what she says, omitting the therapist's linkages:

> I find if I'm with somebody at a concert, somebody who I know is enjoying it as much as I am . . .
>
> It is 50 to 100% more enjoyable, I'm sure . . .
>
> When you look at the face of someone who's into it, and you pick up, you pick up, uh, what do you pick up? (*pause*). You pick up their enjoyment, you pick up what they're experiencing. Yeah . . .
>
> You can see the inspiration on the face and you know that they're getting out of it what you . . . different if you're with somebody who comes along just for company—forget it.

Julia speaks without mentioning the therapist or apparently being aware that she might be talking about the present relationship. Nevertheless, she is looking into the therapist's eyes as she speaks. She is describing the experience of the kind of relationship necessary to the emergence of self.

Chapter 7

Particular Issues and Situations

Joan Haliburn

THIS CHAPTER CONCERNS the actual language and therapist attitude that arise in particular situations, around certain issues and forms of presentation that we see in day-to-day clinical practice. The case of Bella in Chapter 4 and the composite cases of Sarah and Sally are used here as illustrations.

ESTABLISHING THE THERAPEUTIC RELATIONSHIP

In this section I emphasize that the therapist should keep in mind the importance of valuing the patient with BPD and facilitating a sense of safety and the development of trust at the first point of contact. The first session is crucial; it is when traumatic memories are usually activated as a consequence of the often-restricted state of consciousness in which these patients are functioning. The importance of a therapist's language, attitude of listening and connecting in the moment, refraining from exploration of traumatic material before the relationship is established, and of undertaking the journey of therapy alongside the patient are dealt with.

Value and Trust in the Therapeutic Relationship

The therapist working with patients with BPD must always be aware that value and trust are crucial issues. Such patients are likely to have been devalued, often in multiple ways—some catastrophically, as in sexual and physical abuse and neglect; others, though they might appear to be less damaging, become potently malign through their repetitive nature. Examples include being subjected to relentless criticism, contempt, and shaming experiences at an early age. Trust has been betrayed by periods of abandonment (whether actual or emotional) and by unreliability and unpredictability of caregivers, oftentimes when the child is of an age where his/her understanding has not yet fully developed.

Because of these early childhood experiences, these patients expect a repetition of such behavior by the therapist, who in turn must be aware of these expectations. They will undoubtedly contribute to a particular therapeutic attitude, in which a joint effort is made to give value to, and develop a narrative that makes sense of, the patient's subjective experience.

It must be remembered that it is the patient who teaches the therapist the style of listening and responding that is best suited at the time. The therapist attempts to attune accordingly, conveying an attitude that will prevent or reduce feelings of shame or humiliation particularly in the early stages.

Patients who are valued experience and develop the capacity to value themselves.

Creating a place of safety, facilitating conversation, and communicating a wish to understand relevant aspects of the process and the frame are discussed. Difficulties that may be encountered within the therapy are identified. The therapist also takes note of his or her capacity to be of help.

The specter of devaluation hangs over those with BPD in the form of stigma. Many patients with BPD have experienced stigmatizing attitudes from health professionals toward their condition. This devaluing attitude retraumatizes them and makes them more distrustful of other mental health professionals. Having experienced attitudes that devalue them, criticize them, and offer no relief of distress, patients with BPD often come to psychotherapy anxious and uncertain, at the same time needing relief from their disabling symptoms. In the words of a patient, "You are seen as a lesser human being, fit for nothing, just because you have a mental illness."

Some patients living in a culture that stigmatizes mental illness come to accept that they are lesser, which in turn leads to diminished self-esteem, beliefs that they are less intelligent, a decreased sense of agency, and a passive attitude toward improvement, sometimes referred to as *self-stigma*.

As a young patient with BPD said, after she was discharged from the hospital subsequent to a suicide attempt, "It's nobody else—it's just me. I feel like a freak. I *am* a freak. People see me as different. I don't blame them—no one wants me as a friend. How could they? I'm different." The additional trauma of stigma and often of hospitalization also impacts on the formation of the therapeutic relationship, and requires careful consideration when a patient comes for psychotherapy.

Demeanor of the Patient and the Therapist in the First Session

Since trust is an important issue for the patient with BPD, who has learned not to trust, anxiety and apparent sensitivity are usually present. This may or may not be shown in the patient's demeanor or facial expressions. The anxiety will cause the effect of traumatic memory systems to be more salient than usual, becoming apparent in the patient's manner of relating, the language used, and either the ease or the lack of freedom with which the interaction follows.

The therapist and patient impact on each other. The transference–cotransference will have an important effect on the development of the therapeutic relationship from the moment of the first contact, whether on the telephone or in person. You will see this in the case of Bella in Chapter 4 when Bella expected to be rejected by the therapist because rejection was her usual experience. Her presentation at the first session created considerable anxiety for the therapist, which affected the therapist's usual composure, of which she was unaware.

It is important that the therapist be aware of this impact and doesn't get caught up in the traumatic memory system, in which the attributes of self and other can operate in unexpected ways. Compensatory mechanisms that have become the patient's usual way of adapting and coping in certain interpersonal situations may be built around the traumatic memory of the original traumatizing situation. As a result the patient behaves in ways similar to the original situation but in a totally different context.

The patient may become wary, fall into silence quickly, or be dismissive, critical, idealizing, accommodating, aggressive, devaluing, or suicidal. The therapist must be aware of these attitudes, so that he or she does not respond to them inappropriately. If the therapist is not aware of these attitudes, the possibility of connection, and therefore of understanding, will be blocked. It is important to engage the patient at his or her level—that is, on the hierarchy of consciousness, which is discussed next.

Hierarchy of Consciousness

Patients with BPD generally present in a state of restricted consciousness, lower down on the hierarchy than the average person. This state can be roughly judged by the verbal and nonverbal demeanor of the patient. The presence of fragmentation, as in language in the form of a script or chronicle—which comprises words with little or no continuity and with loss of coherence—is an indication that the patient is lower down on the hierarchy.

Such a patient is likely to be in a state of mind that is more primitive, constricted, and lacking in freedom than higher-order consciousness.

In order to connect with this state of mind the therapist must use a language that is appropriate to that level of development—brief and simple—very often that of the patient. Words can be omitted, monosyllabic utterances and verbal intonations can be used, and sentences can be incomplete. The omission of personal pronouns and the use of neutral words, such as "*It* seems difficult" or "*It's* hard to trust," may enable connection with a rather sensitive and disconnected patient more readily than a direct approach, as in "*You* find it difficult" or "*You* find it hard to trust."

The aim of this kind of language is to enter into the immediate experience of the other and to transform a disconnected form of consciousness into another form of consciousness that is larger and more connected. The aim of the therapist, then, is to work, from this lower level, toward transforming this conversation into one of a different kind in which the elements of selfhood will emerge.

Of importance is that language is used as a vehicle for expression based on feeling. Hence the sound of the voice becomes vitally important. In addition, nonverbal facial expressions, gestures, and body movements of the therapist also indicate to the patient that he or she is being listened to.

This attitude helps the patient develop a better sense of self before any attempt is made to explore his or her traumatic experiences. Even though the patient may mention traumatic incidents, the therapist is advised to respond but go no further in this early stage, unless the patient does. Even then, deeper exploration by the therapist is best avoided.

Attempts to explore the trauma in the early stages of therapy often have the effect of destabilizing the already unstable patient, resulting in increased anxiety, depression, self-harm, or suicidal ideation. When a better sense of self-in-relationship is achieved, the patient will be in a position to process the trauma with less of a tendency to fragment.

In-depth exploration of traumatic experiences in the early stage of therapy is best not attempted.

Patients sometimes want to know if they have been abused, as in the following example:

Patient: I must have been sexually abused—otherwise there would be no reason for me to be in this pathetic state (*looking to the therapist for an answer*).

Therapist: (*carefully*) Let's keep talking, so together we can reach a better place where the reasons for your situation will become a whole lot clearer. Can we do that?

The therapist does not have a role in telling the patient whether they have been abused or not.

Particular Difficulties in the Beginning

The forms of presentation of the borderline patient are many, making it difficult, particularly for the novice therapist, who may become aware almost immediately of experiencing cotransference. The patient may refuse to sit down and may stand in a corner of the room. This would naturally create anxiety for the therapist, who may wonder how this behavior has come about. The therapist's verbal and nonverbal language becomes immensely important in this situation; there would be little point in trying to work out what standing in the corner might mean at this point.

In such situations, the therapist may make an observation and perhaps try again to convey, in a quiet voice, that the patient might like to be seated so that they can start to talk. If the patient still appears reluctant, this feeling may have to be identified explicitly, as in "There seems reluctance about coming here?" The tentative question is often helpful, as it indicates that the therapist is not all-knowing. It therefore leaves room for both partners of the dyad to look at, and try to understand, what is happening.

Some of the more difficult situations that confront the therapist are briefly discussed here; however, it must be remembered that a mix of features of the different presentations is likely to be seen.

The Silent Patient

Sometimes a patient may come to the first session and say a few words, perhaps why he or she has come, and then fall into silence. This silence can be quite difficult for the therapist, who might make an attempt to pick up what was stressed by the patient, or what seemed most important. The therapist might respond with something like this:

- "You said you were feeling awful. I wonder if we can talk about how long that's been so." Or—
- "It's difficult to go into issues when you meet someone for the first time, particularly when you're feeling awful—it's understandable."

It is important to try to make the patient feel less anxious, and to not let silences increase. The aim is to create a bridge for the patient to bring him or her out of what seems to be a sense of alienation. More importantly, the therapist must not lapse into asking questions, as doing so might increase the sense of alienation.

Silences can also become problematic during the course of therapy and must be understood and responded to, in the context of what has just happened. The case of Bella in Chapter 4, wherein the therapist experienced great difficulty with silences, provides a useful illustration here. "It's difficult sometimes to talk" may be one way in which the therapist can attempt to deal with the silence. Comfortable silences however, must be identified as such, and allowed, as they may indicate a time for reflection.

The Avoidant Patient

The patient brings his or her usual way of interacting to the therapeutic relationship. This usual way is a consolidation and transformation of previous interactions with significant others. The therapist's demeanor at this time is most important.

Avoidant patients are just one example; they generally present in a very agreeable manner. The conversation may be easy, except when the patient touches on something personal and the attuned therapist picks it up. The patient reacts by changing the topic or by avoiding any further discussion. The therapist must take note of these changes and respect the patient's need for privacy. It may be too early to find out what the reasons for this avoidance may be. Therapists must also be self-aware. An avoidant therapist who is unaware may collude with an avoidant patient, and the patient may not return. This may happen with a variety of presentations.

The topics that are being avoided and particularly the affects that might inherently create this avoidance will gradually become clearer at a later time. Avoidance may be due to the patient's effort to avoid appearing needy or burdensome. It might also be due to the patient's fear of being rejected, of being responded to with aggression, or of being seen as insignificant.

Thus the patient, through avoidance, maintains a distance in the therapy and forgoes any sense of intimacy. The following example illustrates what I mean.

> Patient: I keep having these moods, but then I guess I'm not the only one. Other people must have moods too. (*In the same breath*) Everything seems to go pear-shaped, but then I'm sure it must happen to other people too.
>
> Therapist: [Takes note that the patient avoids discussing the very issues she brings up but does not refer to her avoidance, "I guess I'm not the only one" and her change of topic, as it is the first session. Instead, the therapist closely aligns with her language and offers this empathic response.] You keep having these moods, but you're unsure about these moods.

Further elaboration may ensue as the patient continues to talk about what appear to be triggers to these mood states.

The Dismissive/Hostile Patient

The patient may sometimes give the distinct impression that he or she thinks that the therapist has little to offer or represents a threat that must be kept at a distance. This response has the effect of diminishing the importance of others. It also betrays the enormous difficulty the patient has in trusting and developing genuine intimacy. This example provides an illustration.

> Patient: I was advised to see you. I'm not sure if you can do anything for me (*in a sarcastic voice*), the others could not. You make promises, but are never around. I might as well kill myself. I'm no good to anyone. What's it to you? You don't even know me.

Even though the patient is meeting the therapist for the first time, the effect of traumatic memory is present in this interaction. She attributes to this therapist her experiences with others who failed to help her.

Such a script contains contradictions and is open to different understandings by different therapists; therefore, the therapeutic responses will vary. However, this kind of patient presentation generally has an unsettling effect. The therapist in this example experiences the patient as rigid, hostile, angry, dismissive, cruel, and rejecting. The therapist feels bombarded and momentarily off balance but regains her composure and tries to stay attuned.

While listening, the therapist is also going through her own thoughts and reactions (this capacity develops with experience and thoughtfulness). She thinks that perhaps the patient has internalized the characteristics of a cruel, rejecting caregiver, and at the same time claims to be deserving of such cruel treatment herself. The therapist also notes feeling humbled, put down, useless and helpless one minute, then she is filled with compassion and concern the next.

In the course of time, the therapist is able to reflect back to the patient these opposite feelings with some success.

Therapist: I understand that you have been let down; it's hard not to feel that it will keep happening. You're not sure . . . what to do?

Patient: (*Avoiding the reference to her uncertainty*) There are many others more deserving.

Therapist: More deserving? [The way this is said is important. It is not a mere repetition. The words are given a certain emphasis conveyed by the tone of voice that serves to represent what the patient is saying.]

Patient: Yes . . .

Therapist: I see. It must also be difficult, seeing that you have been let down. It's understandable, though . . .

Patient: You bet (*continuing to sound angry and sarcastic*)!

The therapist feels as if she were trapped. Whatever she says is met with sarcasm, but she does not take it personally. Instead she begins to wonder silently whether perhaps the patient has often felt this way herself: trapped. Thinking in these terms helps the therapist stay with the patient and avoid a struggle for control. It stops her from taking a dominant position with the patient, which would lead to arguing the point or submitting to her challenging attitude. Rather, she tries to meet the patient in the moment.

Therapist: It makes you angry. [The therapist tunes in to the patient's affect and uses what is given.]

Patient: Yes—why shouldn't I? [Her anger serves to distance.]

Therapist: Yes, I can see the difficulty when people let you down—trust—

Patient: (*interrupting*) Why should I?

Therapist: Yes, why should you? It's confusing . . . it's hard . . . it's difficult— it's. . . .

The patient seems to soften a little and starts to talk about her attempts to get help since she was 15 years old. It gradually becomes clear that the disorganization experienced developmentally is re-created in the therapeutic relationship. It is only some time later that the therapist is able to make a link in their relationship as in:

Therapist: It's reasonable to suggest that there's difficulty in trusting me too.

The Devaluing Patient

Another patient may attend the first session expecting nothing from the therapist, but behave as if she is doing something *for* the therapist, as in the following example:

Patient: (*in a sarcastic tone*) And what is it you want to know?

Therapist: (*Though taken aback, replies in an understanding and empathic tone.*) I wonder if you could tell me your reasons for being here.

Patient: It's a waste of time and money—nobody seems to know what to do for me. I might as well be sitting somewhere else and doing nothing, at least I would be enjoying myself (*continuing her tone of sarcasm*).

Therapist: Yes, time and money are precious, but you have taken the time to keep your appointment—it's a good thing (*in a positive tone*).

Such patients may think too well of themselves and badly about others. They shield themselves from their unmet needs, daring not to risk exposure, sometimes seeing themselves as perfect and others as not mattering, so they devalue them. They have internalized criticism, and in becoming critical, they maintain a distance.

Certain patients may be so provocative and contemptuous in their behavior that they provoke hateful, even despicable feelings in the therapist. Such contempt often reflects their internal world, which must be understood in the context of their trauma. It is indeed difficult to maintain a sustained interest in the patient who berates you early in the therapy, but trying to stay attuned and responsive will help to achieve connection.

The Idealizing Patient

The patient may come to the session and start to praise the therapist, making the therapist feel special, as in this example wherein the therapist accepts the patient's idealization:

Patient: Your certificates are very impressive. You must be very intelligent—I heard from people too . . .

Therapist: Thank you. There's a lot of training to be done before we start to practice.

Another therapist may find it difficult to accept and may ignore the patient's idealization, treat it indifferently, or laugh off the praise—which would not be helpful. It is important that the therapist note his or her own discomfort or pleasure in being idealized, so that responses may be adjusted accordingly.

Idealizing may simply be an attitude that the patient takes in attempting to make contact with the therapist; however, it may also be a way of accommodating, which is described next. Idealizing and devaluing may happen alternately in the same session, as the patient experiences different states of mind. Bella, as we have seen in Chapter 4, provides a good example of this attitude when she has expectations of the therapist being there for her, but at the same time does not have the experience of anyone being there for her, so she devalues and idealizes the therapist alternatively. When this happens, the task of therapy is to transform a limited, repetitive state of mind into one that is larger and involves a sense of freedom.

The Accommodating Patient

Some patients pathologically accommodate most of their lives to their environment, in order to please and be seen as pleasing, to avoid being rejected, punished, criticized, or devalued. This accommodation may tend to carry over into their ongoing relationships, including the therapeutic relationship. It is important for the therapist to take note of it and talk about it at a later stage, as in the following example:

Therapist: I am sorry to have kept you waiting. I was called away and could not get back on time.

Patient: There's no need to be apologetic. I know you are very busy—I can wait.

Therapist: I wondered if you would be upset, being made to wait.

Patient: Why should I be upset?? (*she sounded surprised but there was an underlying tone of accommodation.*)

The therapist registers this tone and silently wonders what it might indicate. Perhaps the patient has never been allowed to assert her needs, but rather has had to place others' needs before her own. The therapist also ponders his own values of "always being on time," then returns to thinking about the patient. She might not dare to express her needs for fear of rejection or rebuke.

Later in therapy it becomes clear that the mother of this patient, who was busy working in several jobs, would always return home late. She would expect that her daughter would have the home clean and tidy and the dinner cooked, so that she could relax. The patient could not talk to her mother about having to anxiously wait. She has learned that by being pleasing and uncomplaining, she could avoid her mother's displeasure, anger, and rejection. She has accommodated from quite an early age.

Therapists often become wary, in such a situation, that all the patient's responses will henceforth be accommodating because that is how he or she relates to people in general. However, the therapist can only trust his or her subjective experience, and when appropriate reflect to the patient something like this: "I wonder if there's something here about pleasing me too?"

Such interventions which link what the patient says with what the therapist says, linking in relationship, often result in a positive shift, increasing a sense of connectedness and developing security in the relationship. The patient will come to experience the therapist as accepting and uncritical, and that he or she does not have to be fearful (see "The Story of A Therapeutic Relationship" on page 45). It is also important that the therapist refrain from entertaining fantasies of rescue and getting into rescue mode. Such reactions will inevitably result in all-too-frequent difficulties. Important times such as separations must be carefully dealt with in such patients, as they may dismiss the notion of having any difficulty with the therapist going away—such is their need to please.

The Dependent Patient

Other patients, having been seriously emotionally neglected, may sometimes relate to the therapist in a rather dependent manner, as in this example of the patient who came in and immediately expressed her gratitude for being referred to Dr. X.

> Patient: I'm so glad I came to see you. I know for sure you can help me. I am a burden to everyone. There are so many people with real problems, and here's me!

The therapist, Dr. X, becomes aware that the patient has already begun to idealize her, but also that she places responsibility on her by her warning that she can be a burden, and yet trivializes her problems. The patient's nonverbal language and tone of voice are taken into account—they have a child-like dependent quality, with an evident need to please and be seen as pleasing.

If the therapist is put off by her manner and tone of voice, she may distance herself, but this will only result in increasing the patient's insecurity, anxiety, and clinginess, or she may withdraw. She may also resort to increased self-harm or drug use, in order to feel soothed. This behavior is illustrated by Bella in Chapter 4, who in the early stages when her attitude was one of helplessness and neediness, responded to her perceived rejection by the therapist with increased self-harm and demandingness.

The Ambivalent Patient

When a patient comes to the first session conveying a sense of wariness or uncertainty, the therapist's task is to try to create some sense of comfort, as in this example of an 18-year-old who presented for therapy. The telephone referral, instigated by his mother, indicated that he was experiencing unmanageable changes in mood, intermittent suicidal ideation, and difficulties at school.

Standing at the threshold of the therapist's office with a grimace on his face, he looked like he would rather not be there. The following conversation ensued.

Therapist: Would you like to come in, Gary? (*He looked uncertain.*)

Therapist: (*Observing Gary, asks in a tentative though questioning way*) Looks like you would rather not be here?

Gary: My mother insisted that I should come.

Therapist: (*Pause, then in agreeable tone*) Yes! You always do what your mother says?

Gary: (*Broke into a smile, a mixture of embarrassment and recognition* [which was talked about a little later], *to which the therapist similarly responded with a smile.*)

Therapist: You're here, that's the main thing. Can we sit down and talk about what's happening?

They both sat down and there was a moment of humor that made Gary feel a little less uncomfortable than he did at the start. The positive aspect of Gary's attendance was also pointed out. Ambivalence, it is to be noted, can be present in a number of different ways.

The Disorganized/Dissociative Patient

When patients become angry in the first session, the therapist is often taken aback. What can this be about, the therapist asks him- or herself. However, when this anger alternates with overwhelming helplessness, superficial cooperation, or even seductiveness or lapses in reasoning or in general discourse, it can be extremely disorganizing for the therapist.

The therapist must maintain an empathic stance and be accepting of the patient's anger, even if it is not understood. The predominant affect needs to be discussed. If the patient is disorganized and dissociating, the therapist will necessarily have to stay with the patient, responding with language that is broken up, in ways similar to the language of the patient. Thus a point may be reached when language changes and there is a capacity, even if short-lived, for a dyadic exchange. Establishing connection is the main aim.

It is important that the therapist stay alert, particularly in areas of the frame such as timeliness, not making him- or herself too available and not becoming prone to rescue fantasies. On the contrary, to become antagonistic toward the patient, as in the case of Bella's therapist in Chapter 4 who described feeling like a mouse that is being played with by a cat, would not be helpful. The therapist here is mindful that she does not act on these feelings.

The Fragmenting/Dissociative Patient

There are times when the patient with BPD is confused and confusing, fragmented and incoherent. It becomes the task of the therapist to attune closely even when the words seem to convey only a sense of confusion. The therapist must try to stay with the words and the affective experiences in the moment, reflecting what is most obvious in the fragments, using nonverbal language or short verbal utterances.

It does not help to try to find out the meaning of what is being said, to try to slow the patient down, or to try to make sense, and least of all to let the patient know that he or she is not making sense and that the therapist is confused. Often these patients are prone to dissociate, as we have seen in the case of Bella in Chapter 4, when at first presentation she was repetitive and angry, but at the same time was requesting help.

As the therapeutic relationship is strengthened, striking differences become apparent in the patient's demeanor as he or she becomes clearer, more easily understood, and conversation takes more of a narrative form. The therapist must actively convey a sense of being present with the patient.

Patients with BPD who are functioning on the psychotic end of the spectrum tend to present in this fragmented, dissociative way. They may have micropsychotic episodes both in the beginning and through the early sessions. Therefore the therapist must cautiously stay with, and respond appropriately to, the patient.

Avoiding the use of personal pronouns such as *you*, *I*, or *me* in such situations is important particularly in the early stages when a sense of self and self-differentiation is poorly developed, and when the patient may be highly sensitive. Using neutral language makes it less likely that the patient will perceive criticism where it is not intended. The primary intention is to understand and connect with the patient. In doing so, impersonal phrases such as, "It seems . . . ," or "There is . . . ," or "It's difficult . . . ," or "It's understandable . . . " may be helpful instead of, for example, "*You* find it difficult."

The Suicidal Patient

Another patient may arrive announcing an imminent suicide (as in the case of Bella, in Chapter 4, at her first three sessions), whereupon the therapist is torn between assessing the level of risk and allowing the conversation to take its course. The therapist may respond with something like "I wonder if we can talk about what's happening—I can see how distressed you are."

Yet another patient may come in helpless and defeated, wondering if anyone can help; in which case the therapist, observing the sense of helplessness, may respond with: "It seems like things are really awful, like nothing can change?"

The therapist empathically resonates with what the patient is feeling. Resonance tends to have a containing effect, reducing anxiety and giving the patient a slight feeling perhaps that someone understands and is prepared to listen. The patient is better able to talk about what is so troubling, as the therapist in Chapter 4 finds a way of conveying her understanding of Bella's plight.

PARTICULAR ASPECTS OF THE THERAPEUTIC CONVERSATION

My emphasis in this section is on the particularities of the therapist-patient interaction. Issues of courtesy, confidentiality, and a conversational rather than a questioning style are dealt with. The need to address promptly (without confronting or criticizing) the patient's coming late or failing to attend regularly cannot be overstated. Important areas of culture and ethnicity must be taken into account in the therapeutic exchange.

Greeting

The agenda of the conversation is generally provided by the patient. The therapeutic relationship starts from the very first contact/session. Ways of greeting the patient will vary from therapist to therapist, but if the patient puts his or her hand out to shake yours, it is important to reciprocate the gesture. Cultural and ethnic differences must be noted not only at the first meeting but through the therapy. It is also good practice to observe the patient's reaction to meeting you, the therapist, and to respond accordingly. Common courtesy should be the general practice.

In the first session the patient may spontaneously start to talk. If not, the therapist, after the initial greetings, may say something like this:

> I wonder if we could talk about what brought you to see me. . . . [A few minutes later] I will be taking down a few notes as we talk, and I will want to know some important details about you, so I will be asking you about them and generally will be more active in our conversation. Later, I may only take down an occasional note, but I will also be listening and responding to you. What you have to say is very important, and together we will try to understand what is and has been happening in your life, so that together we can help you feel better.

The patient must be included as a collaborator. It is not a good idea to have one's face buried in notes to the point where face-to-face contact is lost; neither is it a good idea to ask too many questions, thereby cutting off the patient. It is also important that the time is given entirely to the patient, and that phone calls are not received or texts looked at during the therapy hour.

At times the patient may be intrusive, in which case the therapist may need to listen and respond appropriately. Responding to personal questions of the patient, early in therapy, may be fraught with risks, so attempting to look beyond the question will be helpful. Rather than respond by asking a question in return such as "why do you ask?" a balance must be found. When it is vital to obtain certain information in the course of the assessment sessions, the therapist may have to say something like this: "I may have to inquire about a thing or two or find out from you some important information before we go on, or before we finish our session today."

Recording Sessions and Confidentiality

Obtaining permission from the patient to record sessions for supervision is often experienced as difficult, particularly by new therapists. Generally, however, when therapists raise the issue that "supervision is intended to help me to help you, and further, we will be listening to snippets of the session" and assure the patient of confidentiality and the security of the recorded material, most patients give permission. It is not necessary to share details of one's supervisor, as some patients will ask, but rather to answer the question in rather general terms.

The therapist must remember that he or she is offering the patient a valuable service, and that the patient must be approached in a way where neither feels extraordinarily indebted. In rare instances when permission is not given, the therapist can tell the patient that the recorder will still be there, but will not be turned on, and that when the patient feels comfortable about recording, he or she can let the therapist know.

Dependent, accommodating, and caregiving traits may become apparent in the patient's responses to this request. The therapist must take note of these traits, or else they can become an impediment to the therapy. For example, some patients take responsibility for attending sessions because the therapist's successful completion of training depends on it. Others may regard themselves as doing the therapist a favor; still others may feel utterly responsible for attending even when unwell, because they may be letting down the therapist.

When therapists reveal that they are in training and require a training case to fulfill the requirements, they are advised to take care of the manner in which such requests are put to the patient. One training therapist put her request in this way:

> I am a practicing psychotherapist with some experience, and as part of this post-graduate course that I'm undertaking, I am required to see a certain number of patients. Now, we have met for two sessions, I would like to ask you to be my training client/patient. I would need to record our sessions, if you were agreeable, for my supervision. My supervisor will listen to snippets of the tape with me, and we will discuss what's happening, how I am working with you, and how you are responding to me as your therapist. Your confidentiality will be preserved, so that who you are is not known. I will be the only one who can have access to our sessions, and I will delete them some time later. [See also Bella in Chapter 4]

The patient usually agrees as he or she becomes aware of the different aspects of the situation, and may clarify issues if needed.

Questions

Questions are the polar opposite to the style of responding described above (Meares 1993). The borderline patient is frequently bombarded with questions from health professionals. This is not simply a consequence of mental health training but also of the state of relatedness. The patient with BPD, having lived characteristically in a state of alienation and subtle disconnection from others, brings this state of disconnection into new relationships in the medical and psychotherapy setting.

The therapist often begins to feel compelled to ask questions in order to connect; otherwise it seems that the conversation is quite barren. This questioning sets up a particular form of relatedness that is unlike that of selfhood. The dyadic relationship may thereby incite a variety of negative emotions in the patient, including a sense of inferiority and devaluation. Asking questions is an impediment to the movement toward a more mature state of mind.

Remember, a form of relatedness is nearly the same as a form of consciousness.

When the therapist feels that it is necessary to ask questions, or finds him- or herself asking questions, this compulsion should be questioned (silently). Questions often lead to a feeling in the patient of not being understood. Further, questions may result in prolonged silences, when the therapist may have to ponder on how this impasse has come about and how it might be overcome, as illustrated in the case of Bella in Chapter 4. Nevertheless, occasional questions, particularly in the assessment phase, are to be expected.

What Happens When Questions Are Asked?

In considering what happens when questions are asked, the following example is offered:

Sarah: I don't know what else to do (*rather distressed*).

Therapist: What have you done so far?

Sarah: Oh! Saw psychologists, counselors, had CBT, took medications—and the lot! (*Silence ensues; the conversation has been foreclosed. The patient once more sinks into a state of alienation and of despair.*)

Here is a possible alternative response:

Sarah: I don't know what else to do (*rather distressed*).

Therapist: Sounds like wanting to give up. You've been trying . . . and now you're here.

Sarah: I just can't stand feeling this way—I'll do what it takes . . .

Therapist: It's difficult. I can see that you have tried. Perhaps we can talk about the way you're feeling, Sarah.

Why Does the Therapist Ask Questions?

There are times when the therapist feels disconnected and unengaged, and hence attempts to establish connection with a question. This question may sometimes take the patient unawares, particularly if it bears little relevance to what was being talked about. At other times, the therapist is lost for words, cannot think of what to say, and so asks a question to fill in the blanks. Therapists sometimes find that the patient's distress momentarily causes them to tune out, and a question feels like a way of making a connection once again. Others describe asking a question as a way out of the boredom of listening to a patient who is going around in circles and often talking about the same issue.

Questions tend to foreclose further exploration and therefore have the effect of distancing the patient.

There may be many other reasons why therapists ask questions during the course of a long-term therapy. However, it is important to know that there is a place for an occasional question.

When the Patient Is Repeatedly Late or Misses Sessions

It is generally helpful to talk about any failure to observe the frame as soon as possible after its occurrence, taking care not to be too confronting or criticizing of the patient. For example:

- "I missed you for your session the other day."
- "It is important that we talk about your not paying fees regularly."
- "When you are often late, I am concerned that you are not getting the benefit of a whole session, because, as you know, we finish the session at the usual time."

In cases where the patient frequently comes late or misses sessions, it helps to look at the last session with the patient to see if there might be a reason to explain this, as in: "I'm wondering if there was something about our last session that perhaps created some difficulty." Each therapist addresses the issue of patients failing to attend without giving notice on an individual basis. The importance of addressing this issue early cannot be overstated, since much of the therapy depends on maintaining the frame and the patient's regular attendance.

Establishing a frame is vital to the conduct of a successful therapy. However, too much flexibility or too much rigidity can be a hindrance.

In the example (above) of Sarah, the therapist tries to address the issue of the frame. Sarah attended three sessions and did not come for the next; the therapist contacted Sarah about her nonattendance. Sarah apologized, gave no really good reason, then came for two more sessions, missing the next. Once more the therapist telephoned and Sarah once again apologized and promised to be there for her next appointment. The therapist attempted to talk about it with her in the following way:

Therapist: I'm really uncertain of what to think when you don't come—because you've never told me you won't come, or that you do not wish to come. I'm really not sure about this!

Sarah: That's how I feel too. I'm not sure each time I see you. I don't feel when I'm here like I don't want to come next time.

Therapist: You feel the same way too! You don't feel like it in the session—perhaps after the session something comes up? It's good we have talked about it. Perhaps we can keep it mind and continue to talk.

Unconscious repetitions of forms of relatedness to significant others are always at play in these circumstances. Disjunctions in the conversation may also go unnoticed. Raising the issue of failure to attend, as early as possible, gives the therapeutic dyad an opportunity to process material connected with such failures. Leaving the responsibility solely with the patient to talk about these matters may, in fact, foreclose any opportunity to get to know what may be happening in the relationship from one session to the next. This may also result in the patient dropping out of therapy.

Those therapists who use a third party to make appointments, etc., are advised that these issues become the responsibility of the therapist and no other person, so that the confidentiality of the patient is preserved. Also, and importantly, the possibility of uncovering the rich dynamics at play will be lost. Hence care and promptness are essential when handling sensitive issues of fees, attendance, holidays, breaks, etc. Leaving these issues to simmer may be interpreted differently by different patients or treated with total indifference.

SPECIALIZED CONCEPTS

In this section I deal with important concepts such as the Expectational Field (Meares, 2000), in which an unwary therapist, in working with the dissociating patient, might find him/herself grappling with reversals and stimulus entrapment, from which the therapist must help the patient find a way out by creating the conditions necessary for the chronicle to be changed. I will also discuss the need to continue to work in the relationship, as soon as safety is ensured and the patient has been able to respond positively to linking statements, and the role of traumatic intrusions in creating disjunctions, which can also be the result of lapses in the therapist and momentary failure of attunement.

The Expectational Field

The patient's unconscious expectations are quite prominent at the beginning of therapy, and may also be noticed some time later. The therapist should be able to monitor his or her personal experience during the first meeting and thereafter. Parallel streams of processing ensue as a result. The therapist's subjective experience of the patient is registered and thought about, while appropriate responses are being made. He or she may notice fleetingly the effect of the expectational field, however slight this feeling may be.

The therapist may begin to sense that he or she has a part to play in a particular form of relatedness, as can be noted in the case of Bella in Chapter 4. Bella has an expectation that she will be rejected in the very first session, which is related to her lifelong experience of rejection and abandonment, which leads her to expect nothing different and the therapist herself feeling undecided about continuing to see her. This indecision may be unconsciously communicated to Bella in fairly subtle ways, and Bella reacts to what she believes will happen anyway, both as a result of her own expectations and the unverbalized expectation of the therapist—who can be described as unconsciously playing host to the feelings of rejection. However, Bella has always experienced rejection, therefore she has no reason to expect anything different. She expects the therapist will reject her after the assessment and is relieved that this is not so.

The negative effect of the expectational field may be averted when the therapist becomes aware of it, as in the following example of Sarah, in which the therapist feels a pressure to call Sarah lazy, but his awareness of this reaction makes him respond differently.

Sarah: My mother is forever saying that I am lazy (*it's not the first time she has mentioned this; her tone of voice is complaining*). I just didn't get going that day—did only one of the tasks I set myself, then I watched TV, had something to eat and went to bed—just didn't achieve anything.

Therapist: I get the feeling that there is an expectation that I too would call you lazy?

Sarah: Of course you should—you would be thinking it anyway!

Therapist: You were just telling me that your mother was always calling you lazy—I guess you expect that I too would think you're lazy. (*The therapist links what is just said with what he said earlier and what the patient also believed as a result of her mother always referring to her as lazy.*)

This exchange, providing a linking in relationship (see "The Story of A Therapeutic Relationship" on page 45), had the effect of opening Sarah up to talking about her experiences and feelings toward her mother's constant devaluing remarks and repeated accusations that she is lazy, which get them into frequent arguments.

Consider how this exchange might have gone if the therapist were caught unaware in the field and responded something like this:

Therapist: Sounds like you were feeling lazy and didn't get much done.

Sarah: (*Taking offense*) So you too think I'm lazy!

A disjunction has occurred that now needs to be repaired. The therapist later realizes that Sarah has an unconscious expectation that she will always be criticized.

Dissociation

When a therapist encounters a patient with severe BPD for the first time, it is not uncommon to also enter into a mild but overt dissociative state, sharing the condition of the patient. The patient characteristically lacks coherence; there is a lack of continuity and loss of sense of time, with a mix of time past and time present.

This mix makes it difficult for the therapist, who may note a subtle sense of discomfort or even a feeling of daze, as experienced by the therapist in the case of Bella in Chapter 4. The therapist seems to be trying to work out what is happening and experiences a sense of helplessness similar to the patient's—a momentary restriction of consciousness. The therapist can be of no help in such a state. In the case of Bella, the therapist was unaware of it until the next day.

A balance must be struck between "being with" the dissociating patient and "getting into" the dissociative state.

Making short verbal utterances, soothing sounds, and the like, will help the patient know that you are there—someone is there—the therapist. The patient who is in a state of alienation needs to be helped to reconnect rather than dissociate further.

Beginning therapists or those who have not had the experience of working with dissociative patients often do not recognize this state. Similarly, dissociation occurs frequently in hospital patients, but is under-recognized. This failure to recognize the dissociation contributes often, and perhaps largely, to the lack of understanding given to those with BPD, in whom dissociation is a characteristic.

Staying on the edge of the dissociation and *being with* is preferable to trying to make meaning of the patient's conversation in this dissociated state. If the therapist gets too far into the dissociative experience, trying to establish what it is about, it will inevitably result in the therapist's also becoming dissociated and therefore of no help. This topic is also discussed later in this chapter under comorbidity.

Reversals

A puzzling kind of presentation involves the phenomenon of reversal in which the patient, caught in the system of unconscious traumatic memory, is as if "inhabited" by the figure of the traumatizing other (Meares, 1993). The patient's demeanor may become somewhat frightening and the voice harsh and domineering, creating an initial feeling ranging from unease to a period of shock, particularly when it happens suddenly. The example below illustrates this experience.

A man with BPD in his 30s sobbed in the first session as he told the therapist of his miserable past. The therapist was touched and responded empathically; a few minutes later the therapist described feeling small and insignificant as the patient said in a harsh voice, "What on earth do you think you can do? You're hardly out of medical school, eh?" In later sessions with this patient, it became clear that his father could not bear to see his son's confidence in himself. He would "shoot" him down whenever his son asserted himself in his presence.

Stimulus Entrapment

Stimulus entrapment (Meares, 1997) is a common problem in BPD. The individual is outer-oriented and speaks endlessly about problems at work, about the family, and about the world around. Although all of these incidents seem important and need to be recounted, there is within the patient a sense of deadness allied with a feeling of nonconnection between the conversational partners.

Rather than just attempt to change the subject or to merely wait, the therapist must "stay with" what is given, try to approach it as if the patient were talking of a dream, and try to elaborate the experience in a similar way. The therapist, then, maintains what Hobson (1985) called a "symbolical attitude." One might begin by repeating the conversation, in a somewhat different tone of voice, as if pondering, trying to find the *shape* of what is being expressed. In listening to the catalogue of complaints that make up the stimulus entrapment, it is easy to conclude that the patient is merely talking about events, "out there" rather than more personal experience.

However, it must be borne in mind that the patient, in giving this account, has made a selection from the multitude of events he or she has experienced. Choices have been made that are necessarily personal. Within these choices the therapist may discern some idea, some image, some feeling that gives him or her an inkling of an underlying state that allows the therapist to work with the patient toward something of an *inner* state. See also the example of Sarah later in this chapter.

Changing the Chronicle

The way in which the therapist arrives at the idea that is expressed when listening intently to the "chronicle" of a stimulus-entrapped patient depends upon the attainment of a particular state of mind in which it is possible to ponder over what is going on between the two partners at a given moment (Meares, 1998). Not only is a catalogue being told—it is being told to somebody. It is clear in the case of Bella, as described by the therapist, that it was difficult to follow her and to attain a state of mind that was necessary for that to happen.

Coupling with something that the patient says may help to interrupt the chronicle. For example: "There is a lot happening; I can see how difficult it is for you." Or "You mentioned your friends. I wonder if we can talk about what it was like with them." This approach is evident in the case of 24-year-old Sarah, described later in this chapter. Sarah presented with multiple somatic complaints and chronic pain. She also had a diagnosis of BPD. Session after session Sarah launched into a litany of complaints about her painful feet and joints, her back pain and the migraines. She was trapped in painful physical stimuli with a total lack of feeling language.

> Sarah: Woke up with a terrible migraine. I simply could not even drag myself out of bed to close the blinds. The sun was making it worse. The back pain also didn't allow any moving. My first thought was to take some medication, but then someone would have to be there to give it to me—it goes on all the time.
>
> Therapist: The back pain . . . must make it very difficult for you . . . moving. I sense it makes you really frustrated . . . not being able to do the things you want to do.

The therapist empathically resonates with the patient here and repeats what is most prominent in the patient's words, putting an emphasis on them and giving them affective expression, by the use of such words as *difficult* and *frustrating*. The patient is unable to put words to affect. It is this lack of affect that creates the sense of boredom that is described by therapists who work with such patients.

Therapists are often bewildered by the lack of apparent distress in the patient who ceaselessly complains. What to say? When to say? How to say whatever is said? These are the questions most therapists find themselves asking when they are faced with a patient who, session after session, continues complaining. The therapist often describes feeling "on the out" with such patients, or worse still, not even there.

In spite of this apparent impasse the therapist must take an interest and try to attune to the patient in both nonverbal and verbal responses, as in "That must make it difficult for you" or "It must be hard to focus on the things you want to do." By adopting this attitude, the therapist often finds that the chronicle of complaints gradually decreases. In the later stages the patient begins to make links with his or her developmental history, as when Sarah said this:

> I remembered one morning as I was getting out of bed—my mother was in a similar situation. She would stay in bed all day, and often when we came home

from school, we would have to keep perfectly silent. We almost looked after ourselves, my brother and I, until my father came from work—which was often quite late—and then again in the morning. I remember this continued till I left home. I remember thinking, my mother doesn't care about anyone but herself. I know you think that's awful, but that's what I felt.

The therapist, in attempting to put words to what might be the predominant affect, helps the patient to experience consciously what has hitherto been unconscious. Sarah has developed a sense that the therapist could be trusted to listen to her and accept her without criticism and is better able to get more in touch with affects that she once avoided.

Staying with and Linking in Relationship

The therapist must stay close to the immediate experience of the patient, linking what the patient says and what the therapist says in the present relationship (Meares, 2005). The therapist's subjective experience of the patient dictates the use of linking. Links are not directly made with past relationships, i.e., "you feel that I think you are lazy because your mother always called you lazy." That is, they are not actively compared with the past relationship, though the nature of the present is, in fact, a result of the past. Linking differs broadly from interpretations in this way. Conflicts and defences are also dealt with in this way, and not interpreted. Linking may be compared with what some models may describe as transference interpretations; the way linking is done may differ, as in the illustration below. Linking is done when a measure of safety has been achieved in the therapeutic relationship. Linking often leads to a shift in the patient's capacity for narrative.

It is important to note that interpretations—genetic, resistance, conflicts, and defense interpretations—are not a feature of CM.

The following is an example of linking in relationship in the case of Sarah, who after a number of sessions characterized by a litany of complaints, mostly to do with pain, seemed to relate to the therapist in a way that was quite different from usual—there was more affect present. Note that it is a step-wise technique. The therapist works gradually with what the patient can manage.

Sarah: What if there's hostility? Because it is too much.

Therapist: It must be difficult to tell, when there's this question of hostility (*tentative, questioning*) because it's too much?

Note the absence of personal pronouns in both the patient's conversation and the therapist's response. Note that the therapist uses the patient's words in a tone that is tentatively questioning, and therefore is not merely a repetition but an amplification of what the patient is saying. The patient then uses a personal pronoun, and the therapist has a subjective sense of being included in what follows.

Sarah: What if I talk about these things and there's hostility because it's too much (*pause*), too much to deal with?

Therapist: It seems that there's a doubt whether I might feel hostile toward you, that you may be too much for me (*By introducing the pronouns "I" and "You" where hitherto only the impersonal "it" was used, the therapist links what the patient says with what she [therapist] says—the subtlety of this technique serves to help the patient open up, as explained later in this chapter, and in this sense differs from interpretation*).

The function of linking is to increase the patient's capacity for self-reflection—a widening of consciousness—and therefore the ability to talk about his/her traumatic experiences. The development of insight is a by-product and is not considered the main aim of therapy.

This linking in the relationship enabled Sarah to couple her fear of hostility in the therapy situation with the memories of hostility that resulted if she needed help from her mother when she was a young child. She recalled memories of abuse and expressed an intense fear of abandonment. Sarah does this without the therapist having to make reference to her trauma. In future, the therapist does make references to her trauma whenever it is necessary for her to connect.

Memories of such experiences are stored in a system of traumatic memory, recorded as facts about oneself and the other, and disconnected from the original events. Making links in the current relationship enables retrieval of memories of relationships that were chronically hostile, in which the patient as a child had to be extremely careful about letting her needs be known (Haliburn, 2011).

I have previously mentioned that this type of linking is preferably not done too early in the therapy, as the patient may not be quite ready to consciously experience the intimacy of the transference relationship. Neither should it be left too late; it may cause the therapy to maintain a kind of impersonality that does not help to move it forward; or one or both partners in the dyad may experience a feeling of being stuck. In either case the therapist needs to examine his or her own attitude. The therapist must examine his/her own attitudes of avoidance of certain issues, so that he/she does not collude with the patient and keep traumatic material out of conscious awareness and therefore out of the conversation.

Working in the relationship after such linking is done is an essential aspect of the model, and the language used from impersonal in the early stages to more personal at this stage is one that fosters a different kind of relationship.

Links can thereafter be made within the same session or with something that might have been said in another session; links can also be made with things and people outside or with things that have been said about the present and the past. It will be noted that more freedom is experienced than previously in the relationship. This linking helps the patient's consciousness to widen to incorporate a number of possibilities. When links are made with what the therapist says and what the patient says (or does not directly say, as in the example above), noticeable shifts are seen, moving the therapy forward.

Disjunctions

There are times in the therapeutic conversation when the therapist may be misattuned—that is attuned to a particular aspect of the conversation, rather than another aspect that is more emotionally significant. The patient may react in a variety of ways. Some patients may react subtly, as in a change of affect, a change of topic, or a brief silence. Others may go on as if they had not noticed—they react by accommodating to the therapist. There is a loss of vitality in all of these patients. However, there are others who may appeal to the therapist in these circumstances by amplifying their distress to a point where it is too conspicuous to ignore. These reactions are often repetitions of similar ways of handling difficult situations/ relationships in the early environment. If this disjunction happens repeatedly in the therapeutic situation, it would not be much different from what the person may have experienced in his or her earlier years.

The experience of not being understood, of not being listened to or taken seriously, is all too common in the life histories of the patient with BPD.

Catastrophic reactions can be particularly difficult when the patient is expressing thoughts of self-harm or suicidal ideation, creating a sense of urgency that can be disturbing for the novice therapist. Here again the therapist must pay particular attention to the frame, avoiding rescue fantasies and incessant availability. Bella, in Chapter 4, is a good example of this dynamic. She threatened to take overdoses whenever she did not feel heard or understood.

If it is noticed, the therapist can repair the disjunction by an apology, as in "That wasn't helpful," or "I missed what you were trying to tell me," or "I'm sorry that wasn't right on my part." Generally, patients value the fact that the therapist is able to offer an apology after he or she has made a mistake—something they have never experienced.

This kind of repair is important as a "corrective emotional experience" (Alexander & French, 1946). It indicates a different form of relatedness to that experienced in the past. A disjunction very often is not merely an "error" on the part of the therapist (though it can be, when the therapist is not listening or otherwise preoccupied) but a marker of unconscious traumatic memory (discussed in the next section).

WORKING WITH THE TRAUMA SYSTEM

Although the therapist must be constantly aware of intrusions of traumatic memory into the therapeutic conversation, and the need to process this constellation of malignant ideation (Meares, 2005), there must also be an awareness of the patient's fear of reexperiencing the trauma and of reentering the trauma zone.

Systems of avoidance are built around this zone in order to protect the person from the extreme anxiety and distress associated with remembering traumatic experience. The therapist must make clear, both implicitly and at times explicitly, that entry into this experience will be determined by what the patient feels he or she can manage. Otherwise the patient may develop a fear of the therapy itself, thereby impeding progress. The patient knows, implicitly, that continuing avoidance is likely to be deleterious but at the same time fears revelation might be even more deleterious and re-traumatizing.

The therapist must be able to manage and balance these two imperatives: the fear of disclosing and the fear of avoiding disclosure.

It is often helpful to give an explanation to the patient of the concept of the unconscious traumatic memory system. The language should be very simple; the model of the hierarchy of consciousness is used to give this explanation. The explanation can be given in the initial outline of the therapeutic objective. It may also be given at a time when a rather mild traumatic intrusion occurs, and when the therapeutic partners are able to discuss what has happened in a way that allows some reflection.

It is the patient's agenda that governs the directions of the therapeutic conversation. The therapist must not feel that every trauma needs to be discovered and processed—in other words, the therapist must not pounce. The therapist does not have to know everything and should not feel that the work is not being done properly unless all traumatic material has been thoroughly worked through.

Therapeutic zeal in the hunt for traumatic memories involves the ever-present danger of retraumatization.

Clinical evidence suggests that integration goes on when the self system is established, and that beneficial change does not depend on insight. What is necessary is the capacity for self-reflection, which develops with the widening of consciousness as therapy proceeds.

In the following section, I alert the therapist to be aware of traumatic memories that become evident early in therapy, and to be cautious about processing these memories before safety is established. With some patients traumatic memories intrude quite early, disrupting the conversation, as in the example below of Sally.

When Traumatic Memory Is Evident Early in Therapy

From the very beginning of therapy, traumatic memory is operative. The therapist's eventual aim is to integrate this form of psychic material, often experienced as alien and intrusive, into the larger system of self, which has a different "shape" (Meares 2005).

Self is a state of mind that is both nonlinear and coherent, whereas the trauma system is linear and fragmented. In order to achieve integration of the trauma, the self system must first be in place. Priority, therefore, is given to the development of the self system. Those moments when traumatic memory shows itself early in therapy are not, in general, processed because at this stage, the patient is unlikely to have access to sufficient reflective function.

Several different courses of action are more usually chosen. They include (1) letting the moment pass; (2) making some acknowledgment that something has changed, as a "marker" opening the way to a later and more extensive and intensive focus; and (3) repair.

An example is useful here. The therapist notices that his patient is almost pleased with herself as she starts to talk about something she has done. But this self-satisfaction is almost instantly overridden by a negative statement that lowers the patient's affect and injects a feeling of helplessness.

If this happens very early in therapy, the therapist decides to register it, but lets the moment pass, because it will happen again. In the case where the patient appears to be receptive, the therapist draws attention to it, as in: "There was a feeling of joy . . . there—a positive feeling there . . . but very quickly there was something negative that changed it." If this statement is inadvertently offered too early, the patient may ignore the response, becoming silent or upset. The therapist must try to repair the situation in ways discussed above.

Evidence of Intrusion of Unconscious Traumatic Memory

Intrusions of traumatic memory can be triggered by the therapist's responses or by internal events. Some of the indications of the emergence of the unconscious traumatic memory system (e.g., change in bodily feelings, bodily posture, and facial expression; change in language; change in subject and content to that which is negative) are described in Chapter 4.

Memories of traumatic events may intrude into the therapeutic conversation quite unexpectedly, creating a sense of shock and sometimes of confusion. The therapist has to be careful not to express these reactions openly, as they may have a negative effect on the patient. The following is an example of internal events in Sally triggering traumatic memories.

Sally was talking about her family when she mentioned her brother. She was immediately overcome by a look of fear as she blurted out: "Don't you ever tell a soul about what we did—you won't hear the end of it." The therapist was confused because what Sally said came "out of the blue"—it had no connection with what she was saying, and did not match how she said it. In addition, it seemed to derail the conversation. It was almost as if she were she was speaking out in the midst of an abusive situation.

The therapist wondered for a moment if Sally was trying to tell her that her brother had abused her, but instead asked no questions, only tuned into Sally's affect, saying, "You are afraid . . . very afraid . . . but you are safe now." Sally looked down and began to weep silently, as the therapist comforted her with soothing sounds. Sally continued: "You don't expect your own brother to do something like that." Sobbing almost uncontrollably, Sally talked of her brother abusing her as a teenager and threatening her to maintain secrecy, knowing that she had also been abused as a child by their father.

When emotion suddenly intensifies in a session, it is a sign that the therapist is dealing with a hitherto unacknowledged trauma.

PROCESSING TRAUMA

The therapist does not attempt processing trauma until a certain level of reflective function is evident. The presence of this reflective function indicates that there has been some positive development in the therapeutic relationship in the form of trust and therefore in the sense of self.

The processing of trauma takes place both in and out of the therapeutic relationship. It is not confined only to traumatic memories that arise in the session; it also involves difficult interpersonal events occurring outside the therapy. There may be fragments of memories that are initially mentioned, followed by scenes of the traumatic episodes, and of people involved. What has just happened between the conversational partners is laid out, beginning with the conversation and the feeling.

This phase might move into more descriptive material, but what is most important is that the therapist does not search out details, as stressed earlier, but rather helps contain the patient while listening to the story. As associations emerge, the patient may remember similar incidents in the past, whereupon the therapist may link affects in the here-and-now with those experienced in the past. Ways of adapting to difficult earlier situations may be repeated in the therapy and can provide really fertile ground for exploration.

Repair of Disjunctions and Restoration

When reflective function is not evident, traumatic intrusions provide an impediment to the conversation. In this case, the therapist's acknowledgment of the part he or she has played in precipitating a negative affect or simply changing his or her manner of responsiveness will tend to restore the relationship. Repeated misattunement, if left unaddressed, can interfere with regulation and self-cohesion. In the case of Bella, in Chapter 4, early in therapy, threats or actual self-harming behavior occurred whenever she did not feel listened to. This was in contrast with the later stage of therapy, when these disjunctions could be understood, talked about, and repaired in the safety of the therapeutic relationship.

The Language of Processing

Recognizing that the patient with BPD is functioning on a lower level on the hierarchy of consciousness, the therapist must closely align his or her language to that of the patient. If the patient's language is fragmented, the therapist responds with single words, phrases, vocal utterances, and nonverbal gestures, expressions, and movement. By closely aligning with the patient's experience, the therapist begins to realize what suits the patient best. As the patient talks about his or her traumatic experiences and the therapist responds appropriately, a space is created in between where things are pondered, looked at, and talked about. The language, which differs from patient to patient, should not be intrusive, nor should it have the effect of shaming the patient.

Failure in Processing

Several factors may contribute to a failure in processing whatever is emerging in the session: a fear of reexperiencing the trauma and consequent avoidance; a sense of overwhelming guilt because disclosure is seen to be tantamount to betrayal; the loss of attachment to the other, even though pathological; and the fear of change. All these factors make the processing of trauma difficult and can lead to impasse, if the therapist is unaware. The case of Marguerite (in Chapter 6), whose depressed parents could not tolerate her vitality, illustrates how she pathologically accommodated in order to maintain attachment (though hurtful) to them.

Particular Difficulties When Processing Trauma

In this section I talk about the processing of trauma, which is about the therapist's responsiveness to the patient's disclosures of past experiences, remembering that working through is being done in the present. It is most often a difficult time for the therapy, which can come up against impasses—both as a result sometimes of an error on the part of the therapist or as a result of the intrusion of traumatic memory. When the patient is attached to his or her traumatic experience (explained below, and also in Chapter 4), or when there is severe separation anxiety even at the thought that therapy will one day come to an end, difficulties are experienced.

Impasse

At times, the conversation may seem to be stuck. This awareness may come from the therapist alone, or both partners may be aware that they have been going around in circles. If the therapist is unaware, particularly if a disjunction has been unnoticed, it creates more difficulty, and the impasse may be prolonged and the possibility of change minimized.

Careful thought on the part of the therapist is vital. The therapist may wonder, with the patient, if he or she has overlooked something important or misunderstood what the patient has said. If it is neither of these, it is still important for the therapist to raise the fact of an impasse occurring, saying something to this effect: "It seems to me that we have been going around in circles. Does it seem like that for you?" This approach may enable both to become more aware that there may be difficult issues to be talked about that have the potential to provoke painful affects such as shame in the patient. When carefully done, intervening in this way helps further exploration with less defensiveness on the part of the patient.

At other times the impasse may be the result of the patient's anxiety about the possibility of change, and therefore paradoxically finding safety in his or her traumatic memories, clinging to them, metaphorically speaking, rather than processing them and moving toward the development of a more self-reflective capacity and a better sense of self.

This issue will need to be addressed carefully, because embedded within the fear of letting go of traumatic experience is often the positive feeling toward the traumatizing yet loving other, leading to ambivalence toward the relationship, which adds to the complexity of the task at hand. The therapist has to provide for another experience in which he or she appreciates the patient's capacity to form a different kind of relatedness that would lead to the capacity to find self. Attachment to the trauma is one of many causes of impasse and needs to be explored and addressed if the therapy is to move forward.

Dependency and Attachment to the Trauma

There is often fear on the part of the therapist that the already-dependent patient will become overly dependent, and that the dependency will become hard to shift. The therapist must accept the dependent patient and be willing to understand him or her. Distancing strategies can only serve to increase the patient's anxiety and therefore produce an impediment to the therapy, resulting frequently in impasse and often premature termination.

Alternatively, when it is difficult for the dependent patient to leave, the therapy may continue unproductively. The way in which the therapist communicates often provides a model for reflective function. When the therapist first becomes aware of the patient's dependent traits, care must be taken to develop an understanding together as to why these traits make sense. Without this understanding, errors and unhelpful attitudes will be likely.

There are times when patients are preoccupied with their traumatic experiences at the expense of other experiences in their lives. They describe a vague sense of apprehension, emptiness, anxiety, and boredom when not involved in activities reminiscent of the trauma. Reliving the trauma repeatedly in therapy may only serve to reinforce this preoccupation.

Aloneness, Fear of Abandonment, and Separation Anxiety

Many patients with BPD describe experiencing deeply painful aloneness, accompanied by intense anxiety and despair that this feeling will never go away. It is often manifest in severe cases, where the patient is unable to manage between sessions. In these cases it would be helpful to temporarily increase the frequency from two to three sessions a week. If necessary, the therapist may also arrange to make contact by telephone at set times between sessions.

Breaks such as weekends and holidays can be fraught with difficulty and will need to be thought about; arrangements must be made to help the patient manage during these times. Feelings of loneliness are often also accompanied by a sense of emptiness; it becomes clear that such patients have not been able to maintain a stable sense of another for all or most of their lives—the therapist included. Physical objects from the therapist's office, such as a visiting card or a message, may help the patient stabilize; in some cases it may be essential to provide contact with another therapist in your absence. These are times when patients more often fall apart, self-harm, or experience escalating suicidal ideation.

Processing the anxiety that these patients experience often reveals that their early environments lacked sensitive and responsive parenting, resulting in the absence of a sufficiently secure sense of relatedness to a significant other. This absence leads to separation anxiety and chronic fears of abandonment, now being repeated with the therapist.

INTEGRATION

The primary aim of the therapist is to help the patient, as much as possible, achieve the stability of integration. In order for this to happen, the development of the self system is the major priority and then the trauma has to be integrated into the self system, so that it is no longer dissociated but woven into the history of the patient. When self is established, autobiographical memory is possible and, with it, the affects experienced. The patient experiences a higher order of consciousness, is more capable of feeling, and gradually becomes more capable of containing hitherto split-off affects.

This section explores the development of a sense of cohesion, the capacity for reflective awareness, and a solid and stable sense of personal existing, which are prominent among those aspects of self that failed to mature as a result of deficits in the early caregiving environment. Self develops *in relationship*, as illustrated well in the case of Bella in Chapter 4, in which the therapist helped Bella achieve integration.

Aspects of Integration

In this section the many aspects of integration are discussed. A sense of cohesion heralds the development of a dualistic consciousness, when the patient can look at and talk about aspects of him/herself in relation to others, and vice versa. Conversation attains mostly a narrative quality and painful memories can be talked about without fear of fragmentation as traumatic affects are addressed and self-regulation improves. The safety of the therapeutic relationship is generalized with improved capacity for engaging safely in other relationships, as maladaptive coping styles are changed and the patient adapts to his/her environment with a sense of agency and autonomy. Integration is also about bringing together the dissociated parts so that they are no longer experienced as separate.

The Development of Cohesion and Self-Reflectivity

As therapy proceeds, there is a widening of consciousness, an ascent up the hierarchy of mental life, and an improved sense of cohesion as the patient develops a dualistic consciousness and is able to link the past, including the distant past, with the present. This is well illustrated in the case of Bella, in Chapter 4, where both she and the therapist ponder the changes Bella has made.

Development of Narrative and Symbolic Transformation

The development of narrative and symbolic transformation allows for the integration of traumatic memories that have been previously split off and identified in earlier sessions. These painful memories can then be talked about without fragmentation, and there is an improved capacity to engage safely in relationships, and an improved capacity to sustain affects previously dealt with by the use of strategies once adaptive, but no longer so.

The development of dual consciousness, involving mental flexibility and awareness of self and other, gives the patient a sense of being actively engaged as protagonist in his or her own life. Ultimately, in a successful therapy the emergence of narrative capacity is part of the larger consciousness of self—the phenomenon of symbolic transformation that allows integration to occur, when the patient can talk about the trauma, albeit with a sense of sadness, perhaps a sense of loss (for what could have been) but without the fear of fragmentation. Bella, in Chapter 4, is a good illustration of this transition from a state of stimulus entrapment to one in which she is capable of narrative and the use of metaphor, as in *The Phantom of the Opera*.

The Capacity to Remember Traumatic Events without Fragmenting

One of the main aims of psychotherapy with patients who have BPD is integration. Trauma that has hitherto been dissociated is remembered and becomes part of the individual's history, but not relived as an actual experience, time and time again. Bella's case is a good example of such a patient achieving this ability.

In this stage of therapy the patient is able to look back at traumatic experiences with sadness, regret, or disappointment but without falling apart. The patient may also consider resolution (1) via forgiveness of a parent or significant other, (2) by coming to terms with his or her experience, or (3) sometimes by separating from those associated with the trauma. Each individual patient resolves such situations in his or her own way.

Retrieval of the core affective memory of the trauma—in the form of fear, helplessness, betrayal, intimidation, and shame—which have been isolated can now be named and worked through. Bella provides a good illustration of what is being talked about. The example of Sally is described here. Toward the end of her therapy Sally was able to put together fragments of memories previously talked about, but in much more of a narrative form, and without the distress that she had first experienced.

She talked of the house in which she had grown up, and with it, feelings of dread as a shadowy figure approached her and abused her time after time, till she was almost 10 years old and her father was removed from the home.

Sally: I was barely 4 years old. I remember, because we each got our own rooms. How could he? He was supposed to take care of us.

Therapist: You were helpless at the time—just 4 years old—there's a sense of being betrayed, when someone who is supposed to take care of you, abuses you.

Sally: (*Looking at the therapist perhaps for some clarification*) I don't understand it—he was really loving.

Therapist: It would have been confusing for you.

Sally: Could I be dreaming? Could I have made this up?

Therapist: You are distressed by this, but you are also questioning yourself. You are wondering how someone, who is supposed to love you and care for you, could abuse you in the ways you have described.

The Capacity to Integrate Affects and Regulate Self

When affect states are unintegrated or unregulated, mental life may become disrupted and affects experienced as threats to one's own psychic life. And, because affects play an important part as an organizing principle in human behavior, it becomes necessary for the patient to become aware of his or her affects, painful ones included.

The threat of annihilation in some situations causes the walling off of affects and the compartmentalization of different states. Sally often presented in different self states, and there was one, which she affectionately called "my baby," to which she clung till well into the therapy. The therapist was able to help her see herself as an adult, looking at and needing to care for and protect herself as a baby—the baby that was abused and neglected instead of being cared for.

Patients become increasingly aware of their need to ward off difficult affects and the ways in which they do so. They become aware, with the help of the therapist, to consider new ways of dealing with these difficult affect states, because previous coping styles have become maladaptive. When Bella becomes aware of her sense of aloneness and talks about it, she recognizes the *shame of her neediness*. Shame is one of those affects that is often experienced as intolerable;

anything that has the capacity to provoke shame is disavowed and walled off from consciousness. With the therapist's help, shame can be recognized and talked about at last.

When there are indications that the patient might be experiencing a sense of shame, the therapist can tentatively ask, "I wonder if that was embarrassing?" If the patient gives the impression that the therapist is on his or her "wavelength," it becomes necessary to tune into the affect whenever it becomes apparent, using a somewhat similar remark, building up to what is seen to be tolerable for the patient, who may reply, "It was really embarrassing—in fact, shameful."

What was previously walled off from consciousness seems to be more available to be recognized by the patient, who is then able to talk about the shame that was experienced earlier. This linking is helpful because it enables the patient and therapist to talk about the patient's strivings to avoid being shamed, and it helps the patient become better able to deal with future situations that provoke shame.

Processing the shame from early life experiences—its repetitions and surrounding contexts—and seeing it from an adult perspective helps the patient understand that his or her current shamefulness in fact originated in situations of being chronically shamed as a child. In past interpersonal situations, when there was no one from whom to seek refuge, the patient may have had to manage in the circumstances. Now the patient has an opportunity to process it and put it back where it belongs—disown it—rather than regard it as part of self—a bad self.

The therapist needs to help the patient retrieve the affective memory of the trauma. This is done by creating safety, by taking care not to inadvertently provoke shame, and by maintaining an ability to think while experiencing emotion. Retrieving affective memory further enables self-cohesion and a further capacity to trust and develop intimacy. With the help of the therapist the patient becomes more capable of experiencing emotion and connecting with affects formerly dissociated, such as helplessness, despair, betrayal, shame, aloneness, and fear.

The Capacity for Integration Expressed as Relatedness

Often in therapy a stage is reached when patients who have had difficulties in relationships, or engaged in promiscuous relationships, become content in a kind of relationship that is different from what they were used to. The sense of safety experienced in the therapeutic relationship and the capacity for intimacy are generalized to the outside world; family relationships experienced as tumultuous now begin to be dealt with differently. Basic trust that was disrupted or undeveloped in the early environment now has the ability to grow, as in this example of Sally's new realization. She was prone to magical thinking, which she used to control a lot of what she said and did, but now she could laugh at herself:

> I never thought it possible. Here I am—I am afraid to say it lest it get spoiled. I feel contented and happy. It seems only a short while ago that I was telling you I had so many relationships—dissatisfying ones, I see now. When things got really bad, I could find relief in the arms of a guy. That lasted for a day, a week, or maybe a month—with any guy I met, who so much as looked at me.

The therapist could see that Sally had indeed developed the capacity to engage safely in a relationship where she also experienced safety, and commented, "You have come a long way. It's good to see that you are sure of this relationship and feeling a lot more confident."

Ability to Change Maladaptive Coping Styles and Adapt to Change

Becoming aware of their maladaptive coping styles, patients at this stage are able to see for themselves how they have coped in the past and what needs to be done in the future. Coping styles develop out of necessity in the early environment wherein the child learns how best to survive—to avoid rejection, cruelty, abuse, or other negative responses from caregivers and to cope with unbearable pain and distress.

These ways of coping are adaptive at first but later diminish in their adaptive capacity, resulting often in the development of problems, including depression and anxiety. Through therapy these unconscious coping styles become conscious and are processed and integrated into the general scheme of things.

The case of Sally, noted above, is an example of a patient who described her manner of coping with unbearably distressing affects by making impulsive and compulsive liaisons, which temporarily gave relief but did not bring about any lasting change. Instead she experienced an accumulation of guilt and anger, and hated herself for her own behavior. She compared herself in the early stage of therapy with how she functioned much later and talked about the difference she experiences in her relationships.

Development of a Sense of Agency, Autonomy, and Personal Existence

In the safety of the therapeutic relationship, the patient's conversation changes from one that is often broken up, with a poor sense of continuity, to one that has the hallmarks of a narrative. There is a widening of consciousness and, with it, a sense of cohesion that enables reflective capacity, which in turn brings with it a sense of agency, autonomy, and a better sense of personal existence. It may help to quote from one of several patients who, toward the end stages of therapy, remarked:

> I find myself doing things without being prompted or assisted by anyone. I can assert myself in the group; this is unlike how I used to be, doing things unquestioningly, as if in a daze. I feel I know who I am. I no longer have those feelings of uncertainty and doubt that threatened me to the point where I didn't want to be seen.

Integration of Split-off Parts of Self

The capacity to bring together and integrate parts that have been split or dissociated can only occur when traumatic experiences have been processed in the safety of the therapeutic relationship. Initially, the patient has to become conscious of his or her other self-states, so that the therapist may continue to hold the patient in his or her entirety. A therapist can explain to the patient that his or her different self-states are ways of adapting to life circumstances that have become maladaptive, and therefore need to come together and be integrated into one system—self.

Processing of trauma can be completed as self-states come together. However there may be a part which the patient holds on to—as in the example of "my baby" referred to in this chapter—where further work would need to be done. Such patients are then able to get a more coherent sense of their traumatic experiences, similar to the patient with BPD who has not actively dissociated parts of him- or herself.

Refer to "The Capacity to Integrate Affects and Regulate Self" (page 238) and "Dissociative Identity Disorder" (page 259).

SELF-HARMING BEHAVIOR

Repetitive, deliberate, direct injury to the body without the conscious intent to die presents in patients in very many different ways. The therapist tries to connect with the patient's experience, not just to what he or she is saying, but also to *how* he or she is saying it, encouraging the patient to talk about the circumstances preceding, during, and after the episode of self-harm. This attempt to connect in a reflective space enables the patient to feel less alone as well as understood and safe from challenge or criticism.

Language in the relationship organizes the nonverbal, implicit aspects of the patient's experience, allowing for the use of empathic reflection, coupling, amplification, and representation, and thereby enabling both partners to begin to develop an understanding of the behavior. This process is clearly shown in the case of Bella's overdoses.

It does not help if the therapist constantly asks questions about the patient's self-harming behavior; neither does it help to ask the patient to make a contract with the therapist not to self-harm. However, empathic attunement, understanding the patient's need to self-harm, and arriving at that understanding together are found to be helpful.

Self-harming behavior may be an attempt on the part of the patient to control a previously unmanageable situation (e.g., a sexual assault). Through the nuances of language the therapist may enable the patient to reflect on his or her behavior and to gradually become aware of the circumstances leading to self-harm. An unsatisfactory approach to self-harm is seen in this example: A 16-year-old patient revealed to her therapist that she felt so frantic the day before that she searched her home to find something poisonous to end her life, but she could not find what she wanted.

Therapist: You felt so frantic, it was difficult to keep feeling that way. We have to let your mother know about this.

The patient became very angry with the therapist and swore that she would never again tell him when she felt suicidal. The therapist reminded her that they had discussed as part of the contract that he would maintain confidentiality, with certain exceptions; one of these was self-injurious behavior. Though she later accepted that it was the right thing for the therapist to do, she still felt very angry. The therapist was able to repair the disjunction and therapy proceeded.

Several factors played a part. Notwithstanding these, the therapist realized that he had been hasty and if he had talked the episode through, he would have learned more about the patient, and also maintained her trust. Then the issue of discussion with her parents could have been raised and followed through as a joint process.

Reasons for Self-Harming Behavior

This section explores the various ways in which severely disturbed patients cope with environmental stress, unbearable affects such as tension, pain, and feelings of deadness, and the need for the therapist to develop a language of understanding and validation.

Relief of Tension

When self-harm provides a sense of relief from painfully difficult emotions, the patient becomes capable of identifying the hitherto avoided emotion and later of tolerating the sensations from which she has sought relief via self-harm, as in the following example:

> Sally: Every time I hear it, I get this tension in my head . . . and then it's almost like it's going to burst . . . nothing helps.
>
> Therapist: Cutting yourself helps you cope with the tension—makes it better—that's what I hear, nothing else helps.

Relief from a Sense of Deadness

When the discomfort of numbness, deadness, or confusion may be the triggering factor that leads to self-injury, the patient most often is in a dissociated state. The therapist's intervention may gradually help the patient get in touch with what is being dissociated, as in this example:

> Sally: There's no one, nothing but numbness all over me. There's nothing.

Similarly, feelings of deadness are described along with a sense of being totally unaware, as in the following:

> Sally: Suddenly I see the blood all over me, and I think to myself, what have I done? Cutting myself is the only way I can feel alive.
>
> Therapist: The only way you can feel alive. [This response is not a mere repetition; the sound of the voice, used in a particular way, makes the remark a representation.]
>
> Sally: It was like I wasn't even there.

Together the therapist and Sally were able to talk about her dissociative experiences and arrive at an understanding of how aspects of her developmental past led to her feelings of worthlessness and uselessness and to her self-harming behavior.

A Form of Reenactment

When self-harm is a form of reenactment of previous trauma, the patient who continues to be ambivalent toward his or her abuser and with no memory of the experience(s) finds that he or she resorts to self-injurious behavior in stressful times. Such experiences, recorded in procedural memory, often come into conscious awareness and can be spoken about, with help, as in the example of Sally who would denigrate herself to the point where she would easily become a target for others to humiliate. In turn, this humiliation would lead to self-harm by cutting. In this conversation, Sally and her therapist are beginning to understand the significance of her repetitive behavior.

Sally: It was common for him [her father] to criticize me in front of the others to the point where I would feel so small, and I would wish I could disappear. No one believed me, and no one really cared. I remember I told Mum about the abuse, and she called me a liar.

Therapist: (*gently*) You were very brave to tell your mother, but you were not believed. That must have been awful, not being believed.

Sally: (*Comparing her mother's and her father's attitudes, and in spite of her father's abuse, she went on*) At least he loved me. At least I think he did. But you could never tell what mood he would be in, I could never understand why he criticized me. My mother disliked me, because I reminded her of my father.

Therapist: You could not be responsible for what happened. Your trust was betrayed.

Feeling validated, Sally proceeded to ponder her behavior while the therapist intently listened. The therapist needs to develop a language around the form of communication set down by the patient, which is an inevitable part of the transference–cotransference.

SUICIDAL IDEATION/BEHAVIOR

Some patients present with acute suicidal thoughts and behavior, whereas others present with chronic and persistent suicidal preoccupation; still others describe images associated with ending life.

The containing function of the therapist is vital here. The therapist is often tempted to ask questions in order to clarify the intent of such ideation. Unless the therapist's anxiety is kept in check, however, the patient will not experience a sense of being heard or "held" but continue to feel unsafe and uncontained. These topics are covered in this section.

Acute Suicidal Ideation

In this section I deal with the therapist's response to the patient. When a patient expresses suicidal ideation in the course of therapy, it can be quite disconcerting for any therapist; however it is important that the therapist convey through language and tone of voice that he/she is being listened to and not rush to do a risk assessment immediately. In this way action can be taken to ensure the patient's safety if necessary by hospitalization; on the other hand the patient may leave the session feeling more contained and safe.

Listening and Understanding

In acutely suicidal patients the therapist's listening and understanding, and then the language used to convey this understanding, provide what is traditionally described as a "holding" (Winnicott, 1953) or "containing" (Bion, 1963) function. The patient feels heard. It may be a mistake *to look for meaning*, to look *under* or *behind* the patient's language. The patient's ability to flexibly experience and express a wider range of thoughts and feelings, and connect with those experiences, is made possible.

The therapist must not immediately rush to conduct a risk assessment, but allow the conversation to go on until he or she feels reasonably assured either that (1) the patient is not actively suicidal—he or she is talking about the future in a positive way, is making plans for tomorrow, or is going to see you again; or (2) that the patient *is* actively suicidal and needs a risk assessment and plans made to ensure safety. These plans may include close supervision by a trusted relative, if that is considered wise, or to be conveyed to a hospital for admission.

The Language of Understanding

The therapist's willingness to be with the patient, in the midst of his or her terrifying experiences for which the patient sees no solution but death, often proves to be life-saving; the therapist may respond "It seems like there's no way out, except by putting an end to your life—it's as if there will be no more pain?"

Anxiety drives the rigidity that we frequently see in acutely suicidal patients, and it is the therapist's capacity to contain his or her anxiety that helps contain the patient's anxiety. It also helps the therapist to be able to decide whether the patient requires more containment than what is current. An example will illustrate this point.

Sally, at the beginning of a session, announced: "There's no point in living; there's no one I can count on, no one who cares. I've been thinking—I'm done thinking—it's time to act."

The therapist was aware that Sally had no social supports and had been unwilling to accept hospitalization. She, however, was now considering admitting Sally against her will—something that she was once afraid would undermine the therapeutic relationship. The therapist spoke: "I am concerned that if I let you go home now, you won't be here for our next session—and I want you to come back."

Sally was struck that the therapist cared about her and was then willing to be hospitalized. In this instance the therapist utilized the transference relationship to cement, so to speak, the real relationship.

Language of Containing

In another instance the therapist said to the patient: "I am here with you, and if you decide to kill yourself, there will be no therapy—I don't want you to kill yourself." The patient had a sense that somebody cared about him, and though his suicidal ideation persisted for some time, he proceeded in therapy and managed his anxiety.

A further example refers to the therapist who said to his chronically suicidal patient: "I cannot stop you from killing yourself, but together we can try to make life more manageable. I am here to meet you halfway—I would like you to give me a chance to do that."

Issues of Safety: Hospitalization

Therapists are often concerned that if they hospitalize an actively suicidal patient who is in psychotherapy, against his or her will, the therapeutic relationship will be disrupted and difficult to repair. However, experience tells us that the opposite may in fact be the case—it depends on how it is said and what is said to such a patient. The following is an example of what a therapist said to a suicidal patient:

I am concerned that you are seriously suicidal and see no point in living. If I al-low you to go home, that might not be the right thing for me to do for you. I would like you to agree to go to hospital for a brief stay . . . to get some respite from the overwhelming stresses you have to cope with. (*pause*) If you don't agree, I would have no choice but to arrange admission against your will. I will be doing it to protect you. I would prefer for us to make this decision together. Would you think about what I've said?

When patients are involved in the decision-making process, they feel heard and valued and are better able to appreciate their needs. The therapist provides a "holding" that serves to bridge the sense of disconnection the patient often experiences in such situations. It gives the patient a sense of someone being there, of no longer being alone, and that the therapist has his or her best inter-ests at heart.

The Chronically Suicidal Patient

Borderline patients who have experienced numerous hospitalizations and sev-eral exposures to unsuccessful therapies tend to be in this category, as in the case of Bella. The therapist may have to be open to constantly emerging possibilities and not focus on meaning, which might become clearer as the therapy pro-ceeds. The therapist may have to accept the patient's preoccupation with suicidal thoughts as providing him or her with soothing and solace in a rather unpredict-able world.

Using stereotypical language is unhelpful because it assumes that the therapist knows what the patient is experiencing, and an assumption of *knowing* makes it easier to direct the patient, rather than to stay with him or her and the unpredict-ability. This may be anxiety-provoking for the therapist as well.

The therapist must contain his or her own anxiety, as suicidal thoughts are spoken about, for it is in the speaking and in the listening that the patient's level of awareness increases. It may become possible to introduce more flexibility where there was rigidity in thinking, and perhaps a willingness to recognize that there may be alternatives.

Language—not just words but the voice and tone—must do for the patient in this relationship what nothing else was capable of doing. It must help release the patient from rigid, pessimistic attitudes about him- or herself, thereby allowing the patient to process his or her experience.

Suicidal Ideation as Images of Dying

Some borderline patients tend to be markedly obsessional in their thinking and in their behavior as a result of their traumatic experiences, and perhaps because of a genetic predisposition. They describe seeing persistent images of themselves, for example, falling under a moving vehicle, using a sharp instrument to cut themselves, or falling from a tall building. These images tend to create anxiety early on, but become soothing the longer the patient experiences them. They also report finding themselves in these precarious situations, sometimes being helped out by someone from such a situation, or even being in a near-miss situation. Dissociation seems to play a part in these individuals.

In these situations the therapist may need to empathically attune to the patient and attempt to link what is happening with what the patient describes currently or in the past, conveying an understanding of the patient's predicament. Repeated hospitalization does not help to any great extent. However, safety issues may need to be stressed while the therapy proceeds. Medication may be useful in these patients in the early stage of therapy; however, it is important that medication is not seen as the answer, as these patients may then experience themselves as a further failure if they do not respond well to medication.

When a patient talks about his or her suicidal ideation, it is bound to arouse therapist anxiety. It is always useful to hear the patient out before drawing conclusions, because such patients can be contained in the therapy by being listened to and responded to in a nonanxious way. They may thereby be able to continue sessions without being hospitalized. This possibility is further addressed in Chapter 5.

THE CLOSING PHASE

It is sometimes said that one of the aims of therapy is to end it. Ending is the necessary sequel of a widening of consciousness, a capacity for reflectivity, and the working through of separation anxiety that is the core of much psychopathology. The therapist's language about the duration of therapy, and how it will end, is an important aspect of the therapeutic frame that is discussed with the patient at the commencement of therapy.

Though its introduction may vary from therapist to therapist, the notion of the patient's fear of abandonment needs to always remain in the therapist's consciousness. Reactions to intervals between sessions and to short breaks during the therapy will be indicators of the patient's separation fears and fears of abandonment, and must be dealt with when they occur. They are the precursors to that ending. (Bella, in Chapter 4, is a good illustration of the emergence of separation anxiety in the early stage of therapy; her behavior then was important information in deciding how the ending of therapy would be structured.)

In ending therapy there is an enormous potential for further emotional and relational growth. It provides a new opportunity to revisit and help resolve separation and loss issues of the past in the present. It allows for a full review of the therapy; it allows for a look at the future; and it allows new possibilities of saying good-bye in a way that has not seemed possible before.

This phase is both evaluative and therapeutic. Ending therapy must be carefully considered. An ideal ending is one wherein the traumatic forms of relatedness (transference) are understood and possibly resolved as the trauma system is integrated into the larger system of self, and the patient is free to live his or her life.

In the post-therapy phase the therapist is required to maintain a therapeutic stance and be available for future consultation, if needed, while acknowledging a continuing respect and admiration.

Patients often wish to know, though they may not directly ask, how the therapist feels about ending therapy. A human approach is necessary, as the therapist cannot deny having tender feelings for this patient whom he or she has seen regularly for, say, 5 years. "I will miss seeing you, but the thought of you doing so well . . . " may be a way of answering the patient's question. As in other parts of therapy, language is used to resonate with the inner experience of what it's like "being with" the patient.

In this end phase patients may become anxious about a recurrence of their problems. This anxiety needs to be addressed, as in saying to the patient: "If you have difficulties that you feel you would like to talk about with me, you have only to call." The case of Bella in the end phase provides a good example of what is talked about and how language is carefully chosen.

Variations in Ending

The question of ending therapy is a mutual one. Both therapist and patient need to be comfortable about bringing therapy to an end. With some patients, the impact of the past on the present may be so severe that though the patient has improved, it may not be wise for the therapy to be concluded. Separation anxiety may play a role here, and regular reviews may have to be arranged so that it can be processed and worked through, after which the therapy can end.

These patients may have had great difficulty tolerating aloneness when therapy started. They may also be fearful that they will relapse. The choice of how to end may differ from one therapist to another. Decreasing the frequency of sessions and setting a date to finish may be a choice; continuing the same frequency and setting a finishing date may be another choice; yet another may be reducing the frequency and then maintaining contact after longer breaks, until a date is set.

Premature Endings

When a patient leaves therapy before attaining a requisite level of improvement or without achieving the goals he or she wished to achieve, both patient and therapist are affected. The therapist may feel that his or her chance of doing a good job has been disrupted, particularly if it happens precipitously, but also if it happens as a result of the patient's changing circumstances. Feelings of helplessness, loss, despair, and demoralization may be some of the feelings experienced by therapists that will need to be worked through in supervision and/or in personal therapy.

Some patients may fear the possibility of dealing with certain issues and choose to leave therapy, but may then return as illustrated in this example: Dan left therapy after 3 years because he was fearful of processing his relationship with his mother, of which he was aware and openly said so. The therapist felt disappointed and expressed her annoyance and anger in supervision at his leaving therapy when he had so much promise. Two years later Dan returned and greeted the therapist with: "It feels like I have come back home." Dan needed to resolve his idealization of the therapist before he could deal with his fear of his mother, and when he did, he was able to deal with the issues that had once filled him with fear. He was then able to bring up the idea of ending, as if it were the most natural thing to do.

Sufficient resolution of forms of traumatic relatedness will allow the real relationship between patient and therapist to gain ascendance. When this resolution has occurred, fewer transference reactions occur, and when they do, they can be addressed and worked through. If therapy is ended before this resolution is achieved, however, the patient's unexpressed feelings toward the therapist or unresolved feelings toward others may continue to be troublesome.

Interminable Therapies

In some instances, the patient may not be able to achieve sufficient integration or function on his or her own (without some therapist intervention), in which case the therapeutic couple would decide to continue contact to suit the particular situation, so that the patient may gradually achieve what was not possible earlier in the therapy. The frequency of contact may sometimes be reduced and in some instances a regular though infrequent review may be suggested, with other supports built into the agreement. In some cases the therapy may continue as before, if the therapist feels that the holding capacity of the therapy is necessary for the patient to function more effectively.

COMORBIDITY

In general psychiatry it is usual to diagnose coexisting conditions if the symptoms meet the criteria for a separate DSM diagnosis, which is a categorical classification system, and to treat each as if it were a separate condition. We realize that it is important to look at the pattern of *comorbidity*, particularly when there are indicators of complex trauma, and to bear in mind what their relationship might be.

Many of these conditions do not fall neatly into any one of the classification systems, diminishing their value in routine clinical practice and particularly in psychotherapy. Often the use of pharmacological treatment based on these systems proves of little use, resulting in these patients coming to psychotherapy on numerous medications (e.g., antipsychotics, antidepressants, combinations of antidepressants, or mood stabilizers) generally used to treat the "comorbid" conditions.

A psychotherapeutic approach requires that we see "comorbidity" as the result of underlying core psychopathological processes of the complex trauma experience and not as separate conditions (Haliburn, 2009).

We find that medication is warranted when symptoms are severe and when they interfere with functioning, creating an impediment to the efficient formation of the therapeutic relationship that seeks to process and work through traumatic experiences (see also Chapter 5). Additional nonpharmacological measures such as relaxation, exercise programs, yoga, etc., may also be advised alongside psychotherapy.

The Cases of Sally and Sarah

The case of Sally, age 18 years, and the case of Sarah, age 24 years, are used to illustrate these points regarding comorbidity. They are composite cases, and pseudonyms have been used in the interest of confidentiality. Illustrations from both cases have been used earlier in this chapter.

Sally was admitted to a university teaching hospital (after several treatments over 2 years in other parts of the health system) in a state of inanition, with bruises and contusions all over her head and body (as a result of self-harming behavior). She was listless, posturing, and mute. She clung to her mother and looked suspicious; she was hypervigilant and startled easily. She also seemed to be responding to voices, which were later confirmed. She had been refusing to eat or drink for some time.

Sally was reportedly engaging in many rituals, cleaning everything around her, checking things several times, and needing to repeat certain actions a particular number of times. She refrained from washing or bathing herself, because if she were to touch or look at herself, she would need to be punished. Catching a reflection of herself in a mirror would cause her to self-harm.

Previous treatments at two hospitals for anorexia, which was diagnosed because of her disturbed body image, were unsuccessful. She relapsed into starvation and continued to hit herself whenever she felt fat or saw her reflection—which, according to her, confirmed that she was fat.

She experienced flashbacks that she was initially unable to describe, but later on were found to be associated with memories of early physical and sexual abuse. She engaged in cleaning rituals, repetitive ordering and reordering rituals, which if they were disturbed ended in her hitting herself. She had numerous somatic complaints and experienced severe dissociative episodes, during which several "self states" became apparent.

On admission Sally met the criteria for a diagnosis of a severe major depressive disorder with psychotic features, according to DSM. She also met the criteria for several comorbidities: somatization disorder; obsessive–compulsive disorder; an eating disorder that included elements of anorexia, bulimia, and binge eating; psychosis; dissociative disorder; dissociative identity disorder; not to mention separation anxiety disorder and posttraumatic stress disorder, according to DSM.

As she stabilized in the psychotherapeutic milieu of the hospital ward, it also became clear that she met all the criteria for BPD and was functioning at the severe end of the spectrum—that is, with auditory hallucinations, depersonalization, derealization, and dissociative identity disorder. She was preoccupied with suicidal images and constantly wished she could die. She often self-harmed.

Treatment from the time of admission included an antidepressant and antipsychotics (for a brief period), and a psychiatry registrar who was also training to be a psychotherapist, who spent a brief period of each day (10–15 minutes to start) getting to know Sally.

The dynamics of such conditions can only become apparent if we care to speak with the patient and find out what is happening, rather than considering only the signs and symptoms and locking him or her into a diagnosis and then treating accordingly. Continuity of treatment is also found to be helpful for the patient and, in the long run, effective in many ways.

After a 3-month stay in the hospital, Sally continued in twice weekly psychotherapy sessions with the same therapist. It became known through the therapy that Sally had been sexually abused from a very early age until one of her two sisters disclosed the fact of the abuse when Sally was 10 years of age. Her father was removed from the home. She also experienced significant emotional and physical abuse from her mother, her sisters blamed her for what happened, and she was often taunted by her older brother after her father left, until he (the brother) left home. A violent incident caused her illness to escalate.

During the first year of a rather difficult therapy, Sally was twice admitted briefly to the hospital after taking an overdose of medication and cutting herself. There were dissociated parts that needed working with, and maintaining an attitude of holding them together was very difficult. Even though no direct reference was made by the therapist to her obsessions and compulsions or her eating behavior, they were part of the conversation, and gradually her symptoms decreased and then stopped. Significant change and lasting improvement were evident after psychotherapy with CM for over 3 years, and continued for a further 2 years, when therapy was brought to conclusion.

Sally resumed studying and worked part time. Antipsychotic medication had been ceased when Sally was discharged from the hospital. Antidepressants were reduced in the course of therapy and ceased when Sally married and decided to have a baby. There was no further return of symptoms on follow-up.

Depression

Sally suffered with depression, which is commonly seen in patients with BPD. It is usually chronic and low-grade, sometimes superimposed by a major depressive episode, as seen in Sally. At other times it is punctuated erratically by changes in mood, with alternating highs and lows, characteristically described as unstable moods.

These patients are more likely to encounter frequent life events and crises that interfere with their ongoing response to psychotherapy, with the result that therapists are often frustrated by their slowness to respond or their failure to maintain a good response once achieved. Developmentally, most of these patients were not appropriately and caringly responded to by early caregivers, with sufficient feeling-based responses to their immediate experiences. Often they have been chronically devalued, criticized, and dismissed, leaving them with persisting dysphoria and feelings of emptiness and deadness that are often mistaken for serious depression.

Such patients are more prone to depressive feelings than others as a result of the extraordinary diminution in feelings of self-worth, which are at the core of their view of themselves. Patients in these circumstances may often experience themselves as a burden to the therapist.

After she was stabilized in the hospital and discharged, Sally returned home to her mother and sisters, whose attitudes had not changed. Family therapy was refused by them. The therapist must keep in mind that families are deeply affected by the illness of one of its members; similarly psychopathology in the family can undermine the therapy, by adding to the despair that the patient experiences, as in this example:

> Sally: I'm not sure, I come and tell you the same thing about myself—nothing changes. I've been through all the antidepressants you can name; I've been on mood stabilizers too. I was even advised to try ECT [electroconvulsive therapy], which my mother refused, before I came for treatment here. That's how bad I am—beyond repair!
>
> Therapist: Beyond repair (*representing the last words of her sentence in a slightly questioning way*)?

It was clear that Sally had experienced a profound sense of failure and saw herself as a failure when there was no response to the treatments offered, or she got worse. It also opened up recollections of her early experiences of being chronically devalued and criticized with such words as "You're just like your father."

In such situations the therapist often feels the patient's despair, but may also feel a sense of rejection and of failure (*nothing changes*). It is important to take note of the cotransference and the countertransference too. The therapist must be patient and try to stay with the patient's affect, remain connected, and maintain a sense of optimism. It is very difficult to remain a therapist and work with difficult patients if one does not entertain a degree of hope.

Anxiety

Anxiety was a constant feature of Sally's experience, particularly in the early stages of therapy. It ranged from generalized anxiety to phobic anxiety with avoidance and panic attacks. Difficulties in self-regulation, fears of abandonment, and separation anxiety contributed to this pervasive sense of anxiety. Abandonment anxiety was often a feature of Sally's presentation and at times seemed quite crippling. It can be constant in some patients, becoming apparent in sessions as well as outside of sessions, and is manifested by clinging behavior as in repeated attempts to make contact with the therapist. Listening and understanding Sally's predicament helped.

On several occasions Sally presented with mini-psychotic episodes that were in fact dissociative. She experienced episodes of depersonalization (feeling that her body or parts of her body were distorted or sometimes missing, or that they were part of someone else's body) and derealization (feeling that the world around her was not real) and often presented in detached, disorganized states with speech that was disordered and fragmented, to the point of being unintelligible at times. She also described auditory hallucinations in the context of her self-harming behavior. What once seemed like a "thought disorder" became clearer and more coherent as the conversation developed into more of a narrative style.

When she stopped self-harming by hitting and punching herself, Sally started to focus on her weight and body size. While talking about her eating behavior, there were hints of disclosures—what were later described as sexual and physical abuse.

Eating Disorders

Sally, not unlike some other patients with BPD, also suffered with anorexia. In anorexia, symptoms are concrete. The body is a concretized metaphor for what is really experienced; it plays a symbolic role, an example of embodiment; it is a tool for communication. Body symptoms are a vehicle for communication, and in Sally's case they were trying to communicate what she could not bear to talk about.

Sally had no language for feelings. Sensorimotor experiences and body experiences such as hunger, weight, size, and shape are physical entities, not merely representations, but *presentations*. Sally's typical descriptions involved states of emptiness or fullness and heaviness or tightness.

The therapist must look for connections with emotions. For example, when the patient feels that she is taking up too much space, it may be the equivalent of not feeling worthy. Concretized metaphors need to be developed into linguistic ones. The therapist needs to develop a language around the form of communication set down by the patient, as in the following example of Sally.

> Sally: I'm so confused, completely filled up; it's simply too much for me. I want to empty myself; but I have never done that before.
>
> Therapist: Things are too much, and you want to empty yourself?

It is as if Sally is stimulus entrapped in her body, and nothing else seems to matter. Coherence is lost, and with it continuity of experience, as fluctuations occur in the conversation. The therapist needs to set up a particular form of conversation that resembles the state of inner coherence.

How does the therapist achieve this? The therapist aims to fit voice, facial expression, and language to the patient's state of mind, staying connected, not moving away from that state or becoming overtly anxious. The therapist's state *fits* with the immediate experience of the patient and provides an analogical relatedness (see page 176) in the therapy, enhances connectedness between two people having different minds, conveys safety, and creates what Robert Hobson (1985) referred to as a state of fellow feeling or aloneness–togetherness.

The following example illustrates Sally's battle. She was thin and tall, but was preoccupied with a view of herself as fat, and felt ambivalence toward her parents.

> Sally: I am a hopeless person, not worth anything. I cannot stand any more of myself—I know I will only get bigger. I was fat when I was little—that's why—that's why my father liked me. That's what Mum said. I feel sick just thinking of it. It's bad as it is—how big can I get? I can't *stand* it, if there's more of me—that's before he was asked to leave home and we were not to see him.
>
> Therapist: It's been difficult . . . this getting bigger, and then feeling hopeless about it. [The therapist notes Sally's confusion, particularly her confusion of times past and present, and her association of her body size with her father.]
>
> Sally: Sometimes I think I want to disappear . . . then I get the urge not to eat.

Therapist: Not eating—yes, I guess it will make you disappear.

Sally: But it's difficult. My mother keeps putting things in the food she thinks will make me fat. I cannot trust them—my mother or my sisters. I cannot trust anyone. They scare me. I can only trust myself—when I can feel my bones— I'm happy, but it doesn't last. There's something else that hangs around. I don't need anyone—but now, I'm—this is extremely difficult (*enveloping her body in a huge gesture*). I cannot feel—it's confusing, it's all blurred. (*She was not fat, but she associated putting on weight with her father's affection for her [reported by her mother] and therefore his abuse of her. Her huge gesture indicated a disturbed body image, as she believed that she was fat, even though she was quite slim. She feared putting on weight. However, sometime later she began bingeing, purging, and vomiting.*)

Therapist: You can't trust anyone or anything, but you can trust yourself, and only when you can feel your bones? [Here the therapist *represents* to Sally in a tone of voice that suggests they might look at this issue together.]

Sally: Yes, then I am in control—it's all me. I cannot take any more changes. There have been so many changes . . . all my 18 years. I know what I'm doing and where I am going. When I punished myself, I felt in control. I did a bad thing—eating—I needed to be punished. I felt safer then because I did not let myself go.

Therapist: You needed to be punished. I wonder if we can look at those times when you said you were in control . . . when you know what you're doing and where you're going?

When the patient is wrestling with food, appetite, and weight, it is useful to involve a GP and a dietitian in the care of these areas, while the patient is engaged in psychotherapy. This distribution of responsibility eliminates the need for the therapist to get entangled in issues of food and weight, which is what often happens in the patient's family, and if not addressed may lead to further difficulties.

Sally disclosed that she was prone to binge eating, then vomiting and purging. Some patients with BPD present with bulimia and at times also with abuse of drugs (illegal or legal) and alcohol. (As noted in Chapter 5, *abuse* of drugs or alcohol is not a contraindication for psychotherapy, but *dependence* would require management by detoxification, if psychotherapy is to be of subsequent benefit.)

This example further illustrates how Sally talked about her eating behavior.

Sally: I couldn't bear to sit still all afternoon and get my work done. All I could think about was how fat I've become—I can't keep it down. And there I was

filling my shopping cart with biscuits and chocolates and bread and buns—
nothing healthy!

Therapist: Sounds like you were restless—couldn't keep your mind on your
work—that seems to happen often, you said.

Sally: After dinner, there was this feeling, which I couldn't get rid of. I had to get
rid of all I had eaten and much more. [Sally could not stay with the inner feeling being named here (i.e., restlessness); instead she goes on to talk about
eating and getting rid of what she has eaten.]

Therapist: This feeling?

The therapist stayed closely attuned and put words to these feeling states. This
helped Sally to gradually talk about these states in feeling words. She talked further about her eating behavior, including nocturnal bingeing, in relation to her
sense of aloneness and feelings of emptiness. Her distress was quite marked when
she realized the vast amounts of food she had consumed by day and particularly
at night, as illustrated in this example.

Sally: I walked into the kitchen this morning and was shocked to see empty choc-
olate wrappers, the leftovers of a whole loaf of bread and empty biscuit packets strewn on the bench. I was overcome by this sense of shame—what would
my partner think if he was here?

The therapist was in a position to empathically attune and resonate with the patient's distress. (She must have dissociated, as she had no memory of the previous
night.) Later in therapy the patient became more aware and as difficulties were
worked through and trauma processed, she was able to stop bingeing during the
day and particularly at night.

Dissociation, Depersonalization, and Derealization

Sally, as I have said earlier, was prone to dissociation and episodes of depersonalization and derealization. Dissociation disrupts consciousness, resulting in a dis-
continuity of experience. This is in contrast to *continuity*, an essential aspect of
self-integrity: the continuity of experience, memory and identity.

Consciousness is inherently integrative. Trauma impacts the individual's sense
of self. Dissociation is an adaptive attempt to lessen the profound pain of traumatic experiences, resulting in the memories of trauma being stored in discrete
states—a fragmented self—which was the case with Sally. When the patient is

dissociated, it is important for the therapist to enter the dissociated state with a language that seeks to maintain the sense of relatedness and that serves to contain and help the patient return to the here-and-now in a manner that is less fragmented. The therapist maintains a fine balance between staying with the patient and not getting engulfed in the traumatic material. To become engulfed is be useless to the patient. Similarly, staying outside the system can be confusing for the therapist, who then becomes incapable of containing the patient's fragmentation.

The patient may feel bereft and alone if the therapist disentangles him- or herself too quickly and abruptly because the closeness in dissociation is akin to fusion. Paradoxically, both distance and fusion can be sustained as the therapist tries to stay with the patient. At times a dream-like state might be experienced by the therapist, who then has to wrestle with the feeling and stay out of it. Examples of dissociation are also seen in the case of Bella, when she describes finding herself roaming the city, trying to find a place where she could overdose, but not remembering how and when she got there; and also in the sessions when the therapist describes herself as feeling confused.

Depersonalization and derealization are disorders of the experience of self. In the former, the person feels that he/she is no longer his/her natural normal self, because something has happened; in the latter the person experiences a sense of unreality and the environment seems unreal. These experiences, which are part of the dissociation continuum, can be very frightening for the patient. In dissociation, the patient may lose his/her sense of time. Continuity can be affected, and so can coherence if he/she is talking. The patient may also do things and then have no recollection later on. This is as a result of lowering of the patient's awareness or level of consciousness.

A brief education of the patient will be very helpful in all these circumstances. Staying with the patient and understanding him or her is important. Dissociative patients in therapy need help to regain the capacity to move, to fight back, and to live fully in their bodies as well as in their minds.

Dissociative Identity Disorder

Sally presented with 3 different self states, which at times were definitely compartmentalized and presenting differently from her usual demeanor. It is an error to see dissociative identity disorder (DID) as referring to the existence of multiple personalities or separate persons. It is a serious therapeutic error to relate to the different self states as if they were separate people, even though sometimes the patient may insist that they are.

The language used must convey to the patient that the different self states are one and the same person. They are highly discrete states of consciousness separated from other states of consciousness, organized around a particular memory/experience that has been dissociated and compartmentalized. When working with these patients in therapy, the therapist must link empathically with the patient's self-perceptions in order to develop a trusting therapeutic relationship. Observing differences in the patient's affects and behaviors (including reversals), his or her responses to different memories, and his or her different presentations in terms of symptoms and complaints is all important.

I illustrate this with a short excerpt from the therapy with Sally. At one point the therapist commented: "It must be hard to find yourself so angry at times, when you are naturally a very quiet person—at the mercy of so many different states of mind." When responding to different self states that made their appearance, the therapist said something like this: "It seems, Sally, that when Anne says you are suicidal, you are afraid to talk about your suicidal feelings. Can we look at those feelings and see what we can do?"

We sometimes see a patient in a particular self state of helplessness take an overdose, while another self state (hitherto split off) with a need to live regrets the action and calls for help. This may come across as ambivalence. Sally described such moments vividly. As therapists, we need to be able to recognize these changes in order to understand the dynamics involved and help patients integrate these split off parts. (For further information, refer to "Aspects of Integration" on page 236 of this chapter.)

Somatization

After 6 years of medical investigations and treatment by several specialists and practitioners, Sarah was referred for psychotherapy. She presented with multiple chronic somatic complaints, including chronic pain, and was also found to have BPD. Somatic complaints are commonly found in patients with BPD.

In fact such patients have spent years trying unsuccessfully to find answers—many have seen several medical specialists, had hosts of investigations, and been told that there is nothing wrong or that nothing can be found to explain their symptoms; they have then unsuccessfully seen natural therapists and psychotherapists of several descriptions. These patients may actually feel that they are being heard, understood, recognized, and accepted when they have been seen in psychotherapy in this model.

It is essential that the therapist provide the patient with a brief education about the nature of somatization and the possible role of psychological factors in the origin and often the maintenance of illness, particularly the mind–body split, at the commencement of therapy. The following excerpt illustrates this therapeutic attitude.

Sarah: My feet hurt. I can't stand for a minute—it hurts really badly—and I have to almost collapse back into my armchair.

Therapist: That would make it really difficult.

Sarah: I was so nauseated, just couldn't get out of bed.

Therapist: Made it hard to get out of bed.

Sarah: These stomach upsets just come . . . whenever—one never knows—just can't go out.

Therapist: I can see how difficult this illness has made day-to-day things, like going out.

The therapist must adopt a paradoxical stance (Meares, 1997) of taking interest, but making no attempt to inquire about symptoms or complaints, and making no active effort to shift the focus from body symptoms to emotions. The common belief is that such an attitude would only reinforce complaints, but that has not been our experience.

A therapeutic attitude of empathic resonance, in which there is persistent curiosity about the patient's emotional life, is recommended. The therapist's countertransference is often a mixture of feelings—of impatience, boredom, being deceived, nonacceptance, as in cases of somatization—that make it difficult to sustain an empathic stance. It is not unusual for the therapist to find him- or herself oscillating between thinking that the patient is telling lies or being histrionic and making a catastrophe of the situation, and believing the patient and his or her complaints. (This point is also described under the heading of "Changing the Chronicle" in a previous section in this chapter.)

Some of these patients tend to be highly anxious and present with features of obsessional and eating disorders. Among the life events of such patients the therapist must not miss a history of early loss/losses of significant others and a history of chronic illness in a parent—or of an error in diagnosis, a missed diagnosis, or a delay in diagnosis of serious illness in a parent or even in the patient.

Sarah, as I have mentioned, also suffered from chronic pain, which had prevented her from working. Chronic pain is not uncommon in patients with BPD. Most often these patients are, and have been, caregivers in their families of origin, as was Sarah. Others' needs have been regarded as more important than their own; they are often pathologically accommodating, have generally not experienced emotional care, and have been expected to live uncomplainingly or without inconveniencing others.

Later in therapy Sarah recollected having been constantly discouraged from expressing neediness or anything negative that would upset her mother. She had an inability to translate affect into words; emotion was rarely expressed and when it seemed to reach consciousness there seemed a fear of letting go.

A high achiever in her teens, Sarah had lost her ability to work as a result of her problems. She remained depressed and anxious that she would "have to live this shameful life until death came" to her.

> Sarah: I am fed up—a completely useless, hopeless waste of space. I'm not contributing, I'm not helping anyone, I'm doing nothing but complaining when I come here, and I go to the doctors expecting there will be a magic cure. I'm in so much pain all the time—and I hate talking about it—it does nothing for me.
>
> Therapist: I can see how fed up you feel. Anyone in your situation would feel that way. [The therapist attempts to attune with the patient and also validate her.]
>
> Sarah: They couldn't feel as pathetic as I do.
>
> Therapist: You are very hard on yourself when you refer to yourself as pathetic, but I guess that's how you feel.

As therapy progresses, Sarah emphasizes her pain to a lesser degree than she had ever done. She also expresses more feeling in place of being preoccupied with the physical level. The patient's vulnerability is understood to be a deficit in the capacity to modulate pain, and the therapist's understanding and acceptance help further exploration and processing, as in this example:

> Sarah: I feel like that all the time. You were never allowed to be sick—you went to school even if you were burning up. You would miss out on a valuable education, they said. But I don't want to blame my parents, though I think they have a role.

COMPLEX ISSUES

In this section I have briefly dealt with "touch" in therapy and remind the therapist that it is the patient's perception of physical touch in the therapy situation that really matters. I have also described when the 50-minute hour is changed and some reasons why this may be so; the pros and cons of phone and Skype therapy and the inadvisability of using these media for disturbed and suicidal patients. I have looked at changing circumstances in the therapist's life, drawing on the therapist's pregnancy, and also illness in the therapist.

The Question of Touch

As therapists we may sometimes tend to think nothing of a touch on the shoulder when an upset patient leaves a session; an outstretched hand when it appears that the patient needs to be comforted; or an embrace or a hug when the patient is upset at the end of a session—these are ways in which some therapists naturally react to their patients' emotional states.

However, it is each patient's perceptions of physical touch in these circumstances that really matters. The congruence of the touch, the ability of the patient to feel in control, the perception of who benefits, and the clarity of the therapist's boundaries need to be considered before a therapist is equipped to decide what is in the patient's interest.

Such gestures on our part may create problems for some patients who see themselves as a burden, or who feel responsible for the therapist's well-being, or experience guilt when they have something done for them. It is important that we always consider the best interests of the patient, when we do or say something that is particular to a situation and for which there are no definite answers.

The Extended or Double Session

The 50-minute hour has never been challenged, as this time frame seems to suit both the patient and the therapist from many points of view. However, there may be important reasons why a double session should be contemplated, without which there may be no good reason to alter the time frame.

It would seem that scheduling a double session may be in the interest of a patient who lives too far away, when treatment frequency may not be a viable option. This decision can be made at the beginning, particularly when services are unavailable in the patient's hometown.

When a patient moves away some distance during the therapy and the idea of changing therapists is considered to be too disruptive, then a double session can be offered, again for the convenience of the patient. When a patient requests a double session in the absence of any of the above situations, the request needs to be considered in the light of what is happening in the therapy, and that needs to be talked about before any decision is taken. The use of phone or Skype sessions as an alternative can always be considered. Phone sessions have the advantage of both therapist and patient being able to hear each other clearly, with less of a tendency to "drop out." Skype sessions on the other hand depend on a good broadband network, and though they have the advantage of therapist and patient being able to both see and hear each other, distortions are unavoidable. It is for these reasons that it would not be helpful to conduct ongoing therapy in this way with seriously disturbed or suicidal patients. These may be the only contraindications for the use of regular phone or Skype therapy. (There is also the question of payment, as phone and Skype psychotherapy may not be funded by the patient's health insurance, and the patient may have to pay for it.)

Changing Circumstances in the Therapist's Life

The Therapist's Pregnancy

The therapist's pregnancy can stir a wide range of reactions in patients with BPD, depending on the patient's background, his or her own reproductive history, the stage of the therapy, and the state of the therapeutic relationship. Frequent patient reactions include themes of anger, rejection, abandonment, sibling rivalry, and identification with either the therapist or the unborn baby.

A therapist must generally respond to knowledge of her pregnancy by making a mental summary of her patients, and giving some thought to how each patient might respond to this news. She may wish that her patients would receive the news joyfully; she may feel very protective of her unborn baby and therefore may wish that no patient would react negatively; she may wish that patients who may have had difficulty conceiving (if any) or have had sexual issues or relationship issues will not be affected.

Therapists need to be aware that they can be confronted with particular challenges with particular patients. It helps for the therapist to disclose news of her pregnancy as early as practically advisable. However, sometimes a therapist might collude with a particular patient and not disclose her pregnancy, for fear that it might be disruptive.

A great many patients handle the disclosure of the therapist's pregnancy with much less difficulty, provided that the therapist discloses it to each individual patient, takes into account the patient's reaction and discusses it in the context of what is already known about the patient, including necessary plans for the patient's care in the therapist's absence.

Following is an example of a patient who learns of her therapist's pregnancy. The patient has a history of abandonment anxiety and has been in therapy for about 6 months, when she notices a change in her therapist's appearance.

Patient: Are you pregnant?
Therapist: Yes, I am. How did you know?

The patient showered the therapist with congratulations, and the therapist felt that they were genuine. However, the following day the therapist was informed that the patient had taken a large overdose and was admitted to the hospital overnight.

The therapist realized that the patient had often talked about her uncaring and rejecting family members who were caught up in their own affairs and had no time for her. She thought that perhaps her own need to celebrate her pregnancy may have blinded her to the fact that her patient might experience her pregnancy as a form of rejection, which she realized when the patient returned and talked about her overdose after knowing about the therapist's pregnancy. Although they were able to talk about it, the therapist spent some time thinking about an alternate response as in the following:

Therapist: Yes, I am. Can we talk about it? I'm wondering how it will be for you, my having a baby, and then my being away?

The patient may have felt cared for by this remark. In such situations adequate time needs to be spent dealing with the patient's feelings toward the therapist's pregnancy, as well as the ensuing separation, and the perceived division of time by which the therapist could be constrained. Earlier issues of neglect, abandonment, and abuse can be triggered, making it all the more important that this issue be dealt with as early as practicable.

The Ill Therapist

Illness in the therapist may forebode many different outcomes for the therapy. It depends upon how ill the therapist is, how his or her ongoing illness will impact the patient, particularly in those therapies where both patient and therapist desire for the therapy to continue despite the therapist illness.

How much is disclosed, when it is disclosed, and what contingencies the therapist can put in place, will depend entirely on the therapist with each of his or her patients. The chronically ill therapist will have to think very carefully when restructuring his or her psychotherapy practice.

The terminally ill therapist will not only go through his or her own grief, but will as a matter of necessity go through issues of grief and loss with each of his or her patients, and patients will have to deal with their own histories of similar experiences. Bringing therapies to a close will be extremely distressing for the therapist, as each will bring up the fact of his or her mortality. Again, though difficult, the interest of the patient must be served as plans are made for his or her ongoing care.

Chapter 8

Discourse Correlates of Therapeutic Methods and Patient Progress

David G. Butt, Alison R. Moore, and
Caroline K. Henderson-Brooks

THE CHOICES A SPEAKER MAKES in grammar and in lexis accumulate in ways that are not clear or accessible to the speaker in a sustained interaction, for example, in an hour of interaction between a psychotherapist and a patient. Yet this consistency—that is, a regularity beyond the typical threshold of human powers for tracking—is what the psychotherapist and the discourse analyst alike attune to in their respective work. The purpose of this chapter is to describe and illustrate tools that can track consistencies and departures in meaning, and to show how such tools can be used to characterize how patients diagnosed with BPD and their therapists talk to each other in therapy based on CM. Our aim is to enhance the resources that practitioners and students possess for interpreting and tracking significant aspects of their patients' states of mind. These resources can then help practitioners predict, promote, and explain changes in inner state on the basis of their own analyses of patients' "outer" language, in conjunction with other forms of meaningful nonverbal behavior, such as gaze.

PARALLELS AND KEY CONCEPTS

Before illustrating useful tools and techniques from linguistics in later sections, we point out some relevant parallels in the history and foci of CM and functional linguistics and outline a selection of crucial theoretical concepts from functional linguistics that will be drawn on below. These concepts and concerns include the notion of *intersubjectivity*, now important across a wide range of disciplines. Concepts brought in from linguistics include the notions of *motivated selection*, and the notion of *meaning potential* as a relation between each specific *instance* of language use and what might have been selected from the shared language *system* of the speaker and addressee. These concepts are less well known outside linguistics but have been shown to be useful in interdisciplinary studies where meaning needs to be tracked, gauged, compared, and explained. The familiar concept of *topic* is also presented, and contrasted with other ways in which consistency of meaning can be either maintained or interrupted.

Similarities in the Psychotherapeutic and Linguistic "Gaze"

In studying the conversation between therapists and their patients, it emerged that the semantic "drift" of unconscious patterns of meaning making is something that an experienced therapist "reads" from their interactions with patients. Furthermore, it seems probable that it is in responding to a bandwidth of latent patterns of meaning in the structure of discourse that psychotherapists find the motivation for the semiotic techniques their practice propounds as theory. The practitioners of CM, in particular, address these semantic responsibilities explicitly. The motivations of CM are not linguistic, per se, but rather organized around the critical psychic values of intersubjectivity, the quality of relatedness, and the centrality of the self as elucidated by William James (e.g., see Hobson 1985; James, 1890; Meares, 2005). Given these core concepts, it should not be surprising that both the leading practitioner and theorist of CM, Russell Meares, and the linguist who developed Systemic Functional Linguistics (SFL), M.A.K. Halliday, have had a collaboration in common—namely, with the psychologist and neuroscientist Colwyn Trevarthen (e.g., 1987). Trevarthen's work on intersubjectivity between neonates and mothers has been congruent with, and supportive of, both CM and SFL. In parallel forms of inquiry, Halliday, Trevarthen, and Meares have explored the intricacy of mindfulness as it is created between two people in a profound relationship of reciprocation (e.g., child to mother, patient to therapist).

Meares and his research team (see the other contributors to this volume, as well as the brain-imaging collaborations, e.g. Felmingham et al., 2008; Felmingham, 2011) have specialized in treating the difficult condition of borderline personality disorder (BPD). Such patients present with what might be called an "inert core," as if their commitment to lived experience has been extinguished or severely compromised (e.g., through trauma). A challenge to psychotherapists is the restoration of *animus* or aliveness by creating an empathic relationship within which the analogical connections between aspects of living can be created. Crucial to this undertaking is a form of narrative in which memory, reverie, and a new form of meaning potential come together. Such "coming together" is the aim of the therapist's discourse, producing a new level of insight about the past and an inclination to the possibilities of the future. Discourse in the therapist–patient relationship must be the catalyst of change, since it is the resource in which the reciprocation can be created semiotically.

Motivated Selection

By identifying linguistic consistencies and departures in a speaker's choices, a case can be made for their relevance to the speaker's states of mind and also to intersubjectivity between patient and therapist and the relative success of therapist responses. In other words, although speakers do not typically select specific choices in words and grammar with full consciousness of all the other relevant possible expressions that could work at that moment, or with a view to how this choice now echoes a choice made the turn before, or the session before, it is possible to demonstrate that speakers engage in a kind of "motivated selection" of language options. This case depends on the implausibility of semantic consistencies being a merely random phenomenon. The possible combinations in words and grammar in a language, even while talking about the same topic, are so great that the chance of accidental semantic consistencies becomes implausible as more linguistic variables are included and more analyzed data are brought to bear.

This issue of language choices that are "unintentional" yet clearly motivated is familiar to linguists and literary scholars from discussions of verbal art: It is part of the debate around Jakobson's (e.g., 1987) claims for "subliminal" patterns, and it underlies the cognate theories of organization in verbal art as enunciated by Mukařovský (1964, 1977) and Hasan (e.g., 1975, 1985a). So too, in Halliday's (e.g., 1971) concepts of "prominence" and "deautomatization" in relation to verbal art, such accumulating patterns are a recruitment of the habitual resources in existing forms of language to a nonhabitual degree of consistency in their semantic consequences. In verbal art it is only in this orienting of the choices to a thematic consistency that one can then go on to account for innovation of forms, or novelty. In psychotherapy, a similar kind of comparison between the observed utterance and what might be otherwise expected is important, such that departures from what is typical or expected could be considered as signs of a disturbed state of mind or, at other times, of therapeutic progress. Some readers may find a useful analogy here with the epidemiological approach of comparing an *observed* distribution of features (such as the incidence of certain symptoms in a certain group or time period) against the typical, *expected* incidence for the population more generally, or over longer periods of time.

Meaning Potential, System, and Instance

The methods of discourse analysis, whether analyzing spoken, written, gestural, or other meanings, share a common task of holding the *instance* of text against the *meaning potential* of the *system*. Note that both the *instance* and the *system* are dynamic phenomena, with no linguistic system ever closed off to variability and change.

In this approach, the actual choices of a semantic interaction are viewed against the *potential*—that is, what might have been said. Establishing the potential, or what is to be selected, to compare it with the actual, is not a simple process. And what is typical will vary for different situations and for different dyads in therapy. Nevertheless, we find that such an approach to text analysis produces immediate opportunities for construing the dominant meanings between therapist and patient. This is possible because an accumulation of analyses of systematic variation changes the depth of the "field" of human interpretation, much as an optical telescope changes human vision by enhancing the process, not by modifying it.

For instance, when a therapist offers an interpretation to his patient, Patricia, that "It's almost like you've been mothering her, as it were," Patricia replies, "I didn't see it like that." Drawing on the notion of meaning potential, it becomes important to consider what the patient might have said instead. One obvious alternative would be "Yes, you're right"—that is, a change in polarity from negative to positive. But many other alternatives are also possible, such as "No, I don't see it like that," or "Well, that's not really the case." These latter, unchosen alternatives are negative, like the patient's actual utterance, but they also incorporate differences in other linguistic systems. The patient's actual utterance includes the selection of past tense ("didn't"), and arguably this suggests that there is potential for changing the way she sees things—at least, to a greater extent than would have been suggested by the words "I don't see it like that," with the present tense selected. There are many ramifications involved in the apparently small differences between these choices. Indeed, 7 months later Patricia has appropriated the therapist's interpretation, telling the therapist, "<u>Like I said, she wants me to be the mother and mother her</u>" (see Henderson-Brooks, 2006). Here, however, we use the example to show the need to consider what has been said in therapy against what might have been said but wasn't, and to show that these choices can be characterized grammatically.

This linguistic approach also offers semantic motifs and threads that can guide the analyst as to what is salient in the text and what might be the appropriate ordering of steps of analysis. By a *linguistic approach to analysis*, we mean taking the strata of language—context, semantics, lexicogrammar, phonology/phonetics (see Halliday & Matthiessen, 2004)—and asking questions that will elucidate how the construction of meaning is dispersed across systems on different strata, as well as how different resources contribute to the ensemble that we take as the "figure" a person makes.

Overt Topic versus Latent Consistencies

Motivated selections of language choices are particularly significant in that they can compose a semantic "drift" quite distinct from the explicit topic being discussed. They can be an index of an "angle" on the topic, a perspective that is relevant to the affective *and* ideational judgments a person is making moment by moment, albeit unconsciously. It is always important to consider the play between topical consistency and these other kinds of consistency and departure, and we outline a number of these other kinds below. We pay particular attention here to consistencies in the way speakers convey stance, certainty, responsibility, and time orientation, but there are many other motifs that can be important to track alongside topic.

All language users have a very strong, shared sense of what constitutes "the same topic," even though we may occasionally dispute what counts as "off topic." Other aspects of meaning are much more difficult to monitor in real time. Although it might be possible during a session to "listen for" the lexical allocation of actor roles, it is very hard to simultaneously track for differences in how clauses are combined, such as shifts between parataxis/aggregation and hypotaxis/subordination. It is harder still to note what has been left "unchosen"—what might have been taken up in the discourse but which has been grammatically neutralized or occluded.

To give an example, when patient "J" talks about forthcoming plans to move house and join a judo class, she says, "<u>Yes, I start Thursday. I'm really excited.</u>" After four short turns directly on the topic of the judo class times and location, the therapist offers "<u>You're going to become very energetic.</u>" In the patient's next turn she talks a little more on the topic of the judo, but then turns to talking about another group, a mothers' group she is thinking of joining, and her turn finishes with "<u>My life could be so good.</u>" One thing happening here is that the therapist's actual wording combines both a definite future "<u>you are going to</u>" (not "<u>you might</u>") with two expressions of potentiality, the process "<u>become</u>" and the attribute "<u>energetic.</u>" An effect is produced that sustains the potentiality of "<u>I'm excited</u>" and bridges to the potentiality of "<u>My life could be so good.</u>" Imagine the therapist had chosen an alternative wording, such as "That sounds very energetic" or "You'll need a lot of energy for all that." This is unlikely to have produced the semantic consistency of potentiality—which is not a topic in itself but an important motif that the patient and therapist associate here with the future. In Chapter 6, Meares makes a similar distinction when he contrasts consistencies in "aboutness" (i.e., topic) with other kinds of consistencies, such as the consistency in emotional tone, which is called "staying with" (#13).

LINGUISTIC TECHNIQUES

In the following sections, we identify and illustrate some techniques of discourse analysis that we have found salient for the goals and methods of CM. These techniques include: mapping the degree to which patients verbally depict themselves as agentive, prominent or, at least, visible social actors; identifying how therapists and patients exploit the meaning of clausal architecture; mapping the generic shape of therapy sessions; and discriminating different techniques of semantic solidarity. A further technique involves displaying patterns of textual cohesion and cohesive harmony in conversations, and we show the particular relevance of these techniques for therapy with patients who experience dissociative episodes. The final illustration acts as a summary of how the techniques discussed above can work together as a strategy for expanding patients' meaning potential, and how expanded meaning potential can be seen as a marker of valued change.

Agency, Visibility, and Prominence

Therapists are often concerned with the degree to which a patient makes him- or herself a background (i.e., gives herself low visibility) in her own discourse.

Another motivating issue could be the degree to which a patient projects him- or herself as agentive, or as the experiencer of feelings, or as the "victim" of inexorable events (of "happenings," rather than the actions of others, or of him- or herself). These ways of representing self are related, but not the same, and it is important to keep separate accounts of each phenomenon. Questions of role allocation and of general textual visibility can be informed by tracking a number of simultaneous but independent grammatical choices in a text from clause to clause: for example, by tracking what is *grammatical agent* (if there is one); what is *grammatical subject* (that which can be argued over in a clause of English); and what is marked for *priority* (the feature "theme") and what for *newsworthiness* (the feature "new"; see Halliday & Matthiessen [2004] for details on each of these grammatical features; see Moore [2005] for an extended illustration of such textual patterns of patient prominence and agency in the context of HIV medicine).

This "polyphony" of grammatical patterns renders a remarkable display of the moment-to-moment construction of unconscious meaning by a persona in an interaction (it could be the persona of the patient or of the therapist, or additionally the "drift" of the dyad as a unit). The meanings are unconscious because (1) they are realized by choices that few people can consciously report; (2) they accumulate and ramify to degrees that even few linguists could monitor (or censor) in real time; and (3) they accumulate and ramify to amounts that require considerable reflective and statistical processing, since the rates (bunchings and dispersions of a linguistic phenomenon) and quantities (numbers of actual instances of a relevant linguistic choice) can be salient both independently and, even more so, when combined.

If we take just one sentence from a common formulation in English for expressing guilt and responsibility, we can demonstrate the potential for a tension between the ostensible topic (the "aboutness") and the emotional consistency that the therapist needs to "stay with" when construing a patient's utterance. There is a tension between the visibility, prominence, and agentivity that a patient can give himself (let us use *him* for this analysis): "I can't help but blame myself for what happened." On the face of it, this statement appears mature, responsible, and unremarkable in any recount. It consists of three clauses each containing selections from several grammatical systems (transitivity, mood, tense, aspect, thematicity, clausal dependency, etc.) and therefore the statement is a combination of numerous choices by the speaker.

In terms of textual *visibility*, the patient is an overt grammatical participant in at least three ways in the action construed:

1. The participant who can't help something ("<u>I can't help</u> *x*").
2. The participant who allocates blame ("<u>I blame</u> *x*").
3. The participant who is given the blame ("<u>I blame</u> *myself*").

In terms of *prominence* or *priority* the patient places himself in a thematic role—that is, the subject/actor is himself, the first person, and this is located in theme position at the front of two of the three clauses in the utterance, giving a sense in the discourse that his feelings and experience are working as a departure point for the messages exchanged. Contrast this with other choices that would not create that particular prominence; for instance, in the case of another person or some qualification of circumstance occupying the thematic position (e.g., "<u>Deirdre</u> blames me for what happened," or "<u>On bad days</u> I blame myself").

In terms of *agency*, however, the picture painted by the patient is somewhat different. The message includes an agentive construction "<u>I blame</u> *x*," whereby the patient is painting himself as the active participant responsible for the important process of interpreting and evaluating the situation. But undercutting this depiction of agentive responsibility are several other features suggesting that the responsibility is elsewhere, or nowhere. In this expression, the "blame myself" is first person, but with "myself" as grammatical target. This combines the concession of his own guilt with the grammatical role of acted upon or even "victim" (note the traditional terms are the "object," or even "patient," in the "accusative" case in Latin).

In addition, "<u>I can't help</u> but do *x*" locates the patient/speaker as under some duress, by way of the modal <u>can't</u> combined with the main verb <u>can't help</u>. Comparing the selection in this instance with alternative potential choices, such as "I blame myself" or even "I refuse to blame myself," we can see that the actual verb selection implies a much more restricted degree of control to the first person.

A further way of downplaying the patient's own responsibility appears in the last part of the utterance, where he chooses to represent his recent situation as "<u>what happened</u>." Crucially, he does not select the directly available alternative wording, "what I did." By choosing neither the active nor the passive but the middle voice (*x* happened), the personal agency is diminished. The events are placed, latently, in the grammatical domain of weather, storms, disasters, and processes that take their natural (rather than human) course.

In this one common case of expression, we can see already how an instance of explicit avowal of self-criticism can be offset by the implicit meanings of grammatical presentation.

The Meanings in Clause Relations

The principle of comparing the instance (actual) to the system (potential) applies not just to which words and phrases are chosen in a clause, but also to the way that separate clauses are combined to make clause complexes or sentences. In Figure 8.1 we display the sentence about blame, discussed above, in terms of its three separate clauses. Each clause, shown in a separate ellipse, represents a discrete action or state of affairs, which combines with the other clauses to create a more complex account of the goings-on. Arrows show the line of subordination between the clauses, with the first clause being the only independent clause.

Note that the "I" referred to above as a visible participant is placed at two grammatical removes from the "what happened." This grammatical depth can be seen as one form of grammatical "insulation" between the "I" and whatever "happened." The insulation provided by this grammatical depth is in step with the

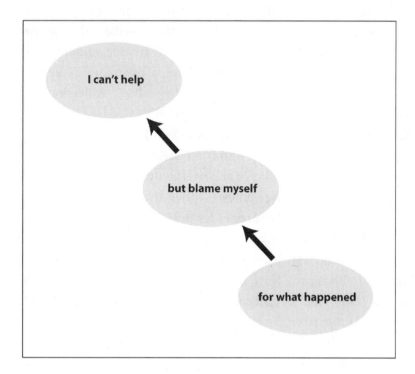

FIGURE **8.1**. Dependency between clauses in "I can't help but blame. . . ."

further insulation provided by the wording that occurs in that element: the choice of "*x* happening" over "what I did." (This third element, i.e., "what happened," is analyzed here as a separate clause from the verbal process of "blame.")

Like the differences between speaker visibility, prominence, and agentivity discussed above, these covert, nonconscious choices in how clause dependencies are organized produce a form of textual counterpoint between guilt and the blaming of others. Such counterpoint in the grammar can be a harbinger of meanings that need to emerge in the therapy session—for example, a patient's shift from self-criticism through to strong claims concerning the role of others in bringing on, or taking advantage of, the patient's illness.

In the extract in Table 8.1 the importance of "reading" for this subtext is readily demonstrable. The linguistic method assists particularly when the experienced therapist needs to be more explicit about what is happening and how it can be presented, and possibly quantified, as clinical evidence or as a training text. The patient, J, has experienced years of profound suffering and mental illness. Some of the motifs of her relationships with others are evident here. The therapist has asked J to expand on the periods when the contending voices and chaotic feelings were not dominating her life. Elaborating on this invitation, J discusses some periods in her marriage, but the text shows that J consistently presents herself without any agency, any effective impact, or role as an independent actor. She typically takes up stative/relational verbs rather than active/material verbs. Although she has been *esteemed* (by others?), she casts herself as a collection of attributes, not actions: *had* (a path)/(hope); *was* (sore) (tired).

After some actions only in association with her partner (moving house; wanting to marry), her only action is that she "would start to hate herself again" (i.e., she acts out an emotion directed at herself only). Again we see the supervening of outside cause—"something comes . . . then there's chaos." To put it crudely, the only independent doing J expresses for herself is a negative action—a failure to be effectual: "and then I *felt like* ‖ nothing [[I *could do*]] *could make* him happy." She takes on the causal responsibility of another's state of mind, as if she had the main obligation in this regard. Note again that J, as even a *nondoer*, is a clause participant only in a clause that is embedded in another clause, as shown by the double square brackets surrounding the clause "[[I *could do*]]". This acts as another form of grammatical insulation, locating J's ineffective action away from the arguable core of the clause: it is as if her ineffectuality is not open for discussion.

Table 8.1. Extract Demonstrating Reading for Grammatical Subtext (Note: ‖ identifies a new clause; << >> indicates a clause that interrupts a clause being spoken; and [[ ]] indicates an embedded clause structure contained within a prior clause.)

37	J	. . . I was esteemed. I had a path. I had hope. You know ‖ what I mean? It seems ‖ when something interrupts the hope, something comes,/mm/ ‖ or interrupts the direction [[I'm going in]] ‖ then there's chaos.
38	T	You were esteemed ‖ and you had a path.
39	J	Like I meet H, I thought ‖ this time it's going to work out. And going to move out to country, wanted to get married, we were gonna have, we were gonna have a number of children. But C she was born ‖ and we moved to F ‖ when C was born. He wouldn't go in and kiss her good night. [[All he wanted to do]] was [[go fishing]]. He was upset ‖ I didn't have sex [[as often with him as I did]] ‖ because I was tired ‖ and I was sore after the birth. It was like [[give me a few weeks to heal]]. And then the chaos would come ‖ and I would start to hate myself again ‖ and um and different, << it's hard to say >> different, obviously different people inside would give a different opinion , and it just gets confusing. I was afraid which part, which one to listen to ‖ and um that's when it . . .
40	T	Those times with H were quite stressful?
41	J	A lot of the time. There were periods when it was really good. We moved, something like six times in 3 years of marriage ‖ and it seemed ‖ after we'd moved ‖ for 2 or 3 months it was wonderful. It was like. I think. Because we had expectations ‖ but then when those expectations weren't met ‖ he'd get edgy and frustrated ‖ and then I felt like ‖ nothing [[I could do]] could make him happy.
42	T	Right. So can you see the difference there? When things are going well with you and H ‖ you felt contented in yourself ‖ you felt esteemed.
43	J	I felt safe. I felt secure.
44	T	You felt safe and secure.
45	J	And there's no need for. And they just sort of seem to come up ‖ when there's chaos ‖ or when there's. I know ‖ it's for protection ‖ or to help out, it's to . . .
46	T	It was, he was causing you a lot of stress /yep/ at times ‖ and it seems ‖ that during those periods of stress you would have all those voices in your head, those noises in your head ‖ and you'd would be trying to sort out one from the other.

One could reasonably respond to our summary of the above conversation: "Well, all that is pretty obvious, so why adopt a stance from functional linguistics?" One of many replies is, as mentioned above, the importance of mobilizing evidence and of taking the method of the therapist into more careful discriminations. For instance, this passage gives the impression of marking some change by J, perhaps a new strength of agency: the opening "I was esteemed. I had a path. I had hope" appears to support this reading. But the grammar does not. It gives a more differentiated sense of motivated selection by the patient, and it displays the motivation for the rare situation of the therapist interrupting the patient's habitual cycle of rationalization (e.g., "something comes . . ."). The patient is still very much the grammatical "patient" (a traditional linguistic term for the one "acted upon"). What is different is the high visibility of her topicality—her position as theme and as subject in the clauses—but the agency is *not* in evidence (she is not an authentic actor in the human affairs reported).

The experienced therapist recognizes this and makes the issue explicit for their ongoing intersubjectivity. She steers the talk toward "the difference" (in 42), and then cuts off the continuation of talk that is vaguely about cause: "they . . . come up . . . when there's chaos" (45). The therapist says: "It was, he was causing you a lot of stress /yep/ at times and it seems that during those periods of stress you would have all those voices in your head, those noises in your head. . . . " Differentiating between prominence of the agentive kind and other means of wording the first person turns out to be crucial in this text and in understanding the therapist's decision to "step in."

The Overall Shape of the Interaction: Generic Structure

A review of the generic structure of an exchange is crucial in that it allows one to establish the value of a choice or of a pattern of choices. For example, an initial discussion on the efficacy of medication may be an obligatory step with many of the patients in our data. But, although important, the linguistic patterns of such a segment may not be a relevant inclusion in the linguistic measure of change in the self-evaluation that develops over the 50 minutes of the therapeutic interaction. In some sessions, the openings and closing "coda" to the therapy can be tightly linked to the therapeutic conversation overall: The patient and the therapist appear mindful of the opportunity for "work" of a symbolic kind. But the relevance of each step of the session to the linguistic measurement of change ought to be adjudicated case by case. This involves the comparison of the structure of a session with the typical cycle of therapeutic treatment overall, with its changing priorities and obligatory procedures. The linguist is always looking for marked (contrastive) choices. These are an index of the options that a person has taken up, of the potential. The degree of markedness is a sign of the motivation in that the interaction has to be turned to the purpose implicit in the language (whether such purpose can be regarded as unconscious or conscious). Figure 8.2 graphically depicts the decision that might be made to separate openings and closings from the relation-building discourse in the body of the conversation (which constitutes the criterial technique of psychotherapeutic interactions in CM).

Although the context of psychotherapy allows a very wide range of topics and angles to be encompassed when compared with other registers, it is clear that practitioners and patients share some expectations about how sessions start, con-

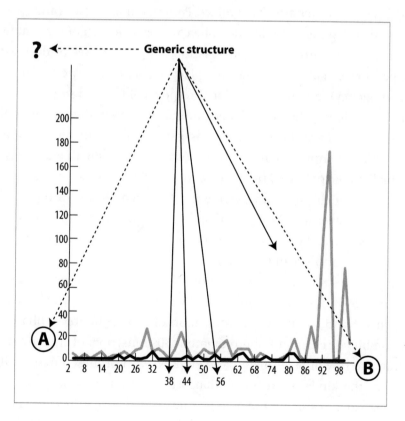

FIGURE 8.2.

tinue, and conclude, and how and where variability is likely to occur. Consequently the session can be conceived of as comprising a sequence of moves or phases that probably do not have distinct boundaries but flow into each other and can be dispersed or revisited.

In tracking and refining one's sense of how these phase changes are organized, it can be helpful to observe changes in the size of the participants' turns. Elapsed time and word length have often been used, but an important index that should not be overlooked is clause rate within turns. One reason this statistic is important is because each clause depicts a whole event or state of affairs, and while they can combine to produce complex depictions, each clause independently selects for key features such as speaker visibility, agency, and priority/prominence (through systems of transitivity and theme). And in each clause the speaker can usually select linguistic features that construe different ideas about his or her sense of obligation or inclination, degree of certainty about something (through systems of mood and modality), and other aspects of affect. Patterns in all these features, when examined, can add to the sense provided by changes in length of turns alone regarding the changing texture of the conversation. Large increases or decreases in clause rate per turn can also suggest a good place to spend energy examining transitivity (action/agency), mood (propositional responsibility), and so on.

The two ellipses shown at the beginning and end of the session indicate procedural zones, where the talk concerns issues such as medication (at the outset here) and appointment dates (at the closure). One issue that arises is whether or not qualitative analysis of the texture in the therapeutic session should, or should not, include such procedural segments. As stated above (in relation to markedness), the answer may be "yes," if and only if they encompass instances that are marked as unusual or contrastive against what is expected as the procedural (or nondiscretionary) use of the potential.

Figure 8.3 is a visual representation of the phases that tend to unfold sequentially in most sessions, as represented by the ellipses titled "Bearings, "Something happened," and so on. The identification of this sequence of phases is based on our combined reading of approximately 30 transcripts of therapy sessions using CM. In the row of boxes below the ellipses, each of these phases is illustrated in terms of the kinds of meanings that occur within them and which, when expressed, usher in and out the phases concerned. The features noted in these boxes attempt to capture the semantic choices available and chosen in a specific session of CM therapy (see Butt et al., 2010).

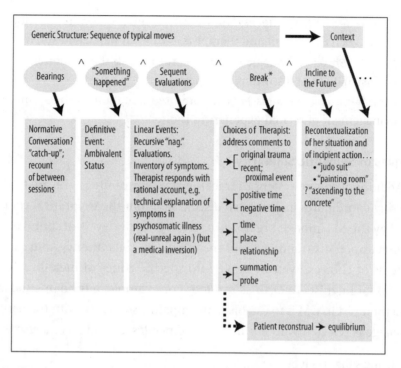

FIGURE 8.3. Generic structure of therapy session shown as a series of moves or "affective cycles," each with typical semantic profiles and choices available.

The therapist's interpretation of patient changes and consistencies in forms of speaking, as identified in CM as *chronicles*, *scripts*, and *narratives*, can be refined against the backdrop of the unfolding moves in a conversation. For instance, a chronicle form may be much more likely to occur in moves at the beginning of the conversation, whose semantic and contextual purpose is to update. But if only chronicles and scripts occur in other phases across the session, where the meaning potential includes more complex nonlinear speech, then this may indicate a restricted range of forms of consciousness in the patient.

Figure 8.3 shows the "moves" or elements that form the generic "backbone" of a therapeutic session. These can also be seen as an "affective cycle," or moves in affective tone and focus.

- *Move 1—Bearings*: The therapist and patient typically exchange procedural information that brings them quickly up to date on logistical and other matters (e.g., medication).
- *Move 2—Something Happened*: The general report is extended to "something happened" that disturbed the tenor of recent days.

- *Move 3—Sequent Evaluations*: There ensues a series of evaluations and reconstruals between the patient and therapists as to what happened and its significance.
- *Move 4—Break*: A strategic step is taken to break the repetitive construal and reconstrual of the disturbing experience.
- *Move 5—Inclination to the Future*: Some reorientation to the future and to the management of related experiences is offered.

Techniques of Semantic Solidarity

Additional concrete steps of tracking also contribute to the analyst's method by offering coordinates in extended discourse. From the theoretical coordinates supplied by the SFL model, organized as it is by strata (levels of sound and grammar), by metafunctions (tendencies of meaning), by constituency, and, ultimately, into systems of choices, we can move into specific zones of meaning making, which functional linguists refer to as *registers*. For example, a fundamental achievement for a therapist in CM is to establish an empathic solidarity with the patient in which language is selected with a number of principles as guidance. These include:

- Using what is given.
- Using the language of the other (incorporating and cocreating an idiom that the patient can "hear" as reflecting his or her immediate experience).
- Attunement to indices of positive value in tone and various layers of expression in the patient.
- Amplification of the experience and emotional value implicit in the reactions of the patient.

Amplification, as the word suggests, involves an "enlargement" of the patient's response to encompass a wider world of actual and imaginable possibilities. It is a response to "what is most alive" in the patient's expression and an attempt to open up the "meaning potential." Something of these strategies can be captured in a network at the semantic level for empathic solidarity (at least as a first step of broad description). The network, shown in Figure 8.4, is read from left to right; in the zone of a move, a number of options are open to the therapist. The aim of this network is to characterize different ways a respondent might choose to reflect back to a speaker that speaker's own preoccupations. These could be evident in the wording, the meaning, or in the enlargement of vision—the dynamic spatialization of a semantic motif created by the patient's discourse.

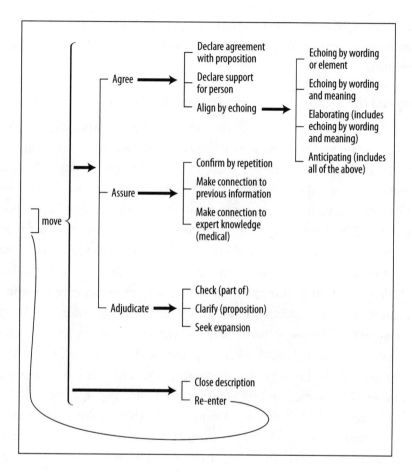

FIGURE 8.4. Techniques of semantic solidarity.

The network can be read as saying that for any interactive move, a speaker must choose from two semantic systems, each of which formalizes a zone of semantic choices. Essentially, the top system characterizes the manner of reciprocation by the therapist. The network for this top system gives more detail as it progresses to the right, in terms of how the reciprocation is shaped. The therapist may *agree* with the patient's view. Alternatively, the therapist may provide solidarity by *assuring* the patient about something relevant to his or her view, such as the clinical feasibility of some symptoms observed and interpreted by the patient. A final group of alternative ways of building solidarity is characterized here as *adjudicate*, a term used to convey the sense that it may fall to the therapist to check or confirm information or understanding; the act of doing this is not adversarial but part of the solidarity. The lower system offers a stop (the move has been described) or an opportunity to reenter (new turns require further alternative descriptions).

Cohesion and the Mapping of Fusion, Fragmentation, and Dissociation

An important discourse analytic method which bears directly upon difficult domains of psychotherapeutic practice is the technique of mapping the cohesive relations in a text, and their semantic interpretation through the technique of cohesive harmony (Hasan, 1984, 1985b) . As shown below, these techniques are particularly relevant for the interpretation of "dissociative" episodes—cases in which the "fragmentation" of the personality of the patient means that he or she may lose touch with the immediate context and reexperience traumatic events, sometimes with details of other times and events "fused" with the relived trauma. Analyzing cohesion in therapeutic talk is a way of visualizing the connectedness of a patient's version of experience, and offers some measures of how well a topic is developed, and how well it is tied in with other topics, or not. By displaying connections between lexical tokens (words used and reused, but with some specific conditions) and repetitions of grammatical roles, we can produce a map and a measure of semantic bonding across an extended passage of text.

A cohesive chain is built out of similarities. These chains are built, then, from "open system" items (i.e., drawn from those dictionary entries for a language known as head words). These are interrelated by way of similarity (synonymy), oppositeness (antonymy), class membership (hyponymy), or part-to-whole relations (meronymy). For instance, if we hear the lexical token *horse* in a recount of an event, and then the token *pony*, we hear these as words that typically keep company with each other. The relation is one of synonymy, and it holds no matter what context the interactants are in, or whether the listener is familiar with the speaker's idiom or history (see Chain 1 in Figure 8.5). Similarly, if we hear the token *real*, then hear the token *made up* (or a different form of the same word, such as *making it up*), we hear these as antonyms (see Chain 2).

A second form of chain is based on the accumulation of words that "point" to an identical person or thing; for example, "he," at the bottom of Chain 1, points back to "the horse." Such words are grammatical items like pronouns and demonstratives, which create threads of identity (known as *identity chains*). These are specific to the given text, but entail grammatical and social limits: "he" for singu-

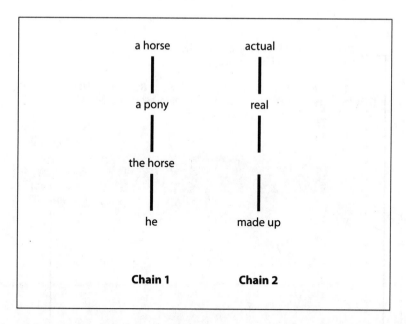

FIGURE 8.5. Fragments of two lexical chains in a therapeutic session with "Jennifer."

lar, male, sentient referent; "it" for nonsentient or gender-unknown referents, including abstract or diffuse ones such as "the situation," etc. Chain 1 in Figure 8.5 is formed using both similarity ties (horse ← pony) and identity ties (horse/pony ← he), where the direction of the arrows shows that when *pony* is heard it refers back to *horse*, and when *he* is heard, it too refers back to *horse*, and also to *pony*.

A third kind of chain can occur that is built from explicit declarations of equivalence in the text, for instance, "the birds, the birds were soldiers . . . " in a war poem by the poet Wallace Stevens. This kind of relation does not carry beyond the text in question—birds are not typically synonymous with soldiers. Such "instantial ties" often capture metaphorical relations that become significant to the logical skeleton of a text. In therapeutic talk, this can include unusual patterns of text chaining that may indicate dissociative experience or other highly personal aspects of a patient's experience.

In Figure 8.6 each long box represents a cohesive chain in the session excerpt. The excerpt starts with J beginning to report on a visit to her sister's place where there are horses, as shown above, using tokens such as *horse, pony,* and *he*. Shortly after, she says, "<u>It's like, it's really disgusting</u>." The conversation, until turn 114, is

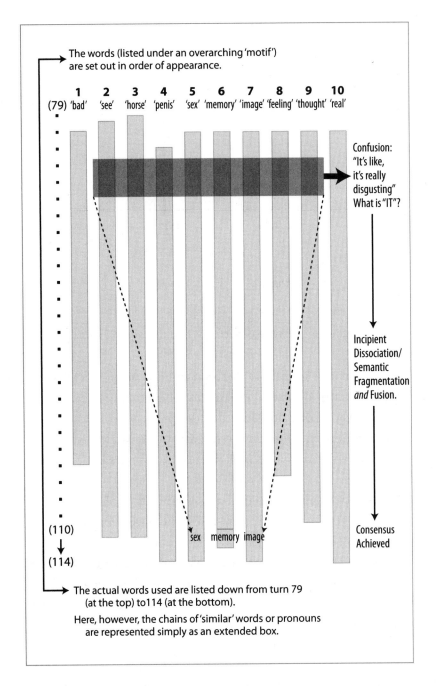

FIGURE 8.6. Selected cohesive chains in therapeutic session with Jennifer (turns 79–114).

taken up with this thread and the patient is in considerable distress. Clinical evaluation suggests that the patient was possibly in a dissociative episode during this part of the session.

There is both fragmentation and fusion between the recent horse episode being narrated, earlier experiences the patient has had, and the current moment of speaking (see Butt, Moore, Henderson-Brooks, Haliburn, & Meares, 2010, for extended analysis). What we draw attention to here is the instrumental value of cohesion analysis and of clinical reflection based on the ideas behind such analysis. The figure shows repeated, shifting, and wide bands of gray running across the chains, including the chains for *horse, penis, sex, memory, image, feeling, thought,* and *seeing*.

What is the "it" that's disgusting and later confusing, perverse, and distressing? The horse, the memory, the images previously seen? Their recollection? Toward the bottom of the diagram the gray banners across the chains narrow and disappear. Here the referential chains become easy for the linguist to resolve, and for the patient and therapist there appears to be considerable resolution and mutual agreement about what "it" is. The patient now appears to be out of the possible dissociative episode. (Note that we are not saying that evidence from the wording of the texts is the only index of how the therapist can judge a patient's language to be dissociative; in fact, quite the opposite: Many forms of gestural and contextual cues form a suite with language, or even provide the signal of a person's experience in the absence of any "wording.")

Furthermore, when viewed as an exchange of rhetorical moves, much is achieved: in particular, the dramatic "closure" (with mutually achieved consensus) in the final turns of 110–114 (see Table 8.2). This reestablished equilibrium, albeit with the perturbing episode now fully integrated in the common "archive" of their relationship, attests to the control in the interaction.

Cohesive Harmony

A further iconic sign of text bonding is the bridging function resulting from what are known as *chain interactions* (Hasan, 1984, 1985b). These are <u>not</u> items that could go in either chain, such as "it" above. Rather these are occasions in the text where items in one chain interact grammatically with items in another chain. For instance, if more than one token from the "horse" chain (*pony, horse,* or their stand-ins *he* or *it*) recurs in more than one sentence with items from the "real" chain (*real, made up, what happens,* etc.) applied to them, then this is heard as sig-

Table 8.2. Excerpt of Session: "Horse" Episode Closure with Patient "J"

TURN	SPEAKER	TEXT
110	Therapist	You see the pony's penis well for that matter one can see, you know, pictures and one can see naked bodies in reality. Mmmm.
111	Patient	Yes.
112	Therapist	But does that mean something sexual? But it seems like the association . . .
113	Patient	It doesn't, it shouldn't but with me it does.
114	Therapist	Yes.

nificant to the drift of the conversation, even if ambiguity or confusion still exists about what the "it" is. Alternatively, does the figure show any chain, or grouping of chains, without a bridge of interaction with other chains? Such "islands" in cohesive chaining suggest a failure of connectedness, or (depending on the genre) such a segment may be indicative of a leap of analogical thinking, a leap that will be interpreted as a parable or excursus. Such leaps may become retroactively relevant if a case can be made for a leap of imagination (i.e., of similarity without explicit identity through a pronominal chain). It should be noted, however, that analogical leaps are important textual phenomena in many registers (e.g., in sciences, in verbal art, in philosophical arguments, and in joking). So too analogical connections in discourse are crucial to CM (as explicated by Meares, 2005); this follows Vygotsky's (1962) emphasis on the value of nonlinearity in discourses of self-reflection.

A Further Example: Meaning Potential, Intervention, and Change

We have suggested that in a therapeutic conversation, although the interaction is very open, each "move" is motivated by a distinct dimension of the social process, by steps in the "business to hand" (Greek: *pragma*). In the session excerpted in Table 8.3, which comes from later in the session between Marguerite and her therapist discussed in Chapter 6, an overarching or long-term purpose appears to be a fresh inclination to a future freer of the sense of a deadened core that is the chief behavioral sign of BPD. This *inclination is to a future* with an extended value, an extended potential to mean.

Table 8.3. Excerpt Demonstrating Overarching Purpose

CLAUSE	SPEAKER	TEXT
1	Therapist	Ha! . . . does that mean
2		If you stopped
3		him doing that to you
4		you would do it less to the children?
5		Is that it?
6	Patient	Well I might feel better about myself
7		Yeah. I might, mm . . .
8		cause he stopped for a few days—
9		I think
10		it was last week
11		or, I don't know
12		I think
13		there was some abatement
14		and then it just . . .
15		just for a couple of days
16		as if it was—
17		I don't know
18		maybe it's sort of delusional, escape
19		it was just living and breathing
20		which was just a little bit easier, y'know . . . er . . .

Session Excerpt: "If you stopped him doing that to you."

Such a breakout into a "freer," more alive space is realized only when the interaction finds a way out of an *aporia*—the conundrum that has entrapped the patient in a loop of hopelessness (Greek: *aporia*, lack or resources; an impasse of material or semantic impoverishment). Such impasses in our data include the logistical and personal constraints of breaking away from abusive relationships. The domestic and emotional reasons "to stay" can appear overwhelming, but the reasons lead to a cascade of problems. For example, in the following extract a mother considers her treatment of her own children as the result of the abuse she experiences from her partner (described earlier as like "acid eating away").

The therapist draws attention to the patient's own agency ("if <u>you stopped him</u> doing that to you," not "if he stopped doing it to you"). This creates a pathway into a meditation—carefully balanced as it is uttered—in which the patient can envisage a different existence, modalized (via *maybe, just, I don't know* etc.) and in small increments though it may be. The mother's realistic review of her own situation has its own discourse correlates. Here, the modalization of her memory and judgments and the balanced clausal architecture are part of a grammatical ensemble, a therapeutic music that realizes the feeling that has emerged: Change can be envisaged. Therefore, change has already occurred.

One can ask: Why should language be given such a central role in the interpretation of a psyche and, particularly, in the characterization of any form of mental disorder? There are many points to consider on this issue and many of those have been taken up by Meares and others in the development of CM. One point we would emphasize here is that language "cuts to the quick" (*quick* is archaic for the core of our living being) in that it is taken up preconsciously in our formative, earliest relationships with carers. Our taking on of personhood and the personalization of our brains (Greenfield, 2008, Chapter 1) are continuous with the meanings we take in and with the meanings by which our intersubjectivities are sustained. In this there is a common theory of intersubjectivity across the work of Trevarthen (e.g., 1974, 1987; see also Bullowa, 1979), Meares (2005), and the functional linguistics of Halliday (1975, 2003). We trust that debate around the status of linguistic evidence will be encouraged by the exemplification in this chapter and related publications by ourselves and others with a similar approach (e.g., Butt et al., 2010; Fine, 2006; Muntigl, 2004).

Future investigations into the discourse correlates of CM are likely to elucidate both the shared and distinctive techniques of psychotherapists, information that should assist in the process of mentoring. Beyond this professional goal, many more global issues are appearing on the horizon: for example, the grammatical construction of the "duplex self," the profound insight by William James that appears to have latent reactances in the most habitual areas of linguistic practices. There is much work to take up, but the linguistic bases of CM and the psychotherapeutic relevance of functional linguistics are well established.

Appendix

AN ADHERENCE SCALE for the CONVERSATIONAL MODEL

THIS SCALE IS DESIGNED to be useful in gauging whether a particular therapist is working according to the Conversational Model (CM). Eight categories of therapeutic response are rated, with four to eight items in each category. There are a total of 40 items. Many of the items can be scored dichotomously. It is suggested that each item is rated 0, 1, 2, with the rating of 1 indicating an equivocal adherence.

In other systems, adherence scales involve scoring a whole session—a highly laborious and expensive procedure. The method we recommend is more generally usable. It involves the rating of only a few minutes of conversation. This approach is consistent with the notion of the "minute particulars," which implies that in the small details of a conversation are embedded the elements of a much larger system.

The conversational sample is randomly chosen at a point about halfway through a recorded therapeutic session. A transcript is insufficient for this purpose because the inflections and tones of voice are crucial. The sample should include at least five conversational units, where each unit is composed of the patient's expression and the therapist's response. An example of such a sample is given at the beginning of Chapter 6, where the opening to a session between Marguerite and her therapist is discussed.

Scoring of the therapist's response should ideally be performed by someone familiar with CM. Alternatively, Chapters 3, 6, and (for some situations) Chapter 7 offer a guide. Examples of most of the items on the scale are given in these chapters.

Before scoring the sample, the rater should study it and calculate what the maximum score could be, since not all items will be applicable to this particular part of the conversation. Traumatic intrusions, for example, may not always be evident. The therapist's responses are then rated. This score, T, is then expressed as a percentage of the ideal maximum score, M—that is, the score equals T/M × 100.

Those using this scale will need to create their own normative data. This scale has not yet been piloted. What is put forward here is a suggested guideline for measuring adherence, and it is capable of development by those who use it.

The categories of therapeutic response and items reflective of each category of response are as follows. It should be stressed that neither the list of categories nor the number of items is exhaustive, but they provide a snapshot view of capable use of CM.

1. Immediacy
   - The therapist's response is closely "coupled" with the expression and the patient, using appropriate emotional tone.
   - The therapist uses that which is expressed by the patient (i.e., the actual words).
   - The therapist responds to that which is most "alive" in this expression.
   - The therapist tends to use the present tense.
   - Trauma is processed as if in the present.

2. Right-Hemispheric Language
   (This term refers to what Vygotsky called "inner speech"; see Chapter 2.)
   - Therapist uses inflections of voice to express feeling.
   - Therapist avoids asking questions.
   - Therapist uses sentences without pronouns.
   - Therapist tends to omit the subject of sentences.
   - Therapist's contribution may be incomplete or asyntactical.
   - Therapist's response has a "shaping" intent.

3. Mutuality
   - Therapist uses language of the patient.
   - Therapist uses speculative tone, as if inviting an elaboration of his or her contribution.
   - Therapist gives evidence of careful listening.

- Therapist respects patient's "agenda" (i.e., subject chosen for discussion).
- Therapist does not "translate" (i.e., turn the expression into his or her own language).
- Therapist "stays with" or "tracks" an evolving theme and feeling.

4. Positivity

- Therapist amplifies positive tone.
- Therapist finds and affirms hidden or muted positive affect.
- Therapist responds to that which is spontaneous.
- Therapist "stays with" positive affect.

5. Representation

- Therapist uses empathic imagination to put into words what is most immediate and essential of patient's experience.
- Therapist uses tone of voice to represent emotional core of patient's experience.
- Therapist uses figurative language (e.g., metaphor, the patient's, and his or her own).
- Therapist gives sensory aliveness to the patient's experience.
- Therapist facilitates the patient's own representing.

6. Reflection

- Therapist potentiates reflective awareness of patient.
- Therapist introduces reflection with appropriate timing.
- Therapist uses propositional speech (i.e., syntactical, including pronouns).
- Therapist's demeanor is one of coparticipant in a reflective process.

7. Changing the Chronicle

- Therapist listens with intent to a boring account.
- Therapist finds what is most "personal" and capable of imaginative development in this account.
- Therapist helps patient elaborate and enlarge this aspect of the account.
- Therapist finds some unifying image in the clatter of details presented to him or her.

8. Processing Trauma

- Therapist identifies and responds to intrusion of traumatic memory.
- Therapist does not proceed with traumatic processing when patient is not ready for it.

- Therapist acknowledges his or her part in triggering disjunction, when this is appropriate.
- Therapist, with patient, builds up the "scene" of the traumatic intrusion into the therapeutic conversation.
- Therapist, with patient, builds up the "scene" of traumatic memory affecting a relationship outside therapy. (Scene includes patient's feelings, self-attributes, tendency to respond, attributes given to the other, expectations of the other, voice/posture/demeanor of patient, and patient's experience of physical attributes of other).
- Therapist, with patient, moves toward changing the script, at an appropriate time when the script and scene have been well laid out.

References

Alexander, F. (1949). *Fundamentals of psychoanalysis: A concise and up-to-date presentation*. London: George Allen and Unwin Ltd.

Alexander, F. French, T. M. (1946). *Psychoanalytic psychotherapy: Principles & application*. New York: Ronald Press.

American Psychiatric Association. (1994). *Diagnostic and statistical manual of mental disorders* (4th ed.). Washington, DC: Author.

Barkham, M., Rees, A., Stiles, W. B., Shapiro, D. A., Hardy, G. E., & Reynolds, S. (1996). Dose–effect relations in time-limited psychotherapy for depression. *Journal of Consulting Clinical Psychology, 64*(5), 927–935.

Beutler, L., Machado, P., & Neufeldt, S. (1994). Therapist variables. In A. Bergin & S. Garfield (Eds.), *Handbook of psychotherapy and behavior change* (4th ed., pp. 229–269). New York, NY: Wiley.

Bilalic, M., Kiesel, A., Pohl, C., Erb, M., & Grodd, W. (2011). It takes two-skilled recognition of objects engages lateral areas in both hemispheres. *PLoS One, 6*(1), e16202.

Bornstein, M., & Tamis Le Monda, C. (1997). Maternal responsiveness and infant mental abilities: Specific predictive relations. *Infant Behaviour and Development, 20*(3), 283–296.

Bowlby, J. (1988). *A secure base: Clinical applications of attachment theory*. London: Routledge.

Brandchaft, B. (1993). To free the spirit from its cell. In A. Goldberg (Ed.), *Progress in self psychology* (Vol. 9). Hillsdale, NJ: Analytic Press.

Brandchaft, B., Doctors, S., & Sorter, D. (2010). *Toward an emancipatory psychoanalysis: Brandchaft's intersubjective vision*. London: Routledge.

Bullowa, M. (Ed.). (1979). *Before speech: The beginning of interpersonal communication*. Cambridge, UK: Cambridge University Press.

Butt, D. G. (1988). Randomness, order and the latent patterning of text. In D. Birch & L. M. O'Toole (Eds.), *Function of style*. London: Pinter.

Butt, D. G., Moore, A. R., Henderson-Brooks, C., Haliburn, J., & Meares, R. (2010). Dissociation, relatedness, and "cohesive harmony": A linguistic measure of degrees of "fragmentation"? *Linguistics and the Human Sciences, 3*(3), 263–293.

Clarkin, J. F., & Posner, M. (2005). Defining the mechanisms of borderline personality disorder. *Psychopathology, 38*(2), 56–63.

Cloninger, C. R. (1987). *The Tridimensional Personality Questionnaire, version IV*. St Louis (Mo): Department of Psychiatry, Washington University School of Medicine.

Felmingham, K. (2011). *The impact of dissociation in postraumatic traumatic stress disorder on electronic brain activity*. Paper presented at the International Society for the Study of Personality Disorders Congress, Melbourne, Victoria, Australia.

Felmingham, K., Kemp, A. H., Williams, L., Falconer, E., Olivieri, G., Peduto, A., et al. (2008). Dissociative responses to conscious and non-conscious fear impact underlying brain function in post-traumatic stress disorder. *Psychological Medicine, 38*(12), 1771–1780.

Fine, J. (2006). *Language in psychiatry: A handbook of clinical practice*. London: Equinox.

Flanagan, O. (1992). *Consciousness reconsidered*. Cambridge, MA: MIT Press.

Freud, S. (1915). Instincts and their vicissitudes. *Standard Edition, 14*, 111–140. London, UK: Hogarth.

Garbutt, M. (1997). *Figure talk: Reported speech and thought in the discourse of psychotherapy*. Unpublished Ph.D. thesis, Macquarie University, Sydney.

Giesen-Bloo, J., van Dyck, R., Spinhoven, P., van Tilburg, W., Dirksen, C., van Asselt, T., et al. (2006). Outpatient psychotherapy for borderline personality disorder: Randomized trial of schema-focused therapy vs. transference-focused psychotherapy. *Archives of General Psychiatry, 63*(6), 649–658.

Greenfield, S. (2008). *ID: The quest for identity in the 21st century*. London: Sceptre.

Gunderson, J. (2011, March). *Basic principles of "good enough" treatment for BPD*. Paper presented at the workshop of the International Society for the Study of Personality Disorders, Melbourne, Victoria, Australia.

Guthrie, E., Creed, F., Dawson, D., & Tomenson, B. (1991). A controlled trial of psychological treatment for the irritable bowel syndrome. *Gastroenterology, 100*(2), 450–457.

Guthrie, E., Kapur, N., Mackway-Jones, K., Chew-Graham, C., Moorey, J., Mendel, E., et al. (2001). Randomised controlled trial of brief psychological intervention after deliberate self-poisoning. *British Medical Journal, 323*(7305), 135–138.

Guthrie, E., Moorey, J., Margison, F., Barker, H., Palmer, S., McGrath, G., et al. (1999). Cost-effectiveness of brief psychodynamic-interpersonal therapy in high utilizers of psychiatric services. *Archives of General Psychiatry, 56*(6), 519–526.

Haliburn, J. (2009). Integration through relatedness in the conversational model: A case study. *Australasian Psychiatry, 17*(1), 29–33.

Haliburn, J. (2011). From traumatic attachment to somatization disorder. *Australasian Psychiatry, 19*(5), 401–405.

Haliburn, J., Stevenson, J., & Gerull, F. (2009). A university psychotherapy training program in a psychiatric hospital: 25 years of the conversational model in the treatment of patients with borderline personality disorder. *Australasian Psychiatry, 17*(1), 25–28.

Hall, J., Caleo, S., Stevenson, J., & Meares, R. (2001). An economic analysis of psychotherapy for borderline personality disorder patients. *Journal of Mental Health Policy and Economics, 4*(1), 3–8.

Halliday, M. A. K. (1971). Linguistic function and literary style: An enquiry into the language of William Golding's "The Inheritors." In S. Chatman (Ed.), *Literary style: A symposium*. New York, NY: Oxford University Press.

Halliday, M. A. K. (1975). *Learning how to mean: Exploration in the development of language*. London: Edward Arnold.

Halliday, M. A. K. (2002). *On the ineffability of grammatical categories* (Vol. 1). London & New York: Continuum.

Halliday, M. A. K. (2002 [1984]). *On the ineffability of grammatical categories*. In J. J. Webster (Ed.), *The collected works of M. A. K. Halliday* (Vol. 1: pp. 291–322). London & New York: Continuum.

Halliday, M. A. K. (2003). The language of early childhood. In J. J. Webster (Ed.), *The collected works of M. A. K. Halliday* (Vol. 4). London & New York: Continuum.

Halliday, M. A. K., & Hasan, R. (1976). *Cohesion in English*. London: Longman.

Halliday, M. A. K., & Matthiessen, C. M. I. M. (2004). *An introduction to functional grammar* (3rd ed.). London: Arnold.

Hamilton, J., Guthrie, E., Creed, F., Thompson, D., Tomenson, B., Bennett, R., et al. (2000). A randomized controlled trial of psychotherapy in patients with chronic functional dyspepsia. *Gastroenterology, 119*(3), 661–669.

Hasan, R. (1975). The place of stylistics in the study of verbal art. In H. Ringbom (Ed.), *Style and text* (pp. 49–62). Amsterdam: Skriptor.

Hasan, R. (1979). Workshop Report No. 6: Language in the study of literature. In M. A. K. Halliday (Ed.), *Working conference on language in education: Report to participants*. Sydney, AU: University of Sydney.

Hasan, R. (1984). Coherence and cohesive harmony. In J. Flood (Ed.), *Understanding reading comprehension* (pp. 181–221). Neward, DE: International Reading Association.

Hasan, R. (1985a). *Linguistics, language and verbal art*. Geelong, Victoria, AU: Deakin University Press.

Hasan, R. (1985b). *Part B. Language, context and text: Aspects of language in a social semiotic perspective*. Geelong, Victoria, AU: Deaken University Press.

Henderson-Brooks, C. (2006). *What type of person am I, Tess? The complex tale of self in psychotherapy*. Unpublished doctoral dissertation. Macquarie University, Sydney, AU.

Hobson, R. F. (1971). Imagination and amplification in psychotherapy. *Journal of Analytical Psychology, 16*, 79–105.

Hobson, R. F. (1985). *Forms of feeling: The heart of psychotherapy*. London: Tavistock.

Jackson, J. H. (1958). *Selected writings of John Hughlings Hackson* (Vol. II). New York, NY: Basic Books. (Original work published 1931–1932)

Jakobson, R. (Ed.). (1987). *Language in literature*. Cambridge, MA: Belknap Press, Harvard University.

James, W. (1890). *Principles of psychology* (Vol. I). New York, NY: Holt.

James, W. (1892). *Psychology: Briefer course*. London: Macmillan.

Janet, P. (1924). *Principles of psychotherapy*. London: Allen & Unwin.

Janet, P. (1925). Treatment by mental liquidation (E. Paul & C. Paul, Trans.) *Psychological healing* (Vol. I, pp. 589–698). London: Allen & Unwin.

Jung, C.G. (1953). Foreword to Frieda Fordham: Introduction to Jung's psychology (R. F. C. Hull, Trans.). *The collected works of C. G. Jung* (Vol. 18). London & New York: Routledge & Kegan Paul.

Kohut, H. (1977). *The restoration of the self*. New York, NY: International Universities Press.

Korner, A., Gerull, F., Meares, R., & Stevenson, J. (2006). Borderline personality disorder treated with the conversational model: A replication study. *Comprehensive Psychiatry, 47*(5), 406–411.

Korner, A., Gerull, F., Meares, R., & Stevenson, J. (2008). The nothing that is something: Core dysphoria as the central feature of borderline personality disorder—implications for treatment. *American Journal of Psychotherapy, 62*(4), 377–394.

Korner, A., Gerull, F., Stevenson, J., & Meares, R. (2007). Harm avoidance, self-harm, psychic pain, and the borderline personality: Life in a "haunted house." *Comprehensive Psychiatry, 48*(3), 303–308.

Leichsenring, F., Leibing, E., Kruse, J., New, A. S., & Leweke, F. (2011). Borderline personality disorder. *Lancet, 377*(9759), 74–84.

Lewis, M. (1992). *Shame: The exposed self*. New York, NY: Free Press.

Linehan, M., Armstrong, H., Suarez, A., Allman, D., & Heard, H. (1991). Cognitive behavioral treatment of chronically parasuicidal borderline patients. *Archives of General Psychiatry, 48*, 1060–1064.

Meares, A. (1958). *The door of serenity: A study in the therapeutic use of symbolic painting.* London: Faber & Faber.

Meares, A. (1961). What makes the patient better? *Lancet, 1*(7189), 1280–1281.

Meares, A. (1967). *Relief without drugs.* New York, NY: Doubleday.

Meares, R. (1976). The secret. *Psychiatry, 39*(3), 258–265.

Meares, R. (1977). *The pursuit of intimacy: An approach to psychotherapy.* Melbourne: Nelson.

Meares, R. (1980). Body feeling in human relations: The possible examples of Brancusi and Giacometti. *Psychiatry, 43*(2), 160–167.

Meares, R. (1983). Keats and the "impersonal" therapist: A note on empathy and the therapeutic screen. *Psychiatry, 46*(1), 73–82.

Meares, R. (1984). Inner space: Its constriction in anxiety states and narcissistic personality. *Psychiatry, 47*(2), 162–171.

Meares, R. (1993a). *The metaphor of play: Disruption and restoration in the borderline experience.* Northvale, NJ: Jason Aronson.

Meares, R. (1993b). Reversals: On certain pathologies of identification. In A. Goldberg (Ed.), *Progress in self psychology* (Vol. 9, pp. 231–246). Hillsdale, NJ: Analytic Press.

Meares, R. (1995). Episodic memory, trauma and the narrative of self. *Contemporary Psychoanalysis, 31*(4), 541–556.

Meares, R. (1997). Stimulus entrapment. *Psychoanalytic Inquiry, 17*(2), 223–234.

Meares, R. (1998). The self in conversation: On narratives, chronicles and scripts. *Psychoanalytic Dialogues, 8*, 875–891.

Meares, R. (1999a). Value, trauma, and personal reality. *Bulletin Menninger Clinic, 63*(4), 443–458.

Meares, R. (1999b). The contribution of Hughlings Jackson to an understanding of dissociation. *American Journal of Psychiatry, 156*(12), 1850–1855.

Meares, R. (1999c). The "adualistic" representation of trauma: On malignant internalization. *American Journal of Psychotherapy, 53*(3), 392–402.

Meares, R. (2000a). *Intimacy and alienation: Memory, trauma and personal being.* London: Routledge.

Meares, R. (2000b). Priming and projective identification. *Bulletin of the Menninger Clinic, 64*(1), 76–90.

Meares, R. (2001). What happens next? A Developmental Model of Therapeutic Spontaneity. Commentary on Paper by Philip A. Ringstrom. *Psychoanalytic Dialogues, 11*, 755-769.

Meares, R. (2005). *The metaphor of play: Origin and breakdown of personal being* (Rev. ed.). London: Routledge.

Meares, R. (2012). *A dissociation model of borderline personality disorder:* New York, NY: Norton.

Meares, R., & Anderson, J. (1993). Intimate space: On the developmental significance of exchange. *Contemporary Psychoanalysis, 29*(4), 595–612.

Meares, R., Gerull, F., Stevenson, J., & Korner, A. (2011). Is self disturbance the core of borderline personality disorder?: An outcome study of borderline personality factors. *Australian and New Zealand Journal of Psychiatry, 45*(3), 214.

Meares, R., & Hobson, R. F. (1977). The persecutory therapist. *British Journal of Medical Psychology, 50*(4), 349–359.

Meares, R., & Horvath, T. (1974). A physiological approach to the study of attachment: The mother's attention and her infant's heart rate. *Australian and New Zealand Journal of Psychiatry, 8*(1), 3–7.

Meares, R., Melkonian, D., Gordon, E., & Williams, L. (2005). Distinct pattern of P3a event-related potential in borderline personality disorder. *NeuroReport, 16*(3), 289–293.

Meares, R., & Orlay, W. (1988). On self-boundary: A study of the development of the concept of secrecy. *British Journal of Medical Psychology, 61*(Pt. 4), 305–316.

Meares, R., Penman, R., Milgrom-Friedman, J., & Baker, K. (1982). Some origins of the "difficult" child: The Brazelton scale and the mother's view of her newborn's character. *British Journal of Medical Psychology, 55*(Pt. 1), 77–86.

Meares, R., Schore, A., & Melkonian, D. (2011). Is borderline personality a particularly right-hemispheric disorder?: A study of P3a using single trial analysis. *Australian and New Zealand Journal of Psychiatry, 45*(2), 131–139.

Meares, R., Stevenson, J., & Comerford, A. (1999). Psychotherapy with borderline patients: I. A comparison between treated and untreated cohorts. *Australian and New Zealand Journal of Psychiatry, 33*(4), 467–472; discussion 478–481.

Meares, R., & Sullivan, G. B. (2004). Two forms of human language. In G. Williams & A. Lukin (Eds.), *Language development: Functional perspectives in evolution and ontogenesis* (pp. 182–195). London: Continuum.

Mukařovský, J. (1964). Standard language and poetic language. In P. L. Garvin (Ed.), *A Prague school reader on aesthetics, literary structure and style*. Washington, DC: Georgetown University Press.

Mukařovský, J. (1977). *The word and verbal art*. New Haven, CT: Yale University Press.

Muntigl, P. (2004). *Narrative counselling: Social and linguistic processes of change*. Amsterdam: John Benjamins.

National Institute for Health and Clinical Excellence. (2009). *Guidelines for borderline personality disorder*. http://www.nice.org.uk/guidance/index.jsp?action=byID&o=11651

Nelson, K. (1992). Emergence of autobiographical memory at four. *Human Development, 35*, 172–177.

Penman, R., Meares, R., Baker, K., & Milgrom-Friedman, J. (1983). Synchrony in mother–infant interaction: A possible neurophysiological base. *British Journal of Medical Psychology, 56*(Pt. 1), 1–7.

Penman, R., Meares, R., & Milgrom-Friedman, J. (1981). The mother's role in the development of object competency. *Archives de Psychologie, 49*, 247–265.

Piaget, J. (1959). *The language and thought of child* (M. R. Gabain, Trans., 3rd ed.). London: Routledge & Kegan Paul.

Saussure, F. (1916). *Course in general linguistics* (W. Baskin, Trans.). New York, NY: Philosophical Library, 1959; London: Peter Owen, 1960.

Schore, A. N. (2003). *Affect dysregulation and disorders of the self*. New York, NY: Norton.

Shapiro, D. A., & Firth, J. (1987). Prescriptive v. exploratory psychotherapy: Outcomes of the Sheffield Psychotherapy Project. *British Journal of Psychiatry, 151*, 790–799.

Shapiro, D. A., Rees, A., Barkham, M., Hardy, G., Reynolds, S., & Startup, M. (1995). Effects of treatment duration and severity of depression on the maintenance of gains after cognitive–behavioral and psychodynamic–interpersonal psychotherapy. *Journal of Consulting and Clinical Psychology, 63*(3), 378–387.

Stevenson, J., & Meares, R. (1992). An outcome study of psychotherapy for patients with borderline personality disorder. *American Journal of Psychiatry, 149*(3), 358–362.

Stevenson, J., & Meares, R. (1999). Psychotherapy with borderline patients: II. A preliminary cost benefit study. *Australian and New Zealand Journal of Psychiatry, 33*(4), 473–477; discussion 478–481.

Trevarthen, C. (1974). Conversations with a two-month old. *New Scientist, 62*, 230–235.

Trevarthen, C. (1987). Sharing makes sense: Intersubjectivity and the making of an infant's meaning. In R. Steele & R. Threadgold (Eds.), *Language topics: Essays in honour of M.A.K. Halliday* (pp. 177–200). Amsterdam: John Benjamins.

Trevarthen, C. (1994). Split-brain and the mind. In R. Gregory (Ed.), *Oxford companion to the mind* (pp. 872–878). Oxford, UK: Oxford University Press.

Trevarthen, C. (2004). Infancy, mind in. In R. L. Gregory (Ed.), *The Oxford companion to the mind* (pp. 455–64). Oxford, UK: Oxford University Press.

van der Veer, R., & Valsiner, J. (1988). Lev Vygotsky and Pierre Janet: On the origin of the concept of sociogenesis. *Developmental Review, 8,* 52–65.

Vygotsky, L. S. (1962). *Thought and language* (E. Hanfmann & G. Vakar, Eds.). Cambridge, MA: MIT Press.

Winnicott, D. W. (1971). *Playing and reality*. London: Tavistock.

Index

balance between work and private life
    for therapist, 156–57
Baldwin, 20
behavior(s)
    self-harming, 241–44; *see also* self-harming behavior
    suicidal, 244–48; *see also* suicidal ideation/behavior
being of "two minds"
    in middle stage of therapy, 83–84
Bethlem Royal Hospital
    London, 11
bipolar disorder
    BPD *vs.*, 114
borderline
    defined, 11–12
borderline personality disorder (BPD)
    aim of treatment of, 20
    bipolar disorder *vs.*, 114
    causes of, 7
    central deficit of, 2–3
    CM for. *see* Conversational Model (CM)
    comorbidities with, 251–62, *see also specific conditions and* comorbidity(ies)
    described, 1, 7
    dissociation in, 3–6
    DSM–IV criteria for, 2–3
    fight–flight system in, 40
    helping family to understand, 126
    identification of, 2–3
    lack of cohesion in, 2–3
    language as basic defect of, 36–37
    morbidity associated with, 1
    outcome studies on, 3–6
    patients with, 110–60; *see also* borderline personality disorder (BPD) patients
    primary disturbance in, 2–3
    relational approach to, 14–16
    right-hemispheric deficiency in, 7
    schizophrenia in, 114–15
    self-triad of, 2–3
    traumatic memories in, 7–8, 29–30; *see also* traumatic memory(ies)
borderline personality disorder (BPD) patients, 110–60
    acutely suicidal, 132–35
    alcohol and substance abuse or dependence among, 146–47
    auxiliary therapeutic techniques for, 143–44
    beginning of therapy with, 111–26
    boundary issues and limits effects on, 140–43
    case example, 126, 144
    chronic pain syndromes in, 114
    chronically suicidal, 130–32
    contraindications to long-term psychoanalytical therapy for, 116–17
    crisis plan for, 122–24

deliberate self-harm by, 128–30
demeanor in first session, 204
developing improved system responses for, 157–60
diagnostic issues related to, 113–16
difficulties in beginning, 206–15; *see also specific issues and* difficult situations confronting therapist
disruptions to therapeutic continuity effects on, 137–40
early information gathering related to, 112
ending of therapy for. *see* ending of therapy
family involvement in therapy for, 126, 145–46
first therapy session with, 112
friends involvement in therapy for, 145–46
general issues in working with, 110–60
holiday effects on, 137–40
joint understanding with, 112–13
medications for, 118–21
multiples diagnoses in, 114
negative feelings about mental health professionals among, 116
physical illness effects on, 137–40
poor attendance/dropouts, 135–37
psychoanalytical therapy for, 116–17
psychoeducation for, 124–25
psychotherapeutic frame for, 117–18
referral for working with, 111–12
separation's effects on, 137–40
somatization syndromes in, 114
stigma related to, 113–16
therapeutic stance for, 127–28
therapist self-care, 152–57; *see also* therapist self-care
"thought disorder" in, 115
transient psychotic states in, 114
during treatment phase, 127–47
boundary issues
    effects on BPD patients, 140–43
BPD. *see* borderline personality disorder (BPD)
brain
    organization of, 30–31
Buber, M., 173

chain interactions, 287–88
change
    adapting to, 240
    in late stage of therapy, 91–95
chronic pain syndromes
    in BPD patients, 114
chronicle(s), 38–39
    changing of, 224–26, 293
clarification
    in middle stage of therapy, 69–70
clause relations
    meanings in, 275–78, 275*f*, 277*t*
Cloniger, C.R., 6

302